MW01069238

REVIVAL AND RECONCILIATION

REVIVAL AND
RECONCILIATION

The Anglican Church and the Politics of Rwanda

Phillip A. Cantrell II

THE UNIVERSITY OF WISCONSIN PRESS

The University of Wisconsin Press
728 State Street, Suite 443
Madison, Wisconsin 53706
uwpress.wisc.edu

Gray's Inn House, 127 Clerkenwell Road
London ECIR 5DB, United Kingdom
eurospanbookstore.com

Printed in the United States of America
This book may be available in a digital edition.

Library of Congress Cataloging-in-Publication Data

Names: Cantrell, Phillip A., author.
Title: Revival and reconciliation: the Anglican church and the politics of
Rwanda / Phillip A. Cantrell II.
Description: Madison, Wisconsin: The University of Wisconsin Press, [2022] |
Includes bibliographical references and index.
Identifiers: LCCN 2021010993 | ISBN 9780299335106 (hardcover)
Subjects: LCSH: Province of the Anglican Church of Rwanda—History. |
Anglicans—Rwanda—History. | Anglican Communion—Rwanda—History. |
Religion and politics—Rwanda. | Rwanda—Church history.
Classification: LCC BX5691.R95 C36 2022 | DDC 283/.67571—dc23
LC record available at https://lccn.loc.gov/2021010993

To my J-loves . . .
Jessica and our children . . . Jacob, Josiah, and Joella

Contents

Preface

Like many Americans in 1994, I knew virtually nothing of Rwanda when the genocide unfolded across the pages of the newspapers and evening broadcasts. My only knowledge of the country came from having seen the 1988 film *Gorillas in the Mist*, recounting the tragic story and murder of naturalist Dian Fossey (1932–85). Although I was enrolled in a master's program in history at James Madison University, Africa remained, as it does in many Western minds still, as a beautiful but undeveloped land filled only with natural wonders and conflicts. My undergraduate institution, a small liberal arts college, had left me no better informed. Since I had no academic background on the country, Rwanda's genocide appeared to me as it was presented in the media: another primitive conflict between two ancient warring tribes, Hutu against Tutsi. Apart from my chagrin at the violence, I put Africa and its challenges out of mind until I found myself undertaking a field in East African history in doctoral school at West Virginia University in 1996. By the time my PhD was awarded in 2004, East Africa was my sole academic obsession. While teaching courses in African history at my first job in 2004, a local Anglican church sought my assistance as an Africa specialist in developing mission opportunities in Rwanda. By then I had traveled to East Africa on a few occasions but never to Rwanda. I leaped at the opportunity.

Devouring as much information as I could before departing, I expected to find Rwanda as it was then being presented in the media: a model of unity, development, and recovery. Nonetheless, I found myself with many questions for the Rwandan pastors and officials who chauffeured us around the country, then amid recovering and rebuilding from the genocide. As soon as I stepped off the airplane in Kigali, I wondered, why did all the Anglican pastors and officials I met speak perfect English when Rwanda was a Francophone country?

The few parishioners and ordinary Rwandans I interacted with spoke French or Kinyarwanda. Why not the pastors, bishops, business owners, and government officials? I discovered that nearly anyone in any position of authority in postgenocide Rwanda had grown up in Uganda as a Tutsi refugee who returned to help "rebuild" the country after the genocide. As a historian, I could not help but wonder what this dynamic meant for the sociopolitical context of the country.

In the years afterward, I delved into Rwanda's history and its Anglican Church, making a second trip to the country in 2007. I spoke publicly, and also privately, with many ordinary Rwandans. I read the secondary literature and made numerous trips to archives in Britain, Belgium, and Uganda. Over time, my research brought me to the conclusion that all is not as it seems with contemporary Rwanda and its Anglican Church. The purpose of this book is to explain how and why. I suspect that not everyone in the Anglican Church will be pleased with the arguments they find here. To those I know in the Anglican Church who may be disappointed, I offer this: the truth will not only set us free, but it will also help, and is indeed necessary, to secure a more stable and inclusive Rwanda.

To many others, I owe a debt of gratitude. I am grateful to Dr. Robert Maxon of West Virginia University for introducing me to a lifelong passion in African history. I am also appreciative of the late Dr. Jan Vansina (1929–2017) of the University of Wisconsin for reading my initial draft of chapter 1 and offering his encouraging feedback. This book has benefited most richly from the insights and constructive feedback of Dr. David Newbury of Smith College, who, in addition to reading the original manuscript, encouraged me several times over the years of its completion. I am also grateful to Dr. Timothy Longman of Boston University, who read and offered feedback on the manuscript. The archival staff at the Cadbury Research Library at the University of Birmingham, the archivists at the Africa Museum in Tervuren, Belgium, the archivists at the Cambridge Center for Christianity Worldwide, and the staff at the Uganda Christian University Library in Mukono, Uganda, were always exceedingly helpful, and I am grateful. I owe Mr. Diron Darst Smith a word of thanks for providing some lodging, transportation, and entertainment during a long research period in the United Kingdom in 2012.

I also owe much to my home institution, Longwood University in Farmville, Virginia, for providing most of the generous financial support to make this book possible. I offer my gratitude to many ordinary Rwandans who shared their frank views with me about their country during my field research. Your names are buried in my files and they will never be shared. To the pioneering men and women of the Ruanda Mission: I stand in personal awe at the work you did. I have tried to tell of your lives and work fairly and admirably, even if at times critically. Lastly, but most importantly, I am eternally grateful to my wife, Jessica Cantrell, for her love, support, patience, and encouragement as I pursued this obsession over the years.

Revival and Reconciliation

Introduction

RWANDA HAS MANY NAMES. It is often referred to in recent years as the "Singapore of Africa" for its intense urbanization and investment in the telecommunications industry and, in a more romantic vein, the "Land of a Thousand Hills" or the "Switzerland of Africa" because of its steep, mountainous topography. Prior to independence in 1959, it was the Belgian Protectorate of Ruanda-Urundi. When European colonialists arrived in the late nineteenth century, they found a smaller kingdom of Ruanda ruled by the Nyiginya Dynasty, perhaps amounting to no more than half to two-thirds of the area of the current state. Regardless of the name, Rwanda is a tiny country, one of the smallest in Africa, most closely approximating in size the U.S. state of Vermont or the European nation of Belgium. Ironically, the word itself, "Rwanda," means "the surface occupied by a swarm or a scattering," semantically suggestive of a "large space."[1]

For most people outside the region, Rwanda was first known as the place where genocide happened, when many hundreds of thousands of people were slaughtered in 1994. Even during the killings, Rwanda remained obscure and its genocide remote. On April 15, 1994, nearly two weeks into the genocide, the *New York Times* described Rwanda as "small, poor, and globally insignificant." Not surprisingly, when the genocide began, it appeared to many observers as a simple, two-sided conflict in which hundreds of thousands of Tutsi, and many Hutu, were massacred while the world watched in horror. Western media outlets cast the genocide as a primitive African war between two ancient tribal groups. In April 1994, the *New York Times* ran a story titled "Tribes Battle for Rwandan Capital." The *Washington Post*, one week after the genocide began, similarly referred to events in Rwanda as "tribal killings." In July, the *Los Angeles Times* summarized what had happened as a government "controlled by the Hutu tribe" carrying out attacks against the "minority Tutsi tribe." Such an overtly simplistic and uninformed view of Rwanda and its people helped the world excuse itself from getting involved in 1994, but it also began a debate over exactly who were the Hutu and Tutsi.[2]

Afterward, popular films like the 2004 *Hotel Rwanda* and numerous books and survivors' testimonials stirred some degree of popular interest but added little academic knowledge about the nation's history, the killings, or why they happened. Few of these accounts, from the early months and years after the genocide, delved deeply into the complex social divisions in Rwanda and how the Europeans racialized the Hutu-Tutsi division during the colonial era. Nor has any scholarly research sought to understand the role of the Anglican Church in abetting these divisions, both before and after the genocide.[3]

During the colonial period, most Western observers, as well as Rwandan elites on both sides, espoused a belief that the Hutu and Tutsi, as well as a tiny minority known as the Twa, were distinct tribes, even different races. The popular narrative of Rwanda's history throughout the twentieth century, a narrative ultimately birthed by nineteenth-century racial assumptions and amateurish observations, held that Rwanda was first populated by Bantu farmers known as Hutu, who were invaded and conquered by Tutsi cattle herders from the north, who founded a Nyiginya monarchy in the sixteenth century. Racist categorizations of African peoples assumed these Tutsi invaders to be from a superior, more advanced tribe and the Hutu farmers to be a backward, less-advanced people. In this view, known in African history as the "Hamitic Myth," it was right and natural that the Tutsi ruled over the Hutu. The Belgian colonialists, along with nearly every voice in the Christian missionary community, including the Anglicans, supported the Tutsi monarchy and ruled the country indirectly through the *mwami* ("king" in Kinyarwanda). When the 1959 revolution occurred, one that was both anticolonial and anti-Tutsi, the Belgians reversed course and supported Hutu majority rule. The former Tutsi rulers, as well as Tutsi commoners, became an oppressed and persecuted minority, victimized by cycles of violence under the Hutu government, violence that finally culminated in the genocide of 1994. This history, as Timothy Longman writes, "played a key role in the 1994 genocide. The ideology used to justify the genocide drew on a historical narrative developed during the colonial period which saw Hutu, Tutsi, and Twa as clear and distinct racial groups and characterized the Tutsi as recent arrivals in the region which had conquered and dominated the other groups."[4]

In the years since the genocide's end and the coming to power of a new Rwandan government, presently under Paul Kagame and the Rwandan Patriotic Front (RPF), a different, but still misleading, narrative has been popularized by the authorities in Kigali. This view insists there never were two tribes nor any such thing as a distinct "Hutu" or a "Tutsi." Rather, what was called Hutu or Tutsi is presented as nothing more than an economic distinction between two groups who supposedly lived in harmony before the country was "racialized" and "tribal-ized" by the Europeans in the early twentieth century. While conducting field research in Rwanda in 2004, it was inaccurately explained to me by an Anglican missionary that the term "Tutsi" meant no more than "one who owned ten cows."[5]

The present narrative emanating out of Rwanda serves two purposes. One, it masks the oppression presently carried out against the majority by the new, and mostly Tutsi, postgenocide rulers in the RPF. Two, by blaming the Hutu-Tutsi conflict on the Europeans, it exacerbates the guilt complex harbored by many Western observers, especially those in the churches and aid industry, for doing nothing to stop the genocide. Presently, the postgenocide Anglican Church in Rwanda and its Western supporters rarely if ever question the RPF's narrative that precolonial Rwanda was harmonious and united between Hutu and Tutsi before the Europeans arrived, obfuscating the nation's history and the true nature of the current political climate in the country. Both views presented here, one of a primordial, "tribal" Rwanda and the other of a "harmonious" precolonial Rwanda, represent false narratives of the past and, in the case of the latter, are dangerous and detrimental to the future. Understanding why requires an exploration into Rwanda's early history and colonial period. Bringing clarity to the Anglican Church's role, both during the colonial and postcolonial eras, and its presently close relationship to the regime, requires an unbiased analysis of its own history as well. Herein lies the purpose of this book.[6]

Such competing narratives and muddled accounts of Rwanda's past are understandable. Prior to the genocide, Rwanda was arguably known only to a few government officials scattered across the Western capitals, a handful of mostly European and British missionaries, and a few college and university professors who harbored an interest in the Great Lakes Region of Africa. Although Rwanda was a "widely researched country, particularly after 1945," the historian Gérard Prunier noted, "the Great Lakes were looked upon as a kind of intellectual backwater up to the 1990s." The small community of scholars and academics who read, questioned, and understood Rwanda's history—occasionally referred to as the "old case-load" scholars—penned many of their books and articles before the genocide. Even here, the vast majority were Belgian or French academics, making them difficult to access for most Americans. Together they constitute a group of professional scholars who understood the country's history and who wrote from primary sources, but with many of their writings coming prior to the genocide, they did not always link Rwanda's early history into what happened in 1994.[7]

When a "new case-load" of historians, political scientists, and researchers weighed in after the genocide, as many have done, they did so with more clarity and insight on the present, yet few of them explained the relationship between Rwanda's precolonial and colonial history, and how its early history set the stage for its postindependence experience and the genocide. Many have offered a critical analysis of the present political climate in Rwanda and observe how many of the same forces that exacerbated the killings are still at work but failed to account for the historical roots of these forces. Nor has there been much dispassionate analysis on the role of the Anglican Church in Rwanda's troubled past. A few academic works by the "new case-load" scholars have addressed the history and role of other church bodies. Among them are J. J. Carney's *Rwanda before the Genocide: Catholic Politics and Ethnic Discourse in the Late Colonial Era* and Timothy Longman's *Christianity and Genocide in Rwanda*, which focuses on the Presbyterian Church. Nor did the "old caseload" scholars pay much attention to the Anglicans and their role in Rwanda's history, and very few recent writings have done so in any academic sense. This book, by a "new case-load" scholar, draws upon primary sources, field research, and the work of the "old case-load" scholars to offer a balanced history of Rwanda and its genocide with a critical focus on the history and role of the Anglican Church in both the past and the present.[8]

History, however, can be a perilous craft in Rwanda's case. History is more than a recounting of past events. More often it is a weapon wielded by those who have power to justify their rule over those who do not. Power in Rwanda is presently in the hands of the ruling RPF, who carefully manages a false narrative of the country's precolonial past because "the government has expressed a clear vested interest" in what is regarded a "highly sensitive topic." Doing so requires the omission of a considerable amount of scholarship, creating a lack of awareness among young Rwandans and casual outside observers of the country's violent and tumultuous history. Knowledge about its past, especially the precolonial past, is difficult to access even by Rwandans, many of whom know little apart from what they are told by the authorities in the church and state. When the RPF took power in 1994, the Rwandan Ministry of Education placed a moratorium on teaching Rwandan history in the country's schools, both for ideological reasons, as this work will demonstrate, and more practically because the education sector was devastated by the genocide. School buildings and supplies were decimated, and nearly 75 percent of its teachers were either killed or jailed for alleged participation. In 2007, at a dinner party in Ruhengeri, seat of the Anglican Diocese of Shyira, former bishop John Rucyahana gathered his staff and asked me to "tell of Rwanda's history" because "these young people do not know their own history."[9]

The caution necessitated by the political climate of present-day Rwanda also compounds the difficulty for professional researchers and writers of its history. Helen Hintjens has documented the risks and challenges for researchers in Rwanda, noting ordinary Rwandans cannot speak frankly about the past. She further claims scholars and researchers must engage in "quiet diplomacy" to avoid risks and accusations. Filip Reyntjens and several well-known scholars are considered persona non grata, and several are no longer allowed into the country. Some researchers have been detained and expelled. In 2006, while conducting field research for her book *Whispering Truth to Power*, American scholar Susan Thomson was detained by the Ministry of Local Government in Kigali for "reeducation" about the "real Rwanda" since her subjects were "filling [her] head with negative ideas." Thomson's passport was confiscated until the government was satisfied that she had been "adequately reeducated."[10]

In 2007, following a previous visit in 2004, I was invited to travel throughout Rwanda with an ad hoc committee called the Anglican Mission Board to scout out development opportunities on behalf of the Anglican Mission in the Americas (AMIA), a U.S.-based province of the diocese of Rwanda under the leadership of then archbishop Emmanuel Kolini. Throughout my travels with the committee, and afterward when I stayed behind to make further investigations, I conducted interviews and made inquiries into Rwanda's history and political climate. I made notes and spoke privately, or so I assumed, with Hutu and Tutsi who shared their frank views about the situation in Rwanda. At the time, my professional status as a historian of Africa was known but my research aim was not fully understood. Yet, very soon after my return in 2007, the Anglican Mission Board was promptly disbanded, and I was disinvited from returning to Rwanda with AMIA, without explanation. My first critical article on Rwanda was published the following year and I became something of a persona non grata myself among numerous AMIA clergymen.[11]

Despite these barriers for current researchers, a generation of professional historians were writing voluminously of the country's history before the genocide. With access to archaeology, linguistics, historical records, and carefully screened oral tales and genealogies of precolonial Rwanda, they have made it possible to unravel the many competing narratives of its past and arrive at an academic analysis of its complex history. Precolonial history in Rwanda is still not an exact science. The culture was preliterate before the European arrival, and its history was maintained through oral tales and traditions. Historians have used these tales to reconstruct Rwanda's precolonial past, exercising the necessary caution required by the inexact nature of oral sources—inexact because names and events were often projected into the distant past and

accepted as part of antiquity because of the legitimacy that adheres to longevity. As a result, some disagreement exists over the exact timing of events or
over the births and deaths of kings, or even if some figures existed at all. Taken
together, however, and with enough academic interrogation, the oral chro-
nologies and genealogies of the Rwandan kingdom provide for a general
reconstruction of its history.[12]

This book also offers a much-needed history of the Anglican Church of
Rwanda, from its beginning to the present. In addition to an academic presentation of its history, the book argues that, from the start, the founders of the
church accepted erroneous myths about Rwanda and its people and, as a
result, were too closely aligned with whomever was in power. As such, the
church endorsed the ruling authorities' misleading account of Rwanda's history and failed to take account of its own history in exacerbating ethnic tensions prior to genocide. The book shows that this tendency persisted through
the postcolonial period of Rwanda's history, and thus left the church culpable
to a degree in the genocide. Lastly, and ominously, the book argues that the
present Anglican authorities are also too closely allied with Paul Kagame and
the ruling RPF, with perhaps dire consequences to come for all.

To do so, I draw upon a rich body of primary sources that includes many
observations, letters, field notes, and essays written by the Anglican missionaries on the ground, printed and made available to supporters in a quarterly
circular titled *Ruanda Notes*, replaced with *Partners Together* in 1971, itself
replaced by *Mid-Africa Ministry News* in 1999. These observations and letters,
which have never been fully used in previous works on the Anglican Church's
history, recount the challenges and successes by the missionaries in the field as
they sought to ensconce themselves in a Belgian Protectorate and build the
first mission stations. The missionary's letters and reports reveal slow but
steady success by the 1930s, as they sought to understand the kingdom and its
people, about whose culture and history they knew almost nothing. Additional primary source material comes from the papers of the Church Missionary Society (CMS) at the University of Birmingham, the CMS Crowther
Library in Oxford, England, and the John E. Church Papers, housed at the
Cambridge Center for Christianity Worldwide at Cambridge University. Other
archival sources come from the Africa Museum in Tervuren, Belgium, and the
Archives of the Bishop of Uganda, housed at Uganda Christian University
in Mukono, Uganda. Lastly, over the course of three research trips, two to
Rwanda and one to southwest Uganda, I conducted numerous interviews and
conversations with Anglican pastors and bishops, as well as ordinary Rwandans. While arguably the views of the Anglican clergy do not necessarily
represent the perspective of all its parishioners, and especially those of non-

Anglicans, the book makes use of the research of numerous other scholars who conducted interviews and reported on their own field research among the populace.

The first chapter of this book, "False Narratives of a Disputed Past: Precolonial Rwanda," is crucial to understanding several themes in Rwanda's precolonial history that impacted the actions and position of the Anglican Church both in the colonial period and presently. First among these was how the Nyiginya Kingdom established a pattern of co-opting new, and sometimes imported, spiritual belief systems to augment its own power and legitimacy. Both the Catholics and Anglicans were used by the ruling figures at various times to enhance their prerogatives, a historical pattern consistently misunderstood by the Western churches and missionaries. This tradition holds true in present-day Rwanda as well, where the ruling RPF uses the Anglican Church and other Western aid bodies to shore up its legitimacy to outsiders. Second, the reign of Mwami Rujugira in the mid-eighteenth century saw the adoption of historical revisionism as a means of centralizing political power and control. In redefining the historical legitimacy of kingship in Rwanda, Rujugira augmented his own power and seized control of historical narrative as the ultimate source of political authority, much as the RPF does today.

This process, of postulating a narrative designed to justify present actions based on revised history, continues in the present with the Anglican Church as a willing accomplice, as the latter chapters will demonstrate. Going further than simply adopting and abetting the RPF's current historical narrative, the Anglicans have espoused a revised version of their own history to make sense of their present position in the new Rwanda. Finally, in refutation of the reigning narrative emanating out of the country today, the first chapter shows that on the eve of European intervention, Rwanda was more conflicted and divided than ever in its history.

The second chapter, "History Intervenes: Colonialism, Christianity, and the Ruanda Mission," starts with the end of the precolonial period and the arrival of the European powers to the region. The chapter recounts the coming of the first Western missionaries to both Rwanda and Uganda, as the latter was the launching pad for the Christian entry into the Nyiginya Kingdom. The approach taken by the Anglicans and Catholics to the Rwandan kingdom was fashioned by their experiences in Uganda and help the reader understand how and why the churches acted as they initially did when confronting the people of the region. In particular, the chapter focuses on the history and arrival of the first emissaries of the Anglican Church Missionary Society (CMS) to

Rwanda, active by the 1920s and known collectively in the earlier parlance as the "Ruanda Mission."

As their work proceeded, the Ruanda Mission responded to the challenges of both interacting with the Belgian Catholics, who arrived before them and who often resisted the presence of English missionaries, and their own Anglican overseers in Uganda, with whom they were often at odds over their distinct beliefs and practices. The beliefs and practices of the Ruanda Mission, shaped in these years, provoked conflicts with the Anglican authorities throughout their history and have left an indelible stamp on the Anglican Church of Rwanda to this day. Lastly, and with great import for the future, the *Ruanda Notes* demonstrate that, from the start and throughout, the CMS missionaries accepted and endorsed the nineteenth-century Hamitic Myth's racial assumptions about Africans. While the missionaries often noted the oppression carried out by the Tutsi overlords against the Hutu, they never in these years or beyond questioned the racist and historically erroneous Hamitic version of Rwanda's history, through which the Belgians ruled over the protectorate. In this light, the Ruanda Mission became complicit, to its own detriment and to Rwanda's detriment for decades to come, in the Belgian racialization of the kingdom. When one considers the *African Rights* report of 1995, which posited that "more Rwandese citizens died in churches or parishes than anywhere else," the role of the missionaries of all church bodies in the country's history must be analyzed closely and critically, Anglicans included.[13]

Chapter 3, "Growth, Revival, and Conflict: The Anglican Church through World War II," continues, as other chapters do, with an account of Rwanda's relevant history from the 1930s through World War II. Woven through the chapter is the story of the Ruanda Mission and the Anglican Church as it continued to evangelize and grow even as it struggled with the machinations of Rwanda's history playing out in its midst. Apart from discussing the continued growth and success of the mission, the chapter focuses primarily on the East African Revival, which originated from the Ruanda Mission. Prior works, mostly by sympathetic participants, have been written on the Revival, but none have done so from a dispassionate academic perspective. The chapter places the Revival within a larger context in the region and discusses its place in Rwanda's history.

Unraveling the meaning and nature of the Revival, much of which has previously been written from a Ugandan perspective, is fundamental to making sense of the Anglican Church in Rwanda presently. The current leadership of the church sees itself as the inheritors of the Revival spirit, and many of the Tutsi returnees after the genocide reference it as the starting point for understanding their place in the new Rwanda. The church frequently recalls the

Revival as a time of unity and often leverages its memory as they seek to build a newly unified country reconciled from the events of 1994. An analysis of the Revival's history, however, reveals a sense of selective memory about what it was and was not. The chapter shows that while, on the one hand, the Revival was a unifying moment for the church, wherein all were "equal at the foot of the cross," the social divisions between Hutu and Tutsi that characterized the colonial period were becoming more deeply entrenched than ever in the 1930s, courtesy of the Belgian colonialists. Caught up in the emotionalism of the Revival, the missionaries of the Ruanda Mission turned a blind eye toward what was politically happening in their midst, in much the same fashion as today. The chapter ends with an assessment of how the practices and beliefs of the East African Revival helped grow the church in numbers yet paradoxically left it ill-equipped to navigate the political storms that engulfed the country after World War II.

The fourth chapter, "The Unraveling: The Ruanda Mission and Independence," starts with the end of World War II and covers the road to independence, continuing through the end of the genocide. The presidency of Grégoire Kayibanda, which ended in a coup in 1973, and the presidency of Juvénal Habyarimana, which ended with his assassination in April 1994, are analyzed. For the Ruanda Mission, these were years of renewed growth, but with eventual consequences. With the independence movement growing in the postwar era, the Belgium and Catholic hierarchies abandoned their long-held support for the monarchy and sympathized with the Hutu masses and their political parties. As a result, many Tutsi turned to the Anglicans for support, which grew their numbers but left them inextricably tied to the royalists. When the violence over independence began, Tutsi refugees fled to the Anglican mission stations. Having little choice but to take them in, the Anglicans soon paid the price for their support of the Tutsi monarchy. Numerous Anglican mission stations were attacked and burned by Hutu partisans. Many of the British missionary leaders were forced to flee for their safety.

The chapter analyzes the Anglican Church in this independence context. The sources reveal a church that tried desperately to remain apolitical in these years. Inclined by theological nature toward political apathy, the church remained fixated on Gospel conversions and Revival, even celebrating, at its Silver Jubilee in 1946, the success it was having among the Tutsi. Rarely did any of the missionary leaders question their support for the monarchy until it was too late. Rank-and-file missionaries persisted in seeing Rwanda's troubles as merely a "tribal conflict" resolving itself for the better; for them, "better" meant the preservation of the Tutsi monarchy. In many of their writings, the main fear of the Ruanda Mission was that independence would lead to communism, an outcome to be decidedly avoided in the Cold War context of the period. For all these reasons, the Ruanda Mission found itself on the wrong side of history at independence and with dire consequences for itself. More ominously, the theological tendency of the Anglicans to remain myopically focused on individual salvation and avoid sociopolitical questioning left it with no indigenous African leadership equipped to lead the church and preserve its own independence under a succession of dictatorial presidents in a Hutu-majority Rwanda. Without exonerating the church for its own actions in these years, the chapter illuminates how the theological tendencies and practices of the Anglican Church from its founding left its African leadership ill-equipped to do otherwise.

The fifth and final chapter, "Revival and Reconciliation: The Anglican Church in Postgenocide Rwanda," discusses the postgenocide Anglican Church and its role in the aftermath. The chapter examines the efforts of the church to aid in the process of reconciliation and rebuilding, including the bringing of considerable amounts of development dollars from Western churches. In a spiritual light, the chapter reveals how the church is leveraging the memory of the East African Revival to process its place in a new but traumatized Rwanda. The church, mostly led by Tutsi returnees from Uganda, arguably does this not only on its own behalf but on behalf of hundreds of thousands of Tutsi returnees from abroad. In this sense, the church has demonstrated it has much to offer the process of healing and forgiveness, albeit with a decidedly selective historical memory at times.

From a political standpoint, the chapter reveals a more troubling position for the Anglicans, insisting that many of the same colonial and postcolonial patterns have continued in the postgenocide Anglican Church, with perhaps another round of dire consequences to follow in the future. Amid promoting spiritual revival in the name of reconciliation, the church has allowed itself, as the church often did in the past, to become complicit in supporting an oppressive regime far from being a model of transparent democracy. In numerous ways, the present Anglican Church espouses the RPF's politicized version of Rwandan history and the genocide, a false construct and misleading narrative meant to bury the regimes' own crimes and its deplorable human rights record since 1994. The chapter further shows how many Western church bodies and aid organizations, with otherwise good intentions, are unwilling to question either the RPF or its supporters in the church, with possibly unfortunate consequences in the future for themselves and Rwanda. The book ends with a concluding chapter titled "History Faces the Present," wherein Rwanda's present situation is discussed along with constructive actions the church should make toward peace and reconciliation.

CHAPTER ONE

False Narratives of a Disputed Past

Precolonial Rwanda

W HILE A CHAPTER on precolonial history might seem distant, and even unnecessary, many of the roots of Rwanda's current troubles can be seen growing early on in its past. Briefly recounting the rise of the Nyiginya Kingdom and its history as the monarchy of what became Rwanda, the chapter further shows how the oppression of the Hutu at the hands of the Tutsi monarchy was the norm—an oppression that did not originate with the colonialists but was exacerbated by them with the collusion of the Anglican missionaries and others. Bringing to light these misleading and ill-informed accounts of the past is necessary to process the various ways in which the first outside observers misunderstood the violent history and politics of the Nyiginya monarchy. These misunderstandings seeded the ground for the killings in the twentieth century and shaped the response of the first Anglican missionaries to Rwanda.

While the remainder of the chapters rely mainly on my field research and primary sources from the Anglican Church, this one makes use of secondary works by earlier historians who wrote from primary sources to reconstruct the precolonial history of the kingdom. First among their number was the late Jan Vansina. A Belgian anthropologist by training, Vansina was sent by the Institut pour la Recherche Scientifique en Afrique Centrale (IRSAC) in Brussels to conduct the first professional studies of Central Africa. Arguing that "oral testimonies not only provided accounts of the past, but when carefully analyzed could be subjected to the same rigor of analysis that applied to all other historical sources," Vansina pioneered the use of oral history in the then-emerging field of African history as he conducted interviews among the Kuba peoples of south-central Congo.[1]

Stationed in Rwanda with IRSAC in 1957, as the independence movement was underway, Vansina recorded the oral narratives of the precolonial kingdom, known as the Ibiteekerezo. The earliest written reconstructions of Rwanda's history were mostly based on these stories, which were arranged in the order of kings and maintained by the official keepers of the dynastic succession lists of the kingdom. Vansina's methodology was to seek out the "experts on each hill," ascertain what they knew, and then send assistants to the various subjects, Hutu and Tutsi alike, from sub chiefdom to sub chiefdom, to record all the traditions "known to the most knowledgeable people." With a historian's mind, Vansina gathered up all the other literary traditions so he could "contrast them with the genres of the Ibiteekerezo and dynastic poetry." Four years later, the "views from the Rwandan past were no longer outrageously one-sided." His sampling method validated the sources and withstood historical scrutiny.[2]

In 2004 Vansina used this research, collected more than fifty years ago in the waning years of colonial rule, to publish *Antecedents to Modern Rwanda: The Nyiginya Kingdom*, a pathbreaking book because it drew upon sources now almost entirely neglected, including ample German sources largely disregarded by the field. Published at a time when little historical depth accompanied the writings on the causes of the genocide, he sought to remind his readers that modern Rwanda and the genocide could not be understood without comprehending its "antecedents" in Rwanda's precolonial history, including his argument that Hutu and Tutsi identities did in fact exist prior to European colonialism, a claim disputed by the RPF, Anglican Church figures, and other apologists for the regime. As evidence, the Institute of Research and Dialogue for Peace (IRDP) in Kigali, "without a single source offered to substantiate" its claim, disputed Vansina's thoroughly researched arguments. Nonetheless, neglecting Vansina's work makes it necessary to revert to earlier, outdated, or incomplete accounts. Other secondary sources used throughout include the works of David and Catharine Newbury, the late Alison Des Forges (1942–2009), René Lemarchand, Jean-Pierre Chrétien, Gérard Prunier, Filip Reyntjens, and others.[3]

Origins

From at least 2,500 years ago, the country known today as Rwanda was populated by Bantu-speaking peoples who had knowledge of both agriculture and cattle-keeping and who also knew how to smelt and forge iron. From the last millennium before Christ, these farming people began to move east and south out of northern Cameroon and southeast Nigeria, both through and around the equatorial forests of the Congo. Rather than being a singular organized movement, over hundreds of years, small groupings settled into a variety of ecological zones throughout the rain forest and adapted their agricultural techniques to newer environments. With iron tools and new crops, they adapted well, living interspersed with earlier inhabitants who relied on hunting, trapping, and gathering. Their population was robust and grew dramatically, forcing each new generation to migrate further in search of additional land to clear and farm. They reached the Great Lakes Region around 500 BC, by which time their language had evolved considerably from the original tongue.[4]

Due to its climate and geography, when Bantu farmers reached Rwanda, they found a place extraordinarily well suited for agriculture. The primary crop of these early farmers, finger millet (*uboro*, in Kinyarwanda), was indigenous to West Africa and brought eastward by the Bantu, along with yams, a tuber crop. By the end of the first millennium AD, the banana tree arrived in the region, coming originally from Southeast Asia. Bananas produce a caloric yield ten times greater than the yam and are ideally suited to evergreen rainforests. Unlike yams, the "absence of a dry season does not hurt them" and they require the clearing of "only about two-thirds of the trees on the field," rather than a complete clearing required for yams and other tubers. As an added benefit of less clearing, banana trees produce a "micro-environment freer of the *Anopheles* mosquito and hence malaria." The forest regenerates faster, and banana trees themselves require very little maintenance. Unlike most crops, they don't deplete the soil of nutrients, thriving year after year without rotation. Useful for both food and beer-making, the banana, more so than any other single crop, occupies a place of agricultural and historical importance for the region, and quickly became the primary crop of Uganda and Rwanda, attested to by more than "sixty terms for banana varieties alone, and another thirty to forty for parts of the plant and stages of preparation."[5]

The coming of the banana tree had social and political ramifications for early Rwanda. Traditionally, the labor required to continually clear fields and cultivate yams was considered the primary task of men. Owing to the less intensive work of raising bananas after planting, and with less work needed for their preparation as a food, society in the region was transformed. The task of agriculture was handed over to women, freeing the men to engage in other pursuits, such as seeking out sources of protein and engaging in warfare, with its concomitant political repercussions like centralized kingdom-building. Early state-building, in the form of kingship, was further encouraged by dramatic population increases because of the bananas' high caloric yield, not to mention the health and longevity benefits of a more malaria-free environment. The region also progressed economically as family heads or chiefs who controlled stands of banana trees could use them to attract followers who were without such lands, forming "significant repositories of lineage wealth transmitted through inheritance." With abundant food, favorable soil and climate, and proximity to forest, pasture, and water resources, the area attracted immigrants from various origins. Over the centuries this became a cultural melting pot, in which many new social forms emerged.[6]

As a result of the social and political changes wrought by these various dynamics, when the first Europeans arrived in the region by 1900, they found a diversity of cultural and political forms. One of these was the Nyiginya monarchy, under the rule of a *mwami*, the ritually consecrated leader of the political community. The closest parallel European position would be "the king," although in most cases in Africa, the leader lacked the executive powers of European kings. The term *mwami* was used in a wide range of political units stretching west of Rwanda; indeed, the origins of the term (and of the office) seem to have been associated with the forest societies east of the Congo River. In accordance with the diffusionist theory of history, the Europeans assumed *superior cultural forms*, such as the Nyiginya monarchy, were brought to the region by outside migrants. In short, the Europeans adopted an overly reductionist, and ultimately racial, vision of the population. They found a Tutsi population, roughly 15 percent, whom they assumed to be the ruling class, when in reality only 5–10 percent of the Tutsi were aristocratic. In the same fashion, they assumed the Hutu, roughly 85 percent, were a servile farming class to the Tutsi aristocracy, when in fact at the time of their arrival, after Rwabugiri's death, many if not most Hutu had become independent of the rule of the Nyiginya royal court. Despite these erroneous assumptions, for the Europeans, the existence of a Tutsi aristocracy ruling over a majority population of Hutu farmers provided a direct confirmation of nineteenth-century Western racial assumptions about Africans.[7]

Informed in no small part by nineteenth-century Darwinian "Race Science," numerous scholars as well as the popular mindset of the time held Africans as an inferior race of people, incapable of advanced civilization and culture, often labeled "Negroid" in the outdated literature of the era. To Europeans, the sophisticated court life of the Tutsi aristocracy, with an undeniably advanced culture and the trappings of regal kingship, begged explanation, which came first from the writings of John Hanning Speke (1827–64). Speke was a British explorer who made several journeys into East Africa and the Great Lakes Region in the 1850s. He later proposed that the kingdoms he encountered in the region were founded by "foreigners, who had invaded and taken possession of them, leaving the agricultural aborigines to till the ground." He argued that this supposedly advanced race originally hailed from Ethiopia, the homeland of the Nilotic peoples who did indeed migrate southward into

East Africa (but not Rwanda), whom Speke referred to as "Gallas or Abyssinians." With no evidence whatsoever, he regarded these peoples as "Christians of the greatest antiquity." With specific regard to Rwanda, Speke contended that the "Watusi" were likewise the descendants of these external conquerors who founded the southernmost monarchy of the Abyssinians.[8]

In 1930 a British professor and ethnologist at Oxford University named Charles Gabriel Seligman (1873–1940) expanded upon the supposedly superior racial origins of the Tutsi. In a book titled *Races of Africa*, Seligman appeared to legitimize what was already in circulation, that the indigenous Bantu Africans were indeed an inferior Negroid race. As such, he argued, any evidence of sophisticated society, including culture, complex social structures, kingship, and even ironworking, were introduced into the Great Lakes Region, including Rwanda, by a race of people he renamed "Hamites," the supposed ancestors of Speke's Abyssinians. The term "Hamites" and the theory that followed were loosely taken from the biblical story of Noah's son Ham, who in the Book of Genesis saw his father unclothed in his tent and was cursed for his indiscretion: "Ham, the father of Canaan . . . saw the nakedness of his father. . . . And Noah awoke from his wine . . . and said, 'Cursed be Canaan: a servant of servants he shall be unto his brethren.'" The Catholic White Fathers, who were the first missionaries in Rwanda, were so convinced of this that, in 1979, they believed that they had found the very tomb of Ham himself in Kintu's sacred woods in Uganda.[9]

Caucasians, according to the theory, descended from Noah's favored sons, Shem and Japheth, while Ham's descendants migrated to the Horn of Africa and Ethiopia (Abyssinia, in earlier times). More recently, in accordance with diffusionist history, the "Hamites" supposedly moved southward into East Africa. There they introduced cattle, ironworking, and the components of advanced civilization and culture. Owing to their supposed superiority, cursed yet still related to the more advanced Caucasian peoples, they established rule over the less advanced Bantu-Negroid farmers—the Hutu, in Rwanda's case.

This notion, referred to at an earlier time as the "Hamitic Hypothesis" but better understood now as a myth, predated both Speke and Seligman. As early as the sixth century BC, and persisting through the Middle Ages, Europeans, Arabs, and Jews had labeled Africans as "Hamites" to account for their supposed inferiority. The concept was used as a justification for African slavery after AD 1500. Speaking of its nineteenth-century manifestation, Edith Sanders explained the Hamitic Myth's central tenant, that "everything of value ever found in Africa was brought there by the Hamites, allegedly a branch of the Caucasian race." Seligman's account provided a modern, pseudoscientific revision of the now-discredited theory, one that allowed Europeans to explain the obvious evidence of advanced civilization in Rwanda, while still espousing the racial inferiority of the Bantu/Hutu majority.[10]

The impact of the Hamitic Myth was considerable and lengthy. Oxford University continued to publish Seligman's book into the 1970s. Throughout the colonial period and beyond in Rwanda, Europeans believed in the supposed Hamitic, superior origins of the Tutsi, whom they incorrectly believed were descendants of cattle-herding Nilotic migrants to the east in Kenya and Tanzania. First the Germans and then the Belgians, who ruled Rwanda after World War I, supported Tutsi rule over the Hutu majority based on the former's alleged racial superiority. That the missionary community in Rwanda accepted the idea as well as the Hamitic Myth is evident in the letters and writings of the earliest missionaries in the field. Leonard Sharp, one of the leading personalities in the Ruanda Mission, wrote to supporters of the mission in September 1922: "All the chiefs are Batutsi, a race distinct from the ordinary African. They are thought to have migrated from ancient Egypt or Abyssinia [Ethiopia]. They own all the cattle and rule the slave race Bahutu."[11]

Although numerous twentieth-century historians and scholars seemed convinced of the outside, Nilotic origins of the Tutsi, *no empirical evidence exists* to suggest this was the case. While the Nilotes did indeed migrate into East Africa from the Ethiopian Highlands with cattle herds and knowledge of ironworking, an erroneous logic followed that they moved into Rwanda and conquered the Bantu-Hutu farmers, bringing culture and kingship with them. Rather, ironworking existed among the original inhabitants' centuries before the Nilotic migrations. As David Schoenbrun notes: "Archeologists working in Buhaya, Rwanda and Burundi have unearthed evidence for early iron production dating to . . . around 500 BC." The presence of cattle in the region also predates the Nilotic migrations, refuting the notion of the Tutsi cattle herds having Nilotic origins. Research has demonstrated that the Bantu farmers in Rwanda were practicing small-scale cattle-keeping by the end of the first millennia.[12]

One misleading corpus of evidence seized upon by proponents of the Nilotic origins of the Tutsi is the physical and genetic differences among Rwandans, such as the greater average height of the Tutsi over the Hutu (typically five inches) or the existence of genetic variations such as the higher capacity of Tutsi to digest the unique milk sugar known as lactose or the higher prevalence among the Hutu of the sickle cell blood gene, which provided greater resistance to malaria. While some take these slight genetic variations as distinct racial markers, they are all explained by centuries of Tutsi inbreeding. Tutsi clans typically married only among themselves, which accounts, along with more reliable access to meat protein and milk calcium, for their height advantage. As Longman writes in refutation, "Even if claims of physical distinctions between the two groups had historical merit, which they do not, the historic flexibility of group membership and the frequency of intermarriage would have eliminated the reliability of judging individuals by their appearance. What distinguishes the two groups, ultimately, is the *idea* that they have *different historical origins*." David Newbury concurs that these "isolated facts [of physical differences among the population] do not amount to a historical reconstruction."[13]

While generations of observers in the church and the colonial administrations of Rwanda believed there was an external invasion by a superior race of Nilotic invaders who established a Tutsi monarchy, the Bantu-speaking agriculturalists who settled Rwanda were never conquered by outsiders until the European invasions of the early twentieth century. The indigenous population already had an advanced culture based on a mix of farming and cattle-rearing centuries before the Nilotic migrations to the north began. The Tutsi were not the descendants of Nilotic-speaking peoples from Ethiopia, and whether anyone ever descended from the biblical Ham is irrelevant here. Hutu and Tutsi were never separate races nor even separate ethnic groups. They were culturally the same people who existed in the same lineages and clans, some of whom farmed and some of whom reared cattle. They spoke the same language, Kinyarwanda, and shared the same space for centuries prior to the Nilotic invasions to the north. As this chapter will demonstrate, the rigid social and political divisions that later came to divide the two groups evolved over a long period of time leading up to the nineteenth century.

Owing to the earlier Hamitic Myth, it is difficult nonetheless to overstate the impact of the Western world's initial and gross misreading of Rwandan history. The thesis that regarded the Tutsi as a separate, superior race of outside invaders was the original poison in Rwanda's well. In the eyes of the colonial world, the Hutu became short, stocky unsophisticated tillers of the soil who knew nothing of kingship and culture. The Tutsi were tall, regal cattle herders who brought civilization and culture to the backward Bantu; more Caucasian than African, admirable cultural cousins of the Europeans who saw themselves as bringing civilization and culture to Africa. In effect, Hutu and Tutsi were typecast into two separate racial groups. As a result, "different identity markers were affixed to Rwandan populations" from the beginning, dictating the terms of "colonial historiography" throughout the nation's history down to the present.[14]

The myth of racial separateness, which lay at the heart of the Tutsi's supposed origins, was taught for decades into the twentieth century in the Rwandan schools and churches. Generations of both Hutu and Tutsi elites accepted this racialized version of their own history, reinforced by the colonial state and the postcolonial governments themselves. This racialized concept of identity, "which still structures the outlook and self-perceptions of many Rwandans," is rooted in this now-discredited notion of the "foreign origins of the Tutsi population." The same narrative, while devoid of its Hamitic racial lingo, persisted through the genocide and beyond in the mind of an uninformed Western public that persisted, and often continues to persist, in seeing Hutu and Tutsi as separate "tribes." Unsurprisingly, when the genocide erupted, it was in part the culmination of a false narrative in which the Hutu majority in 1994, encouraged by "Hutu Power" fanatics, saw themselves as the true and original Rwandans and the Tutsi as non-Rwandan outsiders—that is, "Nilo-Hamite" invaders deserving to be expelled after the revolution and ultimately eradicated in 1994.[15]

Yet still, by the time the Europeans arrived in Rwanda in the last years of the nineteenth century, a clear social and political division did exist between Hutu and Tutsi, a division favoring the Tutsi and fraught with violence between the two. As such, Rwanda, in the centuries leading up to the end of the nineteenth century, was not united and harmonious. Since the genocide, the current Rwandan government publicly maintains there was never any meaningful difference between Hutu and Tutsi for the purpose of masking its own Tutsi origins and blaming the genocide on the West. With the force of law, the authorities in the church and state depict the country as having been harmonious and united before the European colonialists caused their troubles. While this argument serves the country well by earning it guilt-capital in the form of aid and resources from mostly American churches and developmental organizations, it obfuscates the divisions and conflicts that still plague Rwanda and the Great Lakes region. The Hamitic Myth is deservedly discredited in the minds of all but the most uninformed. But the vision of a Rwanda united and harmonious before the Europeans arrived must also be discredited before the nation can experience the reconciliation and healing brought by a true and accurate accounting of history. To do so requires another return to the more recent past.

By the seventeenth century, the people who inhabited Rwanda were organized into family lineages and clans. Lineage refers to specific patrilineal family lines encompassing roughly three to six generations within a clan. These clan groups, mostly identified by the geographic region where they lived, intermingled, traded, and shared many of the same cultural patterns. Nor were lineage and clan identities permanent as they moved and evolved over time. Additionally, membership was not "exclusive," as a "variety of ways" existed for people to be "incorporated into family groups different from that of their birth." Most of these early agriculturalists also kept small numbers of cattle. Occasionally they moved in search of better lands, but by nature farmers were less inclined to leave already-tilled fields, unless a drought or an ecological catastrophe forced them to move. These farming clans constituted most of the population, and an agricultural way of life was the norm across most of western, southwestern, and central Rwanda. Lastly, for most of Rwanda's history, these farming clans were *not* known as "Hutu."[16]

Rather, the term "Hutu" has unclear origins from an earlier time and from beyond what is considered Rwanda, referring to people in Burundi, parts of northeastern Congo, Angola, and the Kigoma region of northwest Tanzania. In these regions, the term "Hutu" has different meanings. In Rwanda's case, the word "hutu" originally meant "servant." As a Kinyarwanda term, the word can still be used in this sense. For instance, "the person carrying my luggage is my *hutu* [servant]," although in postgenocide Rwanda, the use of the term is uncommon and discouraged by legal imperative because of its political implications. The term "Hutu" as a social class identifier in Rwanda "developed gradually among the peasant population to denote their common social position." As late as the eighteenth century, the oral chronicles of Rwanda draw no political or social distinction between "Hutu" and "Tutsi." Only after roughly 1800 did the terms "Hutu" and "Tutsi" come to identify exclusive political and social categories.[17]

In the northeast of Rwanda, the region was occupied by a smaller number of clans who were primarily pastoralist cattle herders. By the time the kingdom of Ruanda came about in the early seventeenth century, most of the cattle breeders referred to themselves as either "Hima" or "Tutsi," who were smaller in numbers. The Hima were known over a much larger area of the Great Lakes Region, with the term most likely originating in Nkore, a kingdom to the north of Rwanda in what became Uganda. Hima cattle keepers could be found across southern Uganda, northwest Tanzania, and in eastern Rwanda.[18]

The founder of the Rwandan monarchy was a Hima king known as Ndori, who originated from the north. Yet within a generation or two, the royal lineages of Ndori's dynasty, the Nyiginya, considered themselves "Tutsi," suggesting the term carried more prestige than the term "Hima," which was seemingly used to designate cattle-herding commoners, whereas "Tutsi" seems to have referred to a class of political elites among the herders. Like "Hutu," the ethnic term "Tutsi" evolved in meaning over time and was also used beyond Rwanda, referring to nonfarming cattle herders in Burundi and parts of Tanzania. In Rwanda, the usage of the word "Tutsi," referring to an elite status associated with the monarchy, gained more prestige. Eventually all cattle herders called themselves Tutsi regardless of their status or position. The designation

"Hima" eventually fell out of common usage in Rwanda. Moreover, the agricultural clans were often intermixed with herders, so those farmers who also owned cattle came to refer to themselves as Tutsi regardless of their origins, to distinguish themselves from their less-wealthy neighbors.[19]

So while clear categories based on lifestyles, then, can be identified in Rwanda by roughly 1600, the Hutu and Tutsi *did not arrive in different waves* to populate Rwanda and the differences between them essentially *developed on site.*" The bulk of the population comprised agricultural clans who farmed the land, *eventually* known as Hutu. The more open areas of the north and east, grazing land par excellence, were inhabited by cattle-herding Hima and Tutsi clans. The various terms and social descriptors at work, based on lifestyles and modes of subsistence, implied no sense of race, historical origins, or inherent ethnic superiority. If any notion of social harmony ever existed in Rwanda, it was then, even while a lack of political organization refutes any idea of unity. No unified Rwanda yet existed nor did any one kingdom dominate the region. Moreover, until "sometime after 1900, there was no general concept even of 'Rwanda.'" The original term "rwanda" was thus not an ethnonym. The awareness by the inhabitants "that they were Rwandan [used as an ethnonym] came only with the colonial period," so one can only correctly refer to the precolonial region as the "rwanda of the Nyiginya," an expansive Tutsi dynasty that forged a kingdom starting in the seventeenth century. As such, it was the Nyiginya Dynasty, not the Europeans, who unraveled the bucolic harmony the present authorities in Rwanda and the Anglican Church claim to be the case.[20]

Ruganzu Ndori and the Nyiginya Dynasty

By the end of the sixteenth century, several small political units emerged among the cattle herders on the open plains of eastern Rwanda, west of the Akagera River on the border with Tanzania. One was associated with a patrilineal descent line of the Nyiginya clan, and over the next several centuries became the founding monarchical line of the Kingdom of Ruanda. Other forms of political organization existed elsewhere in the country, but it was this region that produced the dynastic core of Rwanda. These eastern kingdoms were primarily formed of alliances between pastoralist peoples, Hima and Tutsi, whose policies during this period were directed more toward the expansion of territory available to their herds than conquering and incorporating people living within their domains, as later Hutu historians would claim. Starting near Lake Muhazi in the east, the dynasty was gradually displaced westward where the Nyiginya Kingdom was refounded at Nduga, in Central Rwanda, in the early seventeenth century by Ruganzu Ndori.[21]

The history of the early kingdom, first known through oral tales, claims Ndori as a single person, though it is possible at such an early date that his name refers to an epoch or period. Either way, Ndori, according to the dynastic tales, came from the north and was Hima, not Tutsi. Eventually, the Nyiginya Dynasty claimed Tutsi origins for itself, increasing the prestige attached to the label as its power grew in the region. Once ensconced at Nduga, Ndori solidified his power through a form of cattle clientship known in Kinyarwanda as *ubuhake*, and here geography played a determining role. Central Rwanda is hilly and devoid of wide-open grasslands. Maintaining large herds of hundreds of cattle, as the Hima did, was not feasible. Ndori subdivided the herds into a more manageable thirty to fifty heads and presented them as loans to a client. When a client accepted the loan of cattle, he entered a form of permanent submission to the patron. The cattle remained the ultimate property of the patron, who in turn assured his client of his protection. The client was obligated to help whenever needed and became a de facto vassal. The relationship was hereditary and could only be dissolved by the patron, who then resumed ownership of all the client family's cattle. Through the institution of *ubuhake*, Ndori created dozens of allies to aid in his subjugation of central Rwanda. At first, the only *ubuhake* patron was Ndori himself, but the institution was adopted by other large cattle herders who sought support from lesser ones. Eventually farmers and even Twa entered *ubuhake* relationships with Tutsi herders, pointing toward the vision of a Rwanda where Tutsi cattle herders held power over Hutu farmers.[22]

While creating allies around himself, Ndori conducted raids, mainly against other Hima and Tutsi cattle herders, not so much to conquer territory but to acquire cattle and women. Belongings were taken and huts were burned. As the raids continued, cattle-herding Tutsi often fled to less accessible areas, frequently among the farmers to the west where they were both out of Ndori's reach and in a position to extend the practice of *ubuhake* themselves to regions where it had been unknown.[23]

In this context, militarism and martial violence permeated the Nyiginya Kingdom and its emergent culture. The Rwandese-born, American political scientist Noel Twagiramungu claims Ndori "introduced the concept of leader (king or president) as simultaneously 'owner' of the army," a role embraced by the language used in Rwanda by Kagame today. Moreover, for the army to achieve success by whatever means justified all sorts of behavior, a justification later deployed by the RPF to defend its violent pacification of Rwanda and Eastern Congo after the genocide. Nonetheless, the enduring strength and discipline of Ndori's army, and the kingdom's cohesion, distinguished the Nyiginya from all its neighbors for centuries to come.[24]

In addition to extending *ubuhake* clientship, Ndori made use of an indigenous, regional belief system known as the Gihanga Cult to legitimize Nyiginya rule. In the mythology of the region, Gihanga was a mythical king who founded the first monarchies, including an account of the origins of Hutu, Tutsi, and Twa. Ndori popularized the Gihanga Cult by constructing a shrine in his court at Nduga, where a fire was maintained, which supposedly was the very fire lit by Gihanga at the beginning of time. He maintained a cattle herd that he claimed was descended from Gihanga's own cattle. By introducing the Gihanga mythology into central Rwanda and maintaining control of the sacred fire, Ndori claimed it as "proof of apostolic succession: the Nyiginya king truly was the direct and legitimate descendant of the great conqueror Gihanga."[25]

Ndori's incorporation of the Gihanga Myth further provides the first illustration of a reoccurring narrative throughout Rwanda's history, and one that persists to the present. During periods of political turmoil and social stress, such as the extension of Nyiginya hegemony, the ruling elites have repeatedly adopted both indigenous and foreign spiritual systems to affirm their legitimacy. As Nyiginya power grew, the Gihanga narrative provided the founding myth for the dynasty, legitimizing its rule and establishing divine origins for itself. Ndori's actions were further buttressed by his adoptive queen mother Nyirarumaga, who reformed the *Ibisigo* to support his sovereignty. The *Ibisigo* were the historical poems that "listed the names and deeds of the past kings, from their origin up to the time of their composition." Nyirarumaga's revisions of the *Ibisigo* were the first of many instances in Rwanda, including presently, where history was revised to support those in power. In the mid-eighteenth century, another *mwami*, Rujugira, drew legitimacy from a belief system known as the Ryangombe Cult, whereby he changed the rituals of royal succession to support his own rule. As Christianity became entrenched in various forms and stages in Rwanda, both the rulers and nonelites sought ways to leverage the new Western faith and its rituals to define and secure their social and political status in the face of change. One of the arguments made later in this book is that the present ruling authorities in postgenocide Rwanda are doing the same with the backing of the Anglican Church.[26]

Mythology also served to reinforce erroneous understandings of history. When the missionaries undertook the Christianization of Rwanda in the early years of the twentieth century, the Gihanga Cult was condemned as heresy, yet when the Europeans claimed the Tutsi to be Nilotic invaders descended from the biblical Ham, the story set well with a Nyiginya dynasty already predisposed toward believing mythological stories about its supposedly venerable and hoary past. In this sense, one false narrative replaced another. The

Hamitic Myth, like the Gihanga Myth, emphasized the unique, and in this case racial, origins of the Tutsi as the legitimate conquerors of the region. The mythology of Gihanga and his sons was replaced by the mythology of racial separateness, falsely taking its justification from the story of Noah and his sons. The descendants of Gihanga became the descendants of Ham, who conquered the region from the north, just as the Gihanga Cult itself came from the north.

In the centuries after Ndori, his successors expanded the kingdom, even amid their own political intrigues and frequent coup d'états. In the mid-eighteenth century, Cyirima Rujugira seized power by force from the designated successor and expanded the number of armies in the northern and western regions of Nyiginya control. Aware of his status as a usurper who came to power in a coup d'état against the designated successor, known as Rwaka, Rujugira revised the royal customs to legitimize his authority. Like other kings before him, Rwaka was an initiate in the Ryangombe Cult, which represented the Rwandan spirit deity Immandwa. Rujugira used this to claim Rwaka was an illegitimate king because he had bowed before a representative of Ryangombe and no Nyiginya king could "be the subject of another." Rujugira claimed the throne for himself and decreed thereafter no king could be initiated into the cult. He further dictated that the king would be represented by a "king of the initiates," appointed by Rujugira from his own lineage and made to reside at the court. Such a move "allowed the king to maintain control over the cult but also disassociated him from it," thereby serving to "strengthen the legitimacy of royal power to the victims of that same power, by making desirable and even to some degree accessible the legitimizing rituals of the very powers that oppressed them." Like Ndori before him, and others who came after, Rujugira made use of spiritual rituals to augment his prerogatives.[27]

With his position secure, and to avoid the crises that plagued the dynasty every time an *mwami* died, Rujugira also reorganized the role of the royal lineages. Like other clans, the Nyiginya Dynasty comprised numerous patrilineal lineages, which claimed ancestry from a male forebearer three to six generations back. Solidarity and unity within the clan was maintained by having the king take several wives, each from a different lineage, and often fathering sons with each. When the time came for a son to take power, bitter intrigues and fighting often occurred, especially among the lineage lines of each queen and their kin, who each wanted the new king to be from their own lineage. Rujugira, with the support of allied lineages, likely came to power himself by exploiting this structural weakness within the dynasty. To avoid future crises and solidify the dynasty's unity, Rujugira appointed his son

Ndabarasa as his successor long before his death and then undertook two revisions to the royal rituals governing succession practices.[28]

First, the number of patrilineal lines allowed to supply queen mothers as wives to the king was restricted to three, the Bega, Kono, and Ha (later raised to four, adding the Gesera to include the clan of Rujugira's adopted queen mother). This reduced the number of lineages who could legitimately claim their own sons as successors to the throne. As the nineteenth century demonstrated, this did little to stop the infighting that occurred with each new succession, but it did have several lasting effects. By elevating the status of the Bega, Kono, and Ha lineages, an elite aristocracy was created among the Nyiginya clan, one that was superior to the other lineages going forward. Among the three, the Bega was given greater status, one that guaranteed that two out of every four Nyiginya kings would come from their lineage alone. To emphasize their uniqueness and ascendancy, the Bega, Kono, and Ha ceased to intermarry, becoming subclans themselves. At this point they began to identify themselves specifically as the children of Gatutsi "who had fallen from heaven, exactly like the supposed forebear of the Nyiginya and in contrast to all others."[29]

Worth observing here is that Rwandans presently are not only aware of whether they, or someone else, is Hutu or Tutsi; many know to which clan and lineage they belong. In seeking to understand the political dynamics of present-day Rwanda, outside observers are often unable to determine whether someone is Tutsi or Hutu without asking probing questions and would not even be aware of the role played by clan and lineage in the politics of the state and society. While many outsiders know that Rwanda's president, Paul Kagame, is Tutsi, very few indeed know that he is of the Bega lineage, giving him royal ancestry and linking him to the feared queen mother Kanjogera of the early twentieth century. While they are not allowed to speak of it publicly, Rwandans are aware of this, and whether or not his ancestry has any real meaning, it most definitely has symbolic meaning considering that he has been in power for more than twenty years with no indication of stepping down any time soon.[30]

Second, in addition to reducing the number of Nyiginya lineages with access to the monarchy, Rujugira recast the entire theory of royal ideology. The starting point for the new theory of kingship was that history is cyclical and repetitive, giving an aspect of predestination to each king's reign. Starting with Rujugira himself, each king took a regnal name to indicate a representative period within two predetermined cycles. The successive regnal names of the first cycle, and used in all odd-numbered cycles thereafter, were Cyirima, Kigeri, Mibambwe, and Yuhi. The names for the second set, to be used in all even-numbered cycles, were Mutara, Kigeri, Mibambwe, and Yuhi. In this scheme, the first and last names in each cycle tightly bound each king to adhere to strict ritual functions. If each king with the first and last name in the cycle performed properly, the cycle was predestined by magic ritual to be secure, and thus the monarchy was made safe. The kings in each cycle with the middle names Kigeri and Mibambwe were safe to act as warrior-kings, always bent on expansion. In addition, the queen mothers of each king at the start and end of each cycle had to come from the Bega lineage, resulting in their higher status over the Ha and Kono lineages.[31]

Under the new theory of kingship, with Cyirima Rujugira as the start of a new cycle, the "mystical authority" of kingship itself increased even as the king became "merely a person fulfilling a role in a sequence of successive actors." Rujugira's intention was to further justify his own legitimacy as a usurper to the throne, but the new theory produced additional consequences. The power of the dynastic lineages increased, and a profound reshaping of historical awareness occurred at the court. The *biru*, the keepers of the court rituals, were elevated to the role of official historians and poets, and their position became markedly more important. If history repeated itself in cycles, then historical precedents could be used to foresee the future and justify present actions by appealing to the past. Regnal names were projected onto past kings to make historical memories coincide with the theory. In a form of historical revisionism, past precedents were invented to justify present actions. In a manner of enforced amnesia, ancestor worship was discouraged so their memory would not obfuscate the obvious historical revisionism underway.[32]

One might fairly wonder what significance this obscure recasting of royal theory has on understanding contemporary Rwanda, and on Rwanda's understanding of itself. In a society that "relied heavily on oral tradition until the arrival of colonialism, and which even today does not have a strong infrastructure of knowledge transmission, including education about its history," the ideological use of historical precedent by the court affected all the official oral traditions as well as the popular tales and genealogies. Historical remembrance and its knowledge became the *ultimate justification for all political actions*—a de facto weapon in the hands of whoever was in power seeking to justify his rule. The acceptance of historical revisionism by those authorized to speak on its behalf, in a society where few had the means or willingness to question the narrative, became endemic to the culture. Every subsequent regime in Rwanda, from this point forward, and including the one presently in power, made use of history to justify and undergird its actions. False narratives became the norm, not the exception, and persist still in Rwanda, with the aid of its Anglican Church.[33]

Finally, Rujugira and Ndabarasa's militaristic policies saw an increase in Tutsi immigration to the western areas. The northern and southeastern kingdoms of Ndorwa and Gisaka were mostly Tutsi and Hima regions, and cattle-raiding, as well as countering the threat from their traditional enemies, was the primary aim of both kings. As a result, many Tutsi fled for the western regions to escape the Nyiginya's attacks. While these migrations integrated Tutsi cattle herders with farmers in western Rwanda, some Hutu historians in the years prior to the genocide claimed the migrations were planned by Rujugira to make way for the Nyiginya conquest of the western regions in the nineteenth century. The purpose of such a narrative was to remind the Hutu populace that the Tutsi were conquerors who were returning with the RPF in the early 1990s to dominate the region again and reassert the monarchy. The same narrative also claimed Ndori originally raided the Hutu farmers rather than other Tutsi cattle herders, which in fact was not the case. One of the most popular proponents of these claims was the Hutu historian Ferdinand Nahimana, a relative of then-president Juvénal Habyarimana, who was writing as late as 1993. Historical analysis reveals these arguments as another false narrative of Rwanda's past, a narrative promoted by "Hutu Power" advocates like Nahimana to further malign the Tutsi in the years just prior to the genocide. The courts of Rujugira and Ndabarasa had neither enough geographic knowledge of the west nor enough power to enforce local living arrangements outside the realm to make this a plausible argument.[34]

When Kigeri Ndabarasa died, the throne passed to his designated successor, Mibambwe Sentabyo, who died only five years later, most likely from smallpox. His death marks the beginning of the nineteenth century in Rwanda and the long reigns of the next three *mwamis*: Yuhi Gahindiro, Mutara Rwogera, and Kigeri Rwabugiri, who died in 1895. Throughout the reigns of these three kings in the nineteenth century, Rwanda underwent significant political and social changes, paving the way toward the events of the twentieth century. Pursuing wars of conquest against their traditional rivals, they expanded a highly centralized monarchy over nearly all of what became modern Rwanda. Mostly because of these wars and the centralizing process, a clear divide emerged for the first time between Hutu agriculturalists and Tutsi elites, who derived their power and status from the monarchy. The nineteenth century was also witness to the first outside interventions into the heretofore isolated kingdom.[35]

Against the backdrop of expansion in the first half of the century was an era of pronounced population growth. By 1800, Rwandan farmers increased their output through irrigation and new food products introduced from abroad, among them the protein-rich American bean and the sweet potato, which matured faster and produced a higher caloric yield than the traditional yam. More food produced more offspring to help with labor, creating population problems. The size of the cattle herds in central Rwanda increased as well. Many herders were tied by lineage to the ruling dynasty, enabling them to requisition land for pasturage, forcing many farmers to move westward in search of new fields. As farmers moved away from the central region to the south and the west, they put more pressure on the increasing population, whose growing number of offspring needed more land of their own as they matured. Over time, the plots of land available to the farming class became smaller and smaller.[36]

Population growth also occurred among the royal lineages, who sought coveted positions in the realm for their sons. With more candidates than available posts, the kingdom undertook more territorial expansion to increase the number of positions in the administrative structure through grants of pasturage land. The result was the extension of greater royal control over the land by court-appointed authorities. Control over pasturage and the use of *ubuhake* clientship was a key element in the acquisition of power and influence at the central court since the founding of the kingdom. Extending control over the land, the key economic resource for most Rwandan farmers, was a new feature in the nineteenth century. With population growth already putting more pressure on the availability of land, the assertion of royal control had a far-reaching effect on the agricultural population and caused yet new forms of clientship to emerge over the course of the nineteenth century.[37]

Traditionally most land in Rwanda was held by patrilineal lines and was farmed corporately. When an individual from a different kin group needed land, he requested it from the lineage head. If the request was granted, portions of his produce were occasionally turned over to the lineage head and he was sometimes required to provide labor on the collective land of the clan. As the agricultural population grew in the nineteenth century, the grants of available land became smaller, and at times unavailable. When Tutsi notables started arriving from the central region, usually prominent army chiefs, favored warriors, or the sons of prominent Tutsi lineages, they came with authority from the king to establish landed domains. This form of land patronage was known as *ibikingi*, which was either land for cattle pasturage alone or included both pastureland and farmers who had heretofore been independent— Hutu, as they came to be called. *Ibikingi* began during the reign of Gahindiro and started a process whereby Rwabugiri later assumed control of all the land and cattle.[38]

Rwabugiri's Rwanda

In the last decades of the nineteenth century, a process that began with Ruganzu Ndori in the seventeenth century culminated in the tenure of Kigeri

Rwabugiri, who reigned from 1867 to 1895. Rwabugiri, seen in many of the histories as an ambitious warrior-king of the middle regnal cycle, augmented the power of the court by pursuing two complementary objectives: the formal subjugation of the peripheral areas surrounding the kingdom, and the centralization of power in the hands of the king. In the process, social and political lines were drawn between Hutu and Tutsi and violence and oppression became more commonplace in every respect.[39]

Military campaigns, led by Rwabugiri himself, occurred almost constantly throughout his reign. Nearly every kingdom or principality bordering Rwanda felt his wrath. New areas were defeated and incorporated, enlarging the kingdom territorially. Sometimes cattle-raiding was the only objective. In regions already under Rwandan control, Rwabugiri strengthened the courts' power through the introduction of new administrative structures in the form of court-appointed chiefs. By displacing the hereditary chiefs, both lesser Tutsi as well as Hutu chiefs, with court appointees, he created vassals who owed their power and position to Rwabugiri alone. Formally autonomous regions found themselves under the direct control of the monarchy. In addition to carrying out royal mandates, the appointed chiefs were charged with the task of collecting tribute in the form of cows and other commodities, greatly augmenting the wealth of the monarchy. By appointing chiefs and officials whose prerogatives often overlapped, he created multiple levels of authority to ensure that no single appointee could acquire his own power base. In this way, Rwabugiri was able to maintain a close surveillance over the kingdom in the same manner that the RPF uses its agents and supporters, many of whom are in the Anglican Church, to keep a close surveilling eye on the Hutu populace in the countryside.[40]

The increased power of the court further allowed the appointed chiefs to demand labor and commodities from those under their authority, resulting in new forms of clientship. The existing forms of clientship, the traditional *ubuhake* cattle clientship and the newer *ibikingi* relationship of Gahindiro's time, were supplemented by the introduction of *ubureetwa*. Under *ubureetwa*, a landed chief could requisition labor from the cultivators under his authority. *Ubureetwa* applied solely to Hutu, although it initially affected only the poorest among them who either had no land or were unable to provide commodities and produce as tribute. In contrast, *ubuhake* had originally existed only among Tutsi cattle owners, but this changed under Rwabugiri, allowing wealthier Hutu to enter *ubuhake* with Tutsi patrons and escape *ubureetwa*. Through this new system, the central court extended its authority and power down to the lowest levels of society.[41]

While increasing the power of the Tutsi rulers, the effect of *ubureetwa* was to cause one of the most significant social transformations in Rwandan history.

Many studies of Rwanda history since the genocide have focused heavily on the institution of *ubuhake* as the defining characteristic governing the precolonial relationship between Hutu and Tutsi. By so doing, the relationship appears to be not so onerous, especially when one considers that wealthier Hutu in an *ubuhake* relationship could acquire their own cattle through reproduction and whose family could eventually be seen as Tutsi over several generations, a socially constructed process known in Kinyarwanda as *kihutura*. Tutsi cattle owners who fell on hard times and lost their herds descended into Hutu status, suggesting that the terms were somewhat fluid. Moreover, *ubuhake* never affected more than a small percentage of the overall population, less than 17 percent by some estimates. Rather, it was *ubureetwa* that became the defining social vector between Hutu and Tutsi in the modern era. Of the various forms of clientship, *ubureetwa* was "the most hated and humiliating. . . . It symbolized the servitude of the Hutu *vis á vis* the dominant minority."[42]

With the imposition of *ubureetwa* servitude upon the rural majority, the term "Hutu" took on new meaning. The origin of the word in Kinyarwanda is obscure. Seeming at times to have referred simply to one with "boorish" or "loutish" behavior, the term was originally only applied to those living within the power structures of the state. Those who lived outside the realm were usually identified by lineage or locale but not by ethnicity. In no sense did the term apply exclusively to those who farmed for a living. During Rujugira's time in the eighteenth century, the term was applied to *noncombatants* serving in the army, as noncombatants were always recruited from the rural population, as opposed to Tutsi *combatants*. As the kingdom's power grew in the nineteenth century, both words became more commonly used, with Hutu referring to those who farmed and Tutsi referring to cattle herders. At this juncture, no sociopolitical rigidity or ethnic differentiations applied. The emergence of *ubureetwa* servitude, however, forcing only Hutu to perform menial labor in contrast to the less humiliating obligations of Tutsi clients to their chiefs, aggravated and poisoned the division. A new social awareness spread across the country, resulting in the emergence of two hierarchical political categories.[43]

For those locked in Hutu servitude, grievances, discontent, and a sense of class consciousness arose by the end of the nineteenth century. Yet social consciousness cannot be equated here in any way with ethnic or racial consciousness. When the Europeans arrived at the end of the century, they incorporated the Tutsi monarchy into their own colonial political structure, adopting words already in use—"Hutu" and "Tutsi"—and then racializing the populace in accordance with the Hamitic Myth. The Belgian colonial state even reinforced *ubureetwa* and adapted it further to suit its own objectives. Marital intermingling was prohibited and identity cards restricted movement among the social categories, all of which magnified an awareness of Hutu servitude and submission to the Tutsi monarchy in a kingdom far from harmonious.[44]

In a culture where historical revisionism had been commonplace since Nyirarumaga's revisions of the *Ibisigo* under Ndori and the adoption of regnal name cycles by Rujugira, the Rwandan authorities presently in power in both church and state have publicly maintained otherwise. As Johan Pottier writes: "Post-genocide leaders regard Rwanda's precolonial past as something of a golden era, a state of social harmony later corrupted by Europeans. Vital to the justification of minority rule, their message is delivered in a well-rehearsed manner and style, marked sometimes by omission (of well-established counterevidence) and sometimes by disregard for context. Complexity and context are continuously screened out of contemporary representations of the 'Old Rwanda.'" Thus, the RPF and the authorities in the Anglican Church, both comprising mainly Tutsi who returned after the genocide, promote a narrative of a precolonial Rwanda that was harmonious, peaceful, and ethnically homogenous before the European arrival. Ethnic homogeneity holds true, but the Rwanda of Rwabugiri, both before his time and afterward, was far from harmonious.[45]

Rwabugiri waged thirteen military campaigns in less than twenty years, inflicting much suffering on the population from the ravages of his armies. Having numerous enemies across the kingdom and within his own court, he used personal violence to secure his power. He ordered the execution of his own mother and father and several prominent members of the court. The violence and cycles of vengeance commonplace in the court were projected across the country. Massacres occurred of entire lineage groups, sometimes of up to twenty people or more. The practice of ancestor worship demanded that family members of his enemies be tortured, usually in front of the shrine of their own ancestors and often lasting for days. The methods used were exceptionally cruel. Enemies were known to be impaled, skinned, and mutilated, and then devoured by dogs.[46]

So thorough was the violence of Rwabugiri's reign, the entire lineage system was undermined. His expansion of power exterminated the "independent lineage-based elite" and resulted in the appropriation of community lands, forcing the majority of the population to become a "dependent peasantry." Even gender relations were altered. Previously, "women enjoyed certain indirect and severely circumscribed rights over land and labor" in the patrilineal system. With Rwabugiri's stripping away of the kin groups' power and land, women lost the right to claim land from their own lineage. The result was men being forced to sell their labor as a client while women were left to tend their husband's land.[47]

The violence of Rwabugiri's reign was not unique. The cattle-raiding and wars of expansion in Rwanda produced a culture of violence long before he came to the throne. From as far back as Ruganzu Ndori's time, cattle were rustled and confiscated, and women and young girls were taken as war brides and slaves. The usual pattern was that once an enemy was in route, hand-to-hand combat ensued. No mercy or quarter was shown, and swords and knives were used both for the killing and for the castration of enemies. The testicles of conquered Hutu clan chiefs were displayed on Karinga, the sacred drum of Tutsi kingship, as war trophies. Typically, every male, young or old, wounded or healthy, was killed and houses and crops were destroyed. Nor did the violence in Rwandan society end with Rwabugiri. Exterminations of entire lineages occurred into the early twentieth century.[48]

By this account, any number of these actions would be defined by today's standards as "crimes of genocide" and human rights atrocities. One cannot help but wonder if such a culture seeded the ground and cultivated a mindset for the collectivist killings and atrocities that occurred in Rwanda in the second half of the twentieth century. Susan Thomson wrote of "Rwandan cultural codes about collective revenge." Danielle de Lame agrees, noting how Rwandan cultural codes emphasize "collective revenge" and that Rwandan society had a long-standing "culture of violence, focused on avenging the losses of one's lineage."[49]

The court and its armies were not the only source of violence. Hutu communities frequently revolted against the depredations of the army and the hated imposition of *ubureetwa*. Sources from Rwabugiri's own court confirm numerous conflicts and clashes between the Tutsi armies and the rural populace. On one noteworthy occasion at Save, where the Catholic Church established its first mission station in southern Rwanda, the rural populace revolted against the royal guards who were pillaging food and raping women at a time when famine was occurring. Reinforcements quelled the revolt, and Rwabugiri had to be dissuaded from exterminating the entire population. Revolts continued into the reign of Rwabugiri's successors, often with the cry, "Free us from the Tutsi."[50]

The death of Rwabugiri in 1895 marks the end of the precolonial period. In 1894 a German explorer, Count Gustav-Adolph von Götzen (1866–1910), became the first European to enter Rwanda. Colonialism was not far behind. The arguments and conclusions in this chapter on precolonial Rwanda contradict virtually every official statement and pronouncement made about the country's past, including pronouncements made by figures in the state and in the Anglican Church. Nonetheless, in a culture where historical revisionism was commonplace and where "the stories they tell of their past tend to be dictated by those who hold power," pronouncements about Rwanda's history, whether from the state or church, must be interrogated against the backdrop of scholarship. As such, the scholarship on precolonial Rwanda demonstrates that while Hutu and Tutsi were ethnically and culturally the same, the two groups existed in clearly defined social and political categories by the end of the nineteenth century, and conflict between the two groups was nearly continuous. Far from being mere economic distinctions, the Tutsi monarchy ruled over a Hutu majority. Oppression was widespread and severe, and the kingdom's history was far from harmonious and peaceful. Rather, it was riddled with violence and bloodshed. This was the Rwanda the European colonialists and Anglican missionaries found.[51]

CHAPTER TWO

History Intervenes

Colonialism, Christianity, and the Ruanda Mission

EUROPEANS WERE NOT the first outsiders to venture into the Great Lakes Region. Arab-Swahili traders and their auxiliaries were traversing the region by the 1830s, increasing after Sultan Seyyid Said (1791–1856) fostered the development of spice plantations on Zanzibar that needed labor. Large caravans from the coast brought trade items such as colored glass beads, porcelain cookware, copper and brass jewelry, cotton from New England (known as *merikani*), and calico textiles. The most sought-after trade good, which the Arab traders first brought into the region, was firearms. In exchange, the caravans were seeking slaves and ivory, as the elephant herds were already decimated on the eastern savannahs.[1]

For the centralized kingdoms of southern Uganda, Rwanda, and Burundi, their military and political formations positioned them to either resist the caravans or receive them on their own terms. During the reign of Mwami Gahindiro in the 1830s, the first merchants from the coast appeared in the region. In the 1850s, an entire caravan reached Mwami Rwogera's court. In the case of both monarchs, the Arab traders approached cautiously, owing to the power of the Nyiginya monarchy. In the same period, a drought struck the region and the king's diviners blamed it on the traders, after which outsiders were banned. Rwabugiri continued to resist unwanted incursions into the kingdom. In 1871 an Arab caravan entered the kingdom uninvited and was entirely destroyed by his army. A famous trafficker in slaves and ivory, known only as Rumaliza, was defeated several times by the Rwandan court in the late 1880s. Despite these instances, Rwabugiri eventually allowed for enclosures to be set up at various sites in the kingdom where young girls, mostly captives from Eastern Congo, were sold along with elephant ivory. However, by the 1890s, a series of ecological catastrophes and epidemics, coupled with the political turmoil following Rwabugiri's death in 1895, crippled the Nyiginya kingdom and left it unable to resist outside intervention.[2]

The Nyiginya Monarchy Unravels

In 1891, as the kingdom was recovering from a two-year drought, a rinderpest epizootic reached Rwanda. Rinderpest is a highly contagious, fatal disease that afflicts cattle with devastating mortality rates (often 90 percent or more of a herd may die). For those people for whom cattle was a source of wealth and a symbol of social status, this had a truly catastrophic impact. In some regions of the kingdom, cattle losses approached 90 percent. Hoof-and-mouth disease killed off many more. At the same time, a locust plague struck the region and destroyed vast amounts of crops. The loss and death of so many cattle, combined with a dearth of food resulting from the locusts, left the region open to famine and human diseases, most notably smallpox and jiggers. Rwanda's population suffered heavily from these diseases throughout the first years of the 1890s. Politically, with most of the Tutsi cattle herds nearly wiped out, many *ubuhake* clientship ties were dissolved. To reconstitute the royal herds, Rwabugiri confiscated most of the surviving cattle and then reparceled them out to favored chiefs, thereby augmenting, and affirming again, the power of the king and monarchy. The net effect was to retrench and deepen the divide between the Hutu majority and the Tutsi elites, many of whom emerged with larger herds when the disease passed. Paradoxically, Rwabugiri thus strengthened the monarchy even while Rwanda was left much weaker from the hardships of the previous years.[3]

Rwabugiri's strengthening of the monarchy was short-lived. When he died in 1895, the Nyiginya kingdom was plunged into a violent succession dispute from which it never fully recovered. Prior to his death, the king appointed his son, Mibambwe Rutarindwa, as co-ruler and designated successor. In accordance with the codes of ritual succession from the time of Rujugira, Rutarindwa's mother was from the Kono clan, in line to provide the next king from their ranks. But when Rwabugiri had Rutarindwa's mother executed several years before his death, he violated the traditional code by appointing his favorite wife, Kanjogera Nyirayuhi, as the adoptive queen mother of Rutarindwa. Kanjogera, regarded in Rwandan culture as beautiful but cunning and deceitful, was from the Bega lineage and used her status as a favored wife to benefit her own kin. In the years before Rwabugiri's death, Kanjogera maneuvered members of her Bega lineage into powerful positions around the monarchy, including the positions of first counselor to the king and the principal military commander of the royal armies. When the king died, Kanjogera and two of her brothers, Kabare and Ruhinankiiko, plotted to overthrow

Rutarindwa and replace him with her own son, Yuhi Musinga, also a son of Rwabugiri.[4]

With his own lineage weakened by Kanjogera's schemes, Rutarindwa and his supporters were attacked by members of the Bega at Rucunshu, in central Rwanda, in December 1896. Easily defeated in what came to be called the Coup of Rucunshu, Rutarindwa and his men committed suicide. A purge of the Kono clan followed wherein Rutarindwa's brothers, uncles, and many of their supporters were either assassinated or forced into exile. In a continuation of the endemic violence surrounding the court, entire family lines associated with the Kono lineage were killed. Musinga was proclaimed the new *mwami* of Rwanda, and the royal positions left open by the purge of the Kono were filled with members of the Bega, significantly increasing its power. With power once again having changed hands violently in Rwanda, and with Nyiginya unity now torn apart between competing lineages, Kanjogera and Musinga's powerful uncle, Kabare, seized upon the European arrival to safeguard their position.[5]

European Colonialism

European interests in East Africa and the Great Lakes Region began in earnest in the 1850s. The region was known about in a general way but with few specifics. One point that fascinated European geographers and "armchair explorers" was finding the source of the Nile River. The Egyptian and Nubian sections of the river had been known since antiquity, but its source had never been identified. The sheer length of the Nile, its numerous cataracts, and the Bahr al-Ghazal swamps blocked a simple traverse southward along its length. With the modern era at hand, the Royal Geographic Society in London committed funds to support expeditions from the East African coast to explore the hinterland and look for the Nile's source. The first known European to enter Rwanda was the Austrian cartographer Oscar Baumann (1864–99), who found the source of the Akagera River in southern Rwanda in 1892. Two years later, in 1894, the German explorer von Götzen arrived at the court. Rwabugiri initially sent a small force against him but was unsuccessful. A year later, Lieutenant Constantin Sandrart of Belgium's Force Publique in Congo, and father of the later Belgian Resident in Ruanda Georges Victor Sandrart (1899–1973), crossed into southwest Rwanda at Shangi, in a disputed region between Germany and Belgium. Rutarindwa, not yet deposed of his throne, sent several thousand warriors to drive him out. The Rwandans, armed with spears and bows, attacked three times but were turned back by Belgian guns. In the last attack, the Rwandan commander, and one of Rutarindwa's most powerful allies, was personally killed by Sandrart. The Battle of Shangi was a disaster for the Nyiginya, symbolizing the supremacy of European weapons over

Rwandan ones and, by implication, European power over Rwandan power. The events at Shangi in 1895, followed by the Coup of Rucunshu in 1896, opened the door for German intervention.[6]

In March 1897, a few months after the enthronement of Musinga, another German, Hans von Ramsay (1862–1938), arrived at the court of the *mwami* and proposed an alliance between Germany and the monarchy. Acting on Musinga's behalf, Kanjogera accepted the proposal. Though successful at Rucunshu, the Bega were greatly weakened by the conflict and its enemies still abounded. The court also remained concerned about Belgium's control of the Congo to the west, having been defeated at Shangi. In exchange for accepting the German flag and promises of its loyalty, Ramsay assured the court of German protection from both the Belgians and any internal threat. Ramsay asked for nothing more than loyalty in return, and in the twenty years of German occupation that followed, the colonial authorities only occasionally intervened in the internal intrigues and conflicts of the kingdom. When they did intervene, it was typically at the request of Musinga and his kin at the court, who used the Germans to help quell the ongoing revolts and resistance in areas on the Nyiginya's periphery. In 1911, for example, German troops assisted Tutsi chiefs in crushing a popular uprising in northern Rwanda, leaving widespread bitterness among the northern Hutu and the Bakiga people.[7]

German observations from this period reveal simmering conflicts between the Hutu and Tutsi. In 1898 a German physician, Richard Kandt (1867–1918), took up residence at Shangi and made numerous commentaries about life in the kingdom. On one occasion, Kandt wrote: "In the presence of their lords, they [the Hutu] were sober and reserved and tried to avoid our questions. But as soon as the Tutsi had turned their backs on our camp, they were willing to tell us everything that we wanted to hear and much that we did not because I could do nothing about the numerous grievances about which they complained, their lack of rights, their oppression."[8]

In other writings, Kandt revealed his scorn for the Hutu, demonstrating the general European belief in their inferiority as compared to the Tutsi, whose regal power they admired. Finally, German occupation provided the opportunity for Christian mission work to begin in Rwanda. Both the Catholics and the Anglicans were already active to the north in the Kingdom of Buganda, and their success among the Baganda inspired them to begin working in the new German protectorate.[9]

Buganda: Training Ground for Mission Work

The Kingdom of Buganda was one of several Bantu kingdoms that formed on the populous and rich soils of southern Uganda. Highly populated from a rich agricultural basis, relatively wealthy, and centralized under a king known as the *kabaka*, Buganda was the object of great interest by numerous outsiders. As in Rwanda in the 1840s, Arab-Swahili merchants arrived from Zanzibar via the overland trade routes, bringing their Islamic faith with them. In 1874 Egypt sent Gordon Pasha (1833–85) to further explore the source of the Nile River, flowing northward through the heart of the kingdom. During his circumnavigation of Lake Victoria in 1875, the explorer Henry Morton Stanley (1841–1904) arrived at the kingdom in April and secured an audience with Kabaka Mutesa I (1837–84). Concerned about Muslim collusion between Zanzibar and Egypt over Buganda's independence, and perceiving England to be a potentially friendlier and more powerful ally than either, Mutesa welcomed Stanley's arrival. Following his reception with the *kabaka*, Stanley reported back to the *London Daily Telegraph* that Mutesa and his people were eager for the Christian Gospel. In no small part because of Stanley's letter, Anglican and Catholic missionaries quickly answered the call.[10]

The Anglican missionaries who went to Buganda were sent by the Church Missionary Society (CMS), established in London on April 12, 1799. Founded in an era of heightened missionary activity from the Western churches, the Anglican-affiliated CMS was positioned under the authority of the bishops of the Church of England and endorsed the Anglican liturgy. Most of its early leaders were influenced by the Clapham Sect, a social reform movement emanating from within the Church of England. The well-known English politician and social reform advocate William Wilburforce (1759–1833) was a key founder and the first vice president of the CMS.[11]

The CMS founded its first mission station in East Africa at Mombasa, on the coast of Kenya, in 1844. In 1876 a party of CMS missionaries, including Shergold Smith and C. T. Wilson, left Mombasa for the courts of Mutesa. Wilson and Smith, minus seven others who died in route, reached Buganda in June 1877. Two years later, the first Roman Catholic missionaries from the Société des Missionnaires d'Afrique arrived in Buganda. Their order was founded in Algiers by the French cardinal Charles Lavigerie (1825–92), who wanted to evangelize North African Muslims across the Maghreb. In the 1880s, Lavigerie abandoned the effort and turned his attention to East Africa, where they were known as the "White Fathers" because of the long white cassock robes they had adopted in Algiers.[12]

Very soon, both the CMS and White Fathers were enjoying surprising success among the Baganda. The stability and initial openness of the kingdom made it a popular destination for the missionaries of both churches. By 1904, the CMS missionaries numbered seventy-nine, and the White Fathers claimed eighty-three workers in the field. What they found among the Baganda was a

people open to new ideas for advancing themselves in a wealthy and sophisticated kingdom-state on the rise. As a result, many young Baganda converted
to either Anglicanism or Catholicism, and the numbers rose steadily. Many
were either clan chiefs, or the sons thereof, and served the monarchy and court
in one capacity or another, and both churches continued the practice in
Rwanda of seeking converts from among the Tutsi royals.[13]

With Islam, Catholicism, and Anglicanism established, the 1880s was a
decade of conflict and turmoil, with shifting alliances at the court. The
Baganda ritualists surrounding the *kabaka* tried to reassert the traditional religious practices of the kingdom even while Muslims, Anglicans, and Catholics
vied for converts among the people and influence over the monarchy. When
Mutesa died in 1884 and his unstable son, Kabaka Mwanga (1868–1903),
acceded to the throne, chaos ensued. Suspicious of outsiders and eager to reassert the traditional religious practices that exalted the king, Mwanga turned
on the Christians. In January 1885, three young converts were murdered in the
Mpimerebera Swamp. Eight months later, in October, Mwanga ordered the
execution of the first Anglican bishop of East Africa, James Hannington
(1847–1885), as his caravan approached the eastern border of his kingdom in
Busoga. The following year, in the summer of 1886, he had more than thirty
young converts of both churches burned alive at Namugongo. Of pertinence
later is the observation that, because of their newfound faith, many of the
young converts around Mwanga were evidently resisting his homosexual
advances, a frequent occurrence in the courts of both the *kabaka* of Buganda
and the *mwami* of Rwanda.[14]

Owing to his persecutions, Mwanga was overthrown in 1888, at which
point conflict erupted immediately between the Muslims and the Christians.
More numerous and better armed after the arrival of the British agent Freder-
ick Lugard (1858–1945), the Christians prevailed. With Islam and the Baganda
traditionalists checked, the Anglicans and Catholics fell into conflict themselves in 1892 at the Battle of Mengo Hill, ultimately resolved by Lugard in
favor of the Protestants. With the mission field of Buganda ceded to the Anglicans, the Catholics started searching for a new evangelical terrain, which they
found in neighboring Rwanda. These turbulent years for the White Fathers
defined many internal policies of the later Catholic Church in Rwanda—such
as the fact that the early catechists were often Baganda converts, and were not
popular among the Rwandans, though the same can be said of the Anglicans
when they ventured southward.[15]

The persecutions of the late 1880s spurred a near mass conversion of the
Baganda to Christianity, known as the "Christian Revolution" in Ugandan
history. The importance of the Christian Revolution in Buganda cannot be

overstated when considering the spread of Anglicanism during the colonial period to Rwanda and beyond. Like with the Catholics, the forms and practices of Anglicanism in Buganda influenced the church throughout the Great Lakes Region and wider East Africa. Arguably it was in Buganda where both churches learned the value of seeking out key converts among the ruling class. Nor could the energy and enthusiasm of the Christian Revolution in Buganda be contained. As Adrian Hastings remarked, "By 1882 a collective movement of conversion was under way which nothing would be able to hold back and over which the [European] missionaries themselves had remarkably little control."[16]

The Ruanda Mission

The Anglican mission to Rwanda was preceded by almost twenty years by the Catholic entry into the kingdom and has always been second behind the Catholics in terms of numbers. In 1890 John Joseph Hirth (1854–1931) was consecrated bishop of the Vicariate of Nyanza Meriodonal, a vast swath of East Central Africa stretching from Mt. Kilimanjaro to Lake Kivu, including German East Africa. Soon thereafter, in 1894, Hirth took charge as bishop of the newly created Vicariate of South Nyanza, divided out by Rome from the larger Nyanza Meriodonal. South Nyanza included the southern shores of Lake Victoria and the kingdoms of Rwanda and Burundi. Buganda was left in the Vicariate of North Nyanza—*nyanza* referring to the earlier European name for Lake Victoria (Victoria Nyanza). After the political setback in Buganda following Mengo Hill, Hirth and the Catholics were looking for a place to evangelize. Rwanda, with its centralized state, seemed the perfect fit: no Muslims, no Protestants, no British, and a centralized monarchy to conform to Lavigerie's dictates, which saw conversion of the elites as essential to the eventual conversion of the society as a whole. The German colonial authorities were also agreeable to the Catholic presence.[17]

Having learned in Buganda the importance of having the consent of the ruling structure, Hirth sent envoys to the court of Musinga, who in turn dispatched its own representatives to the White Fathers. To reinforce its approval, the Germans accompanied Hirth and his delegation with two armed soldiers when they arrived at Musinga's court in 1900. Despite an amiable reception, the court was skeptical of Hirth and his escorts, many of whom were Baganda catechists. The Rwandan court assumed the Catholics were agents of the Germans, charged with overseeing their own spiritual matters, and failed to recognize the extent to which the missionaries would become involved in colonial politics. Still recognizing the potential for "spiritual diviners" to cause trouble, Musinga's uncle, Kabare, tried to push the Catholics far from the court. After

negotiations, Hirth agreed to establish his first mission station on seven hundred hectares at Save, in the southern region of Bwanamukari, a region viewed
by the court as "troublesome and inhospitable to outsiders." Save was an
impoverished region whose Hutu inhabitants had suffered multiple attacks by
Rwabugiri. Kabare hoped the Catholics would find it such a miserable place
they would become discouraged and leave.[18]

As it happened, Kabare's attempt to undermine the Fathers failed. When
the mission station was founded on Save Hill, soldiers from Tanzania and
catechists from Buganda served as guards, and the mission had the distinct feel
of an armed encampment. Initially afraid of the newcomers, local residents
refused to provide food, water, or wood. One of Musinga's brothers, Cyitatire,
who commanded the region but who also "feared assassination," ordered the
Hutu to provide materials and help with the building. When the mission
started providing aid and assistance, and following an alleged miraculous healing, converts trickled into the station. In what became a typical response
across the region, the oppressed Hutu saw the mission as a potential source of
aid in difficult times and a means of protection from the depredations of the
Tutsi court. Baganda catechists combed the area for additional recruits, often
proclaiming them to be *intore*, or "chosen ones." Viewing their initial success
as divine confirmation, the White Fathers pushed further, opening four more
mission stations within three years: Zaza (in the southeast) and Nyundo (in
the extreme northwest) in 1900, and Rwaza (in the far north) and Mibirizi (in
the far southwest) in 1903. Though the stations were located in peripheral
areas far from the court, they also ringed the kingdom and later on became
sources for the expansion of "Rwandan" norms into areas outside the firm
control of the court. The next mission station, at Kabgayi (in 1906), was different because it was located in the very heartland of court domination, only
thirty miles from the court itself at Nyanza. Thereafter, Kabgayi became the
"center of Catholic life in Rwanda." With the expansion of the mission, a new
church territory, the Vicariate of Kivu, was carved out of the Vicariate of
South Nyanza in 1912, where Hirth continued as the vicar. By the end of
World War I, in 1918, Catholic conversions in Rwanda numbered roughly
thirteen thousand, almost all of whom were Hutu, including five ordained
Hutu priests.[19]

The early success of the White Fathers is surprising when one considers that
virtually none of the priests nor their Baganda catechists were fluent in Kinyarwanda. To the court and many observers, the missionaries and their auxiliaries seemed foreign and strange. Musinga's court continued to harbor an
abiding suspicion of the missionaries' intentions. The court explicitly forbade
religious instruction for Tutsi, and only Hutu and Twa could attend mission

schools. In many respects, though, while Musinga had "aimed to keep the missionaries at a distance while using them to extend his own influence over restive local populations," the initial exclusion of the White Fathers from the Tutsi court worked to the mission's advantage. With Zaza in the far southeast, Nyundo in the far northwest, Rwaza in the far north, and Mibirizi in the far southeast, they were working in regions with long traditions of resisting Nyiginya control. The paradoxical effect was to find Hutu populations eager for the protection the Fathers seemed to offer, even while the mission stations also "served as a statement on the extent of the territorial aspirations of the dynastic court in the larger region. In other words, even while exiled from the court the missionaries in these stations—and their loyal converts—were seen as extensions of court power."[20]

With the Catholic mission underway, the Anglican incursion into Rwanda was more modest. In December 1916, two doctors from Mengo Hospital in Uganda, Leonard Sharp (1890–1976) and Algernon Stanley Smith (1890–1978), along with a Rev. H. B. Lewin, traveled through Rwanda, where they were "impressed by the beauty of the country, the density of the population, the almost entire lack of medical services, and the wide-open door for the preaching of the Gospel." Smith was the only son of Stanley P. Smith (1861–1931), one of the CMS-celebrated "Cambridge Seven" who ventured to China in 1885 with Hudson Taylor's China Inland Mission, making him a well-known figure in the Anglican missionary community. Both men's initial interest in Rwanda had been piqued by their reading of a book by the German Duke of Mecklenburg called *In the Heart of Africa*.[21]

By the time they arrived, Rwanda was under the occupation of Belgian forces from the Congo. In 1914 the European powers became engulfed in World War I, with small-scale fighting occurring in East Africa between the British, with their Carrier Corps of Kenyan porters, and German forces in Tanzania, with their own troops and indigenous forces known as *askaris*. During the war, the only skirmishes in the region occurred sporadically between 1914 and 1917 in Kigezi on the northern frontier with British Uganda, where the Resident of German Ruanda, Captain Max Wintgens, made use of Tutsi raiding parties to incite revolts among the Bakiga on the British side of the border. The district commissioner of British Kigezi rebuffed the raids and restored order with a Baganda police battalion. In 1916 the British sent the South African general Jan Smuts (1870–1950) into Tanzania to finally route the German forces. With Germany struggling to remain in Tanzania, Rwanda was abandoned to the Belgians. Kigali was occupied by Belgian forces under Philippe Molitor (1869–1952) on May 6, 1916. When the war ended in Europe, the 1919 Paris Peace Conference stripped Germany of its colonies. The British assumed control of Tanzania, and the Protectorate of Ruanda-Urundi was awarded to Belgium by a League of Nations mandate.[22]

Smith and Sharp's trek through Rwanda came to the attention of the Belgian authorities in 1917. Correspondence from the commissioner general of the Belgian occupation forces to the Anglican bishop in Uganda suggests the Belgians were unaware of the missionary's entry into the protectorate. When they arrived at Kigali, Smith, Sharp, and Lewin further disobeyed instructions to wait there for official recognition by the authorities. Of most concern to the commissioner general was the alleged investigations Smith and Sharp made into how Rwandans were being treated by the Belgian forces. The observation that Smith and Sharp wore military attire on their trek, as both men had engaged in wartime service, no doubt heightened fears that the party was trying to "defame Belgian rule and make it possible for Britain to claim colonial authority in Rwanda."[23]

The commissioner cited three examples of inquiries made by the missionaries, including, "Was it correct that in the course of the campaign certain Belgians had committed atrocities against the natives? Was it true that a number of [Rwandan] porters had died of hunger at Kibati? Did we treat our soldiers severely when they killed or injured the natives, and did we authorize them to carry off native women?" The commissioner insisted that such initiatives must not occur in the future. When confronted in writing by the bishop over their actions, Smith and Sharp both maintained that most of what the commissioner general alleged was a misunderstanding in communications but never denied the inquiries they made over native treatment.[24]

The CMS was founded with social reform in mind, and Smith and Sharp reflected this impulse. Their criticisms of colonial actions in Rwanda conjured up for the Belgians memories of the campaign of atrocities in the neighboring Congo at the beginning of the century, where they had acquired a decidedly less-than-admirable reputation as colonizers. When King Leopold II of Belgium (1835–1909) began his exploitation of Congo, his soldiers, known as the Force Publique, committed well-documented human rights violations against the population, including the enslavement of Congolese women to force men to gather wild rubber from the jungle. Often the hands of their children were cut off to terrorize the population. Brutal beatings were commonplace, and hunger ravaged the region. The population declined by millions. Known as the "Rubber Terror," or "Red Rubber" in Belgium, Leopold's actions came to the world's attention by 1908. An international crusade against the atrocities in the Congo ensued, based in part on the testimonies of Protestant missionaries, adding again to the commissioner's suspicions about the CMS. As a result, Leopold was forced to cede control to the Belgian government. The situation improved somewhat afterward, but Belgium's reputation was tarnished and suspect in the eyes of the reform-minded CMS missionaries. Their reputation was not helped when reliable reports surfaced of Congolese soldiers under Belgian command robbing and raping numerous locals when they made their initial occupation of Rwanda. This was the context in which Sharp and Smith were making their investigations.[25]

Undeterred by the controversy, Leonard Sharp wrote to CMS Africa secretary G. T. Manley in April 1917: "You have doubtless heard much lately about . . . opening missionary work in any new country. . . . But with Ruanda it is much more than that—a Medical Mission is imperative." His letter correctly notes, "The Batutsi have withstood for 15 years all the efforts of the Roman Catholics to make converts from among them," and a medical mission was critical to reaching them. His letter also reveals, for the first time, the admiration many Anglican missionaries had for the Tutsi. As he wrote, a medical mission would "rapidly become self-supporting as the Batutsi are a generous race who own all the wealth of the country in the shape of thousands of head of cattle." His letter reveals no awareness of the rampant exploitation suffered by the Hutu under Tutsi rule.[26]

Lacking funds and resources because of World War I, Smith and Sharp were rebuffed and remained at their posts in Uganda. With the war over in 1919, both men were in England raising money independently from private sources to start their medical mission. With funding secured from a group of supporters known as the "Friends of Ruanda," Sharp initially wanted the Ruanda Mission to function independently of the Uganda Mission. Manley was not open to the idea, insisting that any future work in Rwanda must remain under the direction of the Uganda Missionary Committee. He further pointed out that Rwanda was in the Diocese of Mombasa, and thus any ecclesiastical matters had to be approved by Bishop Richard Heywood (1867–1955). Sharp's desire to work independently of Uganda foreshadows the tension that later characterized the relationship between the Ruanda Mission and the Anglican Church, including tensions within the CMS itself. Manley and the CMS General Committee yielded in November 1920, authorizing Sharp and Smith to pioneer an independent medical mission, first in Uganda but also in Rwanda when possible. They were to remain under the direction of the Uganda Missionary Committee, which was directed to negotiate with the Belgian authorities for access to Rwanda.[27]

Like the Catholics, their original intent was to open a mission hospital at the court of Musinga, and a school for the chief's sons. As it turned out, they were unable to obtain access to Rwanda but found a way in via "British Ruanda," as the Kigezi region was called. Kigezi was a region straddling northeast Rwanda and southwest Uganda and populated by a people known as the Bakiga. The Bakiga were a regional subgroup who spoke Kinyarwanda, essentially making them Banyarwandan people but who had effectively resisted any incorporation into the Nyiginya polity. When the British and Germans finalized the agreement in 1911 over the border between Uganda and Rwanda, the Bakiga were divided between the two spheres.[28]

In February 1921, Smith and Sharp, along with their wives, Lillian Zoe Smith (1891–1980), sister of Leonard Sharp, and Esther Sharp (1893–1962), took up residence at Kabale, in the Ugandan section of Kigezi, to begin medical and evangelistic work among the Bakiga. Along with the first ordained missionary to Kigezi, Rev. Jack Warren, they were joined in 1923 by the first unmarried woman to the field, Constance Hornby (1884–1972). In addition to others, they were joined in 1931 by another key participant in the early days, Rev. Warren Orpwood, who married a fellow pioneer missionary, Margaret Forbes, in 1937. From the start, Zoe and Esther started work among the women while their husbands began evangelistic work, constructed new facilities, and scouted the border region. In an encouraging letter to their supporters, addressed to the "Ruanda Friends," Smith noted that they were only a two-hour walk from Rwanda. He does not say in his public letters whether he crossed over, but he routinely provided detailed descriptions of the geography of the area. Considering the uncontrolled nature of the border in that era and their prior adventure into Rwanda, without the full consent of their activities by the Belgian authorities, Smith's frequent and widespread travels through the region lead one to suspect that, in his zeal, he likely crossed into Belgian Ruanda on occasion.[29]

Smith reported success in making some initial converts and in creating a positive impression among the Bakiga, whom he referred to as "Ruandan people." He claimed to have made friends with "the ruling Tutsi chief of British Ruanda, Samson Inyarubuga, and several of his Batutsi retainers." Apart from making contacts, the missionaries' time was spent in building their houses and compound, providing medical aid, and learning the language. By May, they had translated portions of the Gospel into Kinyarwanda with the help of an early convert. Smith and Sharp wrote routine letters describing their activities and progress to their financial backers and supporters, known more formally as the "Friends of Ruanda."[30]

Their letters provide a wealth of insight into the activities and successes of the mission's early years and reveal some of the controversies and divisions that beset the CMS and the Church of England in that era, divisions that spilled over into the Uganda and Rwanda missions throughout much of their history. Smith and Sharp had both studied medicine at Cambridge University in 1910 at a time of heightened tensions between evangelical conservatives and liberals over Scriptural authority. The tensions led to the withdrawal and formation of the conservative Cambridge Inter-Collegiate Christian Union (CiCCU) from the national Student Christian Movement (SCM). Joe Church, later a key figure in the Ruanda Mission and the East African Revival, was from the CiCCU camp, as were most of the Ruanda missionaries.[31]

The division at Cambridge reflected wider tensions within the CMS, which, in 1922, led the conservatives to form the Bible Churchman's Missionary Society (BCMS) over the same issues. The supporters of the Ruanda Mission were largely sympathetic to the BCMS position and agreed to remain within the CMS as its parent society only if they could have their own governing body in London with the freedom to insist upon "uncompromising conservative evangelical loyalty" from its missionaries. From the outset, nearly two-thirds of the doctors and clergymen sent to Rwanda were from Cambridge and reflected the CiCCU/SCM and BCMS/CMS divisions. As it was, the SCM and CMS missionaries were mostly in Uganda while the Ruanda Mission was represented by the CiCCU and BCMC faction, who took a "more conservative attitude to Scripture . . . emphasizing evangelism rather than engagement with the public life of the nation or critique of the sociopolitical context." Their inclination toward disengagement with social issues and politics was a hallmark of the Ruanda Mission, especially so when the East African Revival began, and remains true of the Anglican Church in Rwanda to this day. Additionally, when the Ruanda Mission became its own governing body within the CMS, an objective of Sharp's since 1919, and was able to provide its own support to its missionaries, endless controversies ensued as the mission was generally free to act in ways that often embarrassed and frustrated the larger church.[32]

By 1922 schools were built in Kigezi and a hospital was under construction, along with a brickmaking industry to provide materials. The mission also extended its reach into the Tutsi population, among whom they saw great potential for converts and whom the mission regarded as a separate social class. While the missionaries themselves were not yet free to venture into Belgian territory, Bakiga converts were able to cross the border. As Smith reported in September 1921, "Two Christian boys are going to Ruanda to start a Christian school for the chiefs' sons and the Batutsi." The practice of training indigenous missionaries who could gain access to regions off-limits to outsiders is a common missional practice among churches and, as it turned out, was an effective one for the station at Kigezi. In 1924 the *Church Missionary Outlook* reported "over 170 little churches or grass reading huts" scattered across Rwanda and led by young converts.[33]

The inroads among the Tutsi chiefs continued. In 1922 the mission befriended a cousin of Musinga's, Nyirimbiringa, who was also the paramount chief of the Bakiga in British Ruanda. The mission's excitement about reaching the Tutsi chiefs and their admiration for them is evident throughout their letters. The mission was very much aware of the success the White Fathers were having among the Hutu and saw themselves as having a special task to convert the Tutsi. The churches and missionaries, Anglican and Catholic alike, conformed to the wider European view of Hutu and Tutsi being separate races, deserving of a different approach. Reflecting the influence of the Nilotic "external invasion" theory, Sharp frequently speculated in his letters about the Tutsi having come from Ethiopia.[34]

On this question, the missionaries reflected the common assumptions of the era that held the Tutsi as the descendants of Nilotic invaders from the north. Engaged as they were in their work, the early missionary community never gave any indication of questioning the widespread racial narrative about the people with whom they interacted every day. For them, their calling to do God's work meant disengagement from local conflicts and problems. The social reform impulse that characterized the CMS meant building hospitals and schools, not engaging in sociopolitical critiques of the environments in which they were at work. Political conflicts, even when seen clearly, were processed solely in spiritual terms. Smith reported in 1921 of hearing about killings and raids by different "tribes" across the border in Belgian Ruanda but doesn't speculate further apart from calling it the "work of the devil." The avoidance of critical inquiry into larger contextual questions about politics can be observed still in many of the interactions of Western missionaries and aid workers in present-day Rwanda.[35]

In 1923 a strip of land in eastern Ruanda was leased to the British to construct a "Cape to Cairo" railway. The region was handed back to Belgium in 1924 when the British abandoned the project, but the interval allowed the mission to make exploratory treks into the territory and establish several village churches that continued after the area was lost again. Sharp later claimed that the "Gospel had been planted in all its strategic centers." The mission also fell into its first conflict with the Catholics during this period, foreshadowing many more to come. During the brief opening in eastern Rwanda, Smith tried to claim several sites for new preaching centers near Nzaza but accused the Catholics of intentionally taking over his proposed sites to keep them out of CMS hands. He further accused them of pressuring the chiefs in the region to forbid local people from visiting with them.[36]

Along with its encouraging, albeit brief, incursion into Ruanda, the mission was enjoying productive and successful work in Kigezi. The hospital at Kabale was completed in 1924 and conversions steadily increased. Churches proliferated across the district. The missionaries endured their share of difficulties and losses too. Injuries and malaria were common. In 1923 Sharp and his wife lost their only son to sickness but remained at work in the field. Jack Warren, the first ordained minister to the field in 1921, died in 1929 from a lung condition caused by a poison gas attack in World War I. Geoffrey Holmes and Joe Church, a missionary doctor who arrived in 1927, were both injured in Rwanda by leopard attacks, and Church was nearly killed by a lion on another occasion. Despite the personal hardships, the Ruanda Mission's focus turned toward the expansion of work beyond Kigezi after Belgium granted full access in 1925. The early years of work by Smith, Sharp, and others at Kabale left behind three boarding schools, a hospital, a 2,000-seat cathedral, more than 150 churches, and thousands of converts by 1927.[37]

With access to Rwanda in hand, Geoffrey Holmes (1894–1964), a former British Army captain and Olympic ice hockey player, ventured into the territory and chose Gahini as the site of the first Anglican mission on a hill overlooking the eastern shore of Lake Muhazi. Accompanying him was a young Tutsi Christian named Kosiya Shalita. The son of a Tutsi chief, he was born in 1901 near Gahini. After a failed uprising against the king in 1906, his family fled to Ankole in southern Uganda, where he converted. In 1924 Shalita was in Kampala finishing a three-year course at Budo College when he met Smith, who was looking for native missionaries to reside and work at Kabale. After a year at Kabale, Shalita accompanied Holmes to Gahini to start mission work in his homeland. He married a girl from the mission named Irene in 1929 and on January 25, 1933, he became the first Rwandan ordained into the Anglican priesthood at Namirembe Cathedral in Kampala, eventually becoming bishop of Ankole.[38]

By the end of 1925, twelve missionaries were serving at Gahini, including a doctor named Herbert ("Bert") Jackson, who began medical work, and Rev. Harold Guillebaud (1889–1941) and wife Margaret. Along with Sharp, Guillebaud was at Cambridge during the CiCCU/SCM controversy. He joined the mission as a translator and by 1926 had translated portions of the Bible into Kinyarwanda. Guillebaud baptized the first converts at Gahini in May of the same year. Several of the Guillebaud's children and grandchildren remained in the mission field in Central Africa long after their parents' deaths. Rev. Cecil Verity (1902–95), who had gone to Kabale in July 1928, also joined the Gahini station to run the boys' school and oversee evangelists.[39]

In 1927 a Cambridge-educated doctor, John E. ("Joe") Church (1899–1989), arrived at Gahini to begin construction of a seventy-five-bed hospital, completed a year later. Within five years, the hospital was performing twenty-two

thousand outpatient procedures a year, and four additional stations in outly-
ing areas were recognized by the Belgian authorities as first aid clinics. In 1930
Church married Decima ("Decie") Mary Tracey (1904–91) at Namirembe
Cathedral in Kampala, Uganda; she then joined him at Gahini. His brother,
William Church, a tropical medicine specialist, arrived in 1934.[40]

Prior histories have generally understated the role of the missionaries' wives
and numerous other women who ventured to the Ruanda Mission. They are
often unfairly given nothing more than passing mention in previous writings.
Among them was Constance Hornby, who served in the Ruanda Mission
until the age of 81 and whose engaging and routine letters back home about
the girls' school she headed made her one of the best-known women in the
field. Decie Church was herself a doctor and worked alongside her husband at
Gahini. By the late 1930s, when Joe Church was frequently away on evangelistic work, she was left in charge of the station, where she performed surgeries
and Caesarian sections. Despite this, John Church, the oldest of their five
children and himself a doctor, reminisced years later in 2008 that he never
heard his mother addressed as "doctor." Leonard Sharp's wife, Esther, was
known for voicing strong opinions about some of the alleged extremism of the
later East African Revival, embroiling her in controversy. She, too, remains a
mostly overlooked figure. Indeed, the role of women in the mission field created one of the first points of friction between the larger CMS and the Ruanda
Mission. The CMS in London insisted that women missionaries receive at
least some of their training at CMS institutions, training that the Ruanda
Mission regarded as too modernistic and "unsuitable for women with no
background in theology." This was the first of many moments of friction
between the Ruanda Mission and the CMS and reflects an orthodox and conservative posture toward woman in ecclesiastical roles, which may account for
the paucity of attention afforded them in prior histories.[41]

Ilaria Buscaglia and Shirley Randell have written on the wider impact of the
church and colonialism on Rwandan women. According to them, the colonial
discourse on women, carried out by the Anglican missionaries and other
church bodies, was that women needed to be freed from "traditional culture
which was seen as a hindrance to their personal and collective development.
In so doing, they would easily become good spouses and responsible mothers."
Accordingly, female promotion went hand in hand with social control by
imposing a European nuclear family model onto society with the expected
gender roles. Rather than seeing this as a form of female emancipation from
traditional society, however, in the Anglican girls' schools, under the tutelage
of the missionaries' wives and other women in the field, Rwandan women
were disempowered. Previous gender power relations in precolonial, rural

Rwanda held forth women as important agricultural workers and producers. Under the new colonial imposition, men were to be the producers and women were domesticated into new family roles. In effect, Rwandan women were expected to go from being "producers to re-producers."[42]

More so than the Sharps, the Smiths, or any other figures, Joe Church and his family became synonymous with the history of the Ruanda Mission. They spent most of their working lives at Gahini, not leaving until 1961 when the violence and unrest of the 1959 revolution forced them back to Uganda. Like the Gillebauds, several of their children entered missionary service, and all were born in Rwanda. After leaving Rwanda in 1961, they remained at Kampala until 1972 before retiring to England. Church is also associated with the start of the East African Revival in the 1930s, making his name the most recognizable one from the early period of Anglican history in Rwanda. His writings also provide considerable primary research material for the early history of the mission.[43]

With the Ruanda Mission underway by 1925, Sharp and Smith wanted a more structured support network to meet the "great needs and opportunities among the Ruanda speaking peoples and the Batutsi tribe," whom they called "one of the finest in Central Africa." In 1926 the CMS Executive Committee authorized the formal creation of the Ruanda Medical Mission, to be known as the Ruanda Mission (CMS Auxiliary). The small circle of financial supporters of Sharp and Smith's previous work, the "Friends of Ruanda," was formalized into a standing subcommittee of the CMS Africa Group. Referred to as the "Ruanda Council," the group was charged with providing oversight and raising funds solely for the Ruanda Mission. The goal was to no longer have need of CMS grants—instead raising money from "sources otherwise not available to the CMS." The assumption of "complete financial responsibility for the existing work and workers in Ruanda" was to be achieved before making any new advances in the field.[44]

Apart from its financial responsibilities, the committee had the power to approve or deny any missionary or clergy sent to the field to ensure they agreed with the strict conservative, evangelical principles upon which the Ruanda Mission was founded. According to Sharp, these principles were to be "Protestant, Evangelical," and along "Keswick lines," in reference to the nineteenth-century Keswick Higher Life holiness movement, which profoundly influenced the beliefs of the Ruanda Mission. Membership on the Ruanda Council was self-selected to guarantee adherence to the same doctrines. With these understandings, the Ruanda Council became the administrative oversight body to the Anglican churches in Rwanda until 1965, under the CMS but also with considerable autonomy to guide the mission.[45]

From the beginning, though, the uneasy relationship between the council and the CMS was evident. The general secretary of the CMS, Bishop William Wilson Cash (1880–1955), wrote to the Ruanda Council in November 1926: "I would like to emphasize strongly the fact that the CMS wants men of like mind with those whom you support, not only in Ruanda but in every Mission of the Society. . . . It would help us very much if you could make this as clearly and as widely known as possible, for the last thing we would like to happen would be that anyone should think that they were peculiar to Ruanda, and were not to be found in our other missions." The often "peculiar" and independent actions of the Ruanda Mission, especially when the East African Revival began, frequently generated consternation within the CMS and on more than one occasion created conflicts with Anglican Church authorities in Uganda.[46]

With the establishment of a formal Ruanda Council, the numerous letters back to supporters were published and circulated in a fundraising and prayer-support quarterly called *Ruanda Notes*. These letters printed in the quarterlies constitute the bulk of the primary source material from the various mission stations and churches in Rwanda. Throughout the late 1920s, they speak of expansion and successful work, while Gahini remained the center of excitement and focus. The pattern and approach mirrored other successful Christian mission stations across Rwanda and the region. The missionaries lived in tents until houses were constructed and a brickmaking yard was established. Medical clinics were founded and expanded into full hospitals. Schools were built, and children, especially those of new converts, were encouraged to attend. The primary objective of the schools was to train and educate indigenous Christian teachers and evangelists, who were then sent into rural villages away from the station to lead "reading huts." Catechists also started primitive "churches on the grass," as they were called.

In the early days of the Ruanda Mission, most of the lay leaders were Baganda teachers, catechists, and pastors who were trained in the formal Anglican colleges in Uganda. Occasionally, their approach sparked local resentment, as they were outsiders who insisted upon instruction being given in their own language of Luganda, not surprisingly when one considers that missionaries across Africa often "made some crucial decisions which privileged certain languages over others and helped familiarize people with a new *lingua franca*." Over time, the mission stations became self-supporting agricultural centers with fields and cattle herds. Indigenous workers, usually converts who were encouraged to serve the mission, provided the labor. In both the Catholic and Anglican missions, medical aid and food supplies were a considerable attraction for residents, who were then evangelized in the process, like the impoverished Hutu at Save, where the Catholics began their work.[47]

Local inhabitants were especially drawn to the mission stations during times of famine, a routine occurrence. Densely populated and almost entirely agricultural, the country suffered greatly when the rains failed. Writing from Gahini, an area hit especially hard by famine, Smith reported a severe episode in November 1928: "The whole work in Ruanda is haunted by the specter of famine. Two seasons of crops have failed and our hopes that the rain would fall and save these hungry multitudes seem destined to be disappointed." In Rwandan history, famines were often remembered by names. The one Smith was writing of was known as the "Rwakayihura." The Rwakayihura famine began in northern Rwanda among the Bakiga and affected most of the country until 1930. Hundreds of thousands of Rwandans became refugees in search of food. The shortage was most catastrophic in the southeast, in Gisaka, where as much as one-third of the regional population either died or fled to British-controlled East Africa.[48]

Joe Church, who also wrote of the famine, partly blamed it on the land-usage policies of the Tutsi chiefs. He noted how the food shortage was compounded by the excessive amount of pasturage land used for the "rich Batutsi's cattle . . . which means that the thousands of Bahutu slaves are left with a very small portion of land on the tops of the hills." Church's observation is a succinct point. The Belgian colonial government, under pressure to provide food aid, rearranged Tutsi landholdings in response to the Rwakayihura famine. When the administrators found that large numbers of Tutsi notables had failed to execute measures designed to end the famine, they removed many of them from their commands and merged their domains with the holdings of others, thereby opening more of the marshy lowlands for crop cultivation. The hardships of the Rwakayihura also provided opportunities to both the Belgians and the Ruanda Mission. In 1926 the Belgian administration tried to solve the seasonal character of traditional crops by introducing nonseasonal crop growing, such as "cassava, in the hot and low regions, potatoes in the high regions, sweet potatoes more or less everywhere." Following the Rwakayihura famine, the Belgian colonial state was able to further extend its reach into the lives of ordinary peasants by requiring the cultivation of new drought-resistant crops and extensive terracing. For the missionaries distributing food aid at Gahini, some of which was provided by the Belgians, the famine was a "blessing in the Lord's hands, because hundreds hear the Word who never would have come near us perhaps, otherwise."[49]

In many respects, Anglican mission practices differed little from Catholic practices, with one significant exception. In its early years, the court forbade the Catholics from evangelizing the Tutsi and kept the Fathers away from the court. Conversely, though, the slow and somewhat inauspicious start of the Ruanda Mission positioned it to reach Tutsi converts, an objective they pursued unapologetically, as revealed in the racial assumptions evident from their letters. This strategy of reaching people through their monarchs and the existing structures of power, a strategy the Catholics first tried to adopt themselves, anticipated the church's frequent and ambiguous relationship with state power in Africa. Moreover, in the northern areas where the Anglican mission began, the machinations of the central court had alienated many Hutu and smaller Tutsi chiefs who saw advantages in allying themselves with the Europeans. By the time the Anglicans arrived, northern Rwanda was controlled by chiefs who refused to acknowledge the suzerainty of Musinga, a situation that inadvertently worked to the missionaries' advantage in seeking converts. One can observe among these chiefs a similarity of the practice adopted by Ndori and Rujugira centuries earlier of accommodating a new spiritual movement, in this case Anglicanism, for social leverage and security amid political uncertainty.[50]

The missionaries' letters reveal an intentional effort to seek out converts from among the Tutsi. While conversions took place among the Hutu, it was always the conversion of a Tutsi that sparked excitement and a description in a letter to supporters. Photographs meant to provoke admiration of the Tutsi appeared regularly in the pages of the *Ruanda Notes*. Against the backdrop of this was a near-universal acceptance of the wider European view of the Tutsi being of a higher racial stock. Tutsi were usually referred to as the "aristocratic" class of Rwanda. While harboring a clearly racial admiration for the Tutsi, the missionaries were also keenly aware of the oppression endured by the Hutu, speaking of them often as "slaves." A lesser-known missionary, identified only as Mrs. Wilkinson, wrote, "Here in Ruanda there are two classes of people: the [Tutsi] chiefs, altogether aristocratic in manner, and the poorer classes [Hutu] who are practically their slaves." On another occasion a photograph was printed of a Tutsi chief with a small boy alongside who was identified as his "Hutu slave." Geoffrey Holmes offered a wider analysis of the prevailing social structure in Rwanda. He wrote that for "hundreds of years" Rwanda had been a place of oppression: "The Bahutu by the Batutsi, the poor Batutsi by the rich, the rich and poor alike by the lesser chiefs, the lesser chiefs by the more powerful, and these by their Mwami, or king." Leonard Sharp was aware too of the status of the Hutu, writing, "The Bahutu for generations have been all but the slaves of the Batutsi throughout Ruanda." Based on their letters and observations, the missionaries were evidently unaware that the people of this region did not always accept or exist within the Hutu-Tutsi social parameters of the kingdom. For example, there was a greater amount of shared identity among the Bakiga, known to the court as the "people of the mountains."[51]

Such commentaries, speaking admirably of the Tutsi on the one hand and noting the oppression and slavery with which they ruled over the Hutu on the other, reveals an inherent moral contradiction within the early days of the Ruanda Mission. Part and parcel to the founding of the CMS was an emphasis on social reform and the eradication of slavery, yet one detects little if any sense of moral outrage leading to action on the missionaries' part—that is, the moral outrage that had once put the CMS at the forefront of abolishing slavery and its trade across the British empire. In a habit that persisted throughout the history of the Anglican Church in Rwanda down to the present, the missionaries displayed a tendency to avoid, in any meaningful political sense, "the crucial issues troubling the society." They were undeniably aware of the oppression of the Hutu. Being theologically disinclined toward political engagement and recognizing their precarious position as British missionaries in a Belgian colony, they sought to resolve the issue through a reliance on personal conversion and change on the individual level.[52]

Evangelical to the core, the Ruanda Mission held forth hope for the Christian Gospel to change Rwandan society by changing the hearts of the believers. Sharp wrote of a Tutsi convert who, having "never done a stroke of work in his life," now is willing to "wash the feet, or worse, of the Bahutu in the hospital." Stanley Smith went further. Speaking of the social divisions plaguing Rwanda, he wrote, "Under the disintegrating forces of civilization and a civilized government this system is steadily losing its power and will rapidly pass away; and then these Batutsi gentry must work or go to the wall." As history unfolded in twentieth-century Rwanda, Smith's faith in the "forces of civilization," a Eurocentric assumption from the start, was misplaced. As Belgian colonial rule accelerated, the precolonial divisions in Rwandan society were deepened and took on an even more overt racial dimension, Christian conversion notwithstanding.[53]

In addition to gaining followers from among the ranks of the Tutsi, the Ruanda Mission benefited by making strategic converts among the followers of the Cult of Nyabingi. Ian and Jane Linden, historians of the early church in Rwanda, write, "It was the CMS in the northeast who inherited the religious traditions of Nyabingi." In the mythology of the region, Nyabingi was a female spirit-deity who communicated prophesies through her priestesses. Known as the *bagirwa*, they were believed to receive communications from Nyabingi and made supplications for the people directly to her, offering protection from evil and relief from curses and cures for illnesses and assurances of good fortune.[54]

The term "Nyabingi" originally meant "one who possesses great riches." According to Rwandan lore, Nyabingi was the title of a queen who reigned over the region of Karagwe until she was beheaded by her husband, Ruhinda, a Tutsi chief from the region of Kigezi. The murdered queen was believed to be an avenging spirit, and public disasters were attributed to her wrath. In the nineteenth century, as the dynasty was consolidating its power, Nyabingi became one of several possession cults in the region, which in turn became "vehicles for opposition to alien rule." In Nyabingi's case, access to her spirit was limited to the *bagirwa* specialists who claimed to communicate with her in the form of a dialogue. Numerous instances of rebellions in the north against the Nyiginya Dynasty, including one noteworthy occasion against Rwabugiri, were attributed to instigations by Nyabingi and her followers—yet another example of a spiritual cult providing the impetus for a "clear-cut agenda of rebellion against [in this case] the central-state structures" of the Nyiginya. The court periodically sent expeditions northward to crush the *bagirwa* for inciting the Hutu against their Tutsi overlords.[55]

When the European colonialists arrived, they became embroiled in Nyabingi activities. In 1907 the Germans aided Musinga by arresting a powerful *bagirwa* priestess named Muhumusa who was conspiring against the monarchy. Muhumusa resurfaced again in 1911 after instigating a series of raids against the British in Kigezi, ostensibly to drive them from the area. She was arrested again and deported, but one of her lieutenants, Ndungutsi, was believed by many in the cult to be Mibambwe, who had been usurped of his throne by Kanjogera and Kabare during the Coup of Rucunshu. By claiming to be Mibambwe, Ndungutsi became popular by manipulating the Tutsi clans on the succession issue and promising to liberate the Hutu. He remained a troublesome and dangerous figure to the Germans until his death in 1912. The Nyabingi Cult, with its anticolonial sentiments, reemerged in Kigezi in 1917, where it became the predominant means of protesting British rule. This time the British arrested Nyabingi followers, not as political prisoners but as sorceresses under the 1912 Witchcraft Ordinance, which had been directed specifically at the *bagirwa*. By 1919 the uprising in Kigezi subsided, but Nyabingi activities continued on a smaller scale, with one final uprising in 1928, by which time Anglican missionary efforts and Christian conversion were sapping the cult of its appeal.[56]

When the CMS missionaries in Kigezi first encountered the cult, they generally processed it through the lens of their conservative, orthodox reading of Christianity, calling it "worship of the personal devil." Yet Stanley Smith still betrays an awareness of the anticolonial motives behind it. Smith noted in 1921, "From time to time there arises a man or woman possessed by Nyabingi and all who are discontent and tired of making the white man's roads or paying the white man's taxes, report to him . . . the people credit him with curing sickness and death . . . cattle, sheep and goats are offered to appease his malice . . . girls will be offered to him . . . the 'handmaidens of Satan.'" Periodic references to Nyabingi appear throughout the Ruanda Mission's letters. The last widespread Nyabingi revolt in 1928 was reported in the *Ruanda Notes* by Leonard Sharp, who claimed indigenous Christians outed the planned uprising to the authorities. Five years later, Sharp reported to the *Church Missionary Outlook* about a former Nyabingi sorcerer who had converted to Christianity. As late as 1947, field missionaries were referring to former *bagirwa* who had converted.[57]

The Ruanda Mission's firsthand observations and reports from the field confirm the argument of the Lindens, who credit part of the initial success of the CMS in northern Rwanda to the conversion of numerous *bagirwa* priestesses, who then directed their followers and supplicants to church. Elizabeth Hopkins, historian of the Nyabingi cult, likewise maintains that a dramatic increase in the number of converts to Christianity by 1928 aided British authorities in their suppression of the movement. Presenting a more cynical argument about why this occurred, Hopkins cites a confidential report from a district commissioner in Kigezi who wrote that "they, the Baganda catechists who were in charge of the Protestant bush-churches, circulated rumors that those who did not become Christians in six months would be considered sympathizers with the Nyabingi and thrown in prison." Considering the chauvinism that Baganda catechists often displayed toward the Bakiga, the report may contain a goodly measure of truth.[58]

Regardless of the politics, the Ruanda Mission displayed a common missional practice when confronted with indigenous belief systems. Church history is replete with examples of missionaries co-opting pagan mythologies and then incorporating them into the Christian narrative. In writing of the history of Anglican missions, Titus Presler argued that the church carried into the modern era Pope Gregory's famous directive to "adapt pagan sites and practices to Christian devotion rather than to destroy them," producing a creative stance toward preexisting religions and cultures. A renowned historian of Christianity in Africa, Thomas Spear, puts this into the context of the CMS efforts in Rwanda.[59]

According to Spear, pre-Christian African belief in the supernatural was common, and as the missionaries sought greater control over their churches, the charismatic teachings of evangelicals, with their emphasis on divine inspiration and the gifts of the Holy Spirit, synthesized the two traditions. Spear writes that African Christians "built on the traditions of the Old Testament

and Christ's ministry as much as on African prophetic traditions and quests
for spiritual power to contest God's word," pointing to the belief in the presence and power of evil spirits and witches in most African cultures. When
traditional church leaders attacked such beliefs as the work of the Devil, they
"inadvertently incorporated African doctrines of evil within Christianity, leading African Christians to adopt prayer and baptism by the Holy Spirit as a
means of combating witchcraft in general."[60]

In this manner, the traditional African religious heritage enabled people to
retain certain elements of their culture that they considered necessary for inte-
gration into their Christian faith. The CMS missionaries and their first converts in Rwanda were no exception. In 1938 M. J. Bessell recorded how *bagirwa*
priestesses would go behind a bark-cloth curtain to invoke Nyabingi, and
those who had brought offerings and supplications would hear the words:
"Lady of the Great Spirit, come, save, cure your people. . . . Save us from evil,
from sickness." Followed by, "My children, I will cure you . . . but your Lady
is not satisfied with your gifts. . . . You must return and bring others. . . . Then
I will intercede for you again before her." For the evangelical-minded missionaries of the Ruanda Mission, it's not difficult to imagine the effectiveness with
which the oracles of Nyabingi were replaced with the revelations of the Holy
Spirit.[61]

With education, medical aid, and conversions proceeding apace at Gahini,
the Belgian governor of Ruanda-Urundi, General Alfred Marzorati (1881–
1955), assured the mission in November 1928 of "no further hindrances to
working in Ruanda." By then, Geoffrey Holmes, Kosiya Shalita, Stanley
Smith, and Joe Church had all visited at one time or another with Musinga
and presumably secured his approval for their work, albeit under Belgian auspices. Evidently the CMS missionaries were unaware that Musinga's power
was waning in the face of the Catholic Church and that he was seeking the aid
of the Protestants to counter their influence, including among the Seventh
Day Adventists, also active in the kingdom. Nonetheless, after years of advances and setbacks with the Belgian authorities and conflicts with the Catholics, the Ruanda Mission was well established by 1931, the same year the Belgians rearranged the political dynamics of Rwanda once again.[62]

The Coming of Belgian Rule

The German occupation of Rwanda ended on May 16, 1916, when Belgian
forces from the Congo, under Molitor, arrived at Musinga's royal enclosure.
From the outset of European colonialism in the region, the Rwandans dreaded
the prospect of Belgian rule. Wagering that continued German rule was pref-
erable to Belgian or even British annexation, Musinga cooperated in aiding

the colonial forces of Germany in any way he could, even while he used the dislocations of the fighting to strengthen his own power. The court remembered the disastrous defeat at Shangi, where one of its finest armies had been destroyed by Belgian guns. Belgian officials in Eastern Congo routinely caused trouble in Rwanda in the intermediary years, and Musinga was aware of the abuses committed by their forces under Leopold. As if to confirm the court's fears, the Belgian forces who entered the *mwami's* compound in May promptly shot and killed two of Musinga's guards. Having little alternative, Musinga hurriedly paid tribute to the Belgians and pledged no further contact or support for Germany.[63]

Throughout German rule, the colonial administrators and Musinga's court had shrewdly made frequent use of each other to accomplish their respective aims. Germany had no desire to destabilize the kingdom by overturning the monarchy. Nonetheless, for the Tutsi chiefs at the court and elsewhere, the White Fathers were a growing and unwelcome nuisance. As Catholic missions expanded, their compounds and buildings became more elaborate, and growing numbers of Hutu laborers were called upon to work in the service of the church. The requisitioning of Hutu laborers offended the Tutsi chiefs, who regarded the levying of peasants as their exclusive right under *ubureetwa*. Often, when workers left their chiefs to work at the mission compounds, they were not allowed to return. Sometimes the chiefs withdrew cattle from wealthier Hutu clients, and the Fathers would subsequently compensate them with grants of their own cows. With such practices, the White Fathers were undermining and threatening the political order of the kingdom. Germany was often called upon to intervene and curb the power of the Catholics, at one point even restricting the building of new Catholic mission stations.[64]

At other times, each side, the court and the Germans, leveraged the support of the Fathers against the other. As each group, the court, the German administrators, and the White Fathers, tried to triangulate the politics of the kingdom to its own advantage, all gained in the process. For Musinga and his allies, German support allowed them to isolate their rivals and increase Tutsi hegemony over the region and their Hutu subjects. Despite initial humiliations inflicted on the court by the Belgian administrators, Musinga and his powerful mother, Kanjogera, adapted to the new arrangement and used the Belgians, as they had the Germans, to successfully protect their position during the early years of the new occupation. Following the British colonial practice in Africa of indirect rule, which preserved the existing institutions of power by placing them under colonial management, Belgium was committed to upholding the monarchy. By the mid-1920s, however, Musinga discovered in the Belgians a much more difficult opponent to manipulate. Being a

Catholic monarchy, they were naturally more closely allied to the White Fathers, set upon the colonial development of the kingdom, and determined to be the final authority in Rwanda.[65]

With the Belgians being a more supportive administration than the Germans had been, increasing numbers of younger Tutsi, previously shielded from the White Fathers' endeavors, saw advantages to be gained in European civilization. By 1923 a Catholic school for young Tutsi men was founded at Nyanza, the location of the court, and Christian instruction was permitted, though at first the school was intended for secular education only. After 1925 the Belgians insisted that only Tutsi with some degree of European education be appointed to official positions by the court, preferably those who were Christian. With a new avenue of advancement open, within three years nearly all the young men at the Nyanza school were either Catholic or in the process of so becoming. The effect was to continue the elite status of the Tutsi around the court even while Christianization was undermining the traditional prerogatives of the *mwami*.[66]

In 1927 rich deposits of tin were discovered in eastern Rwanda, and several large banks and business firms in Belgium were planning commercial investments. The colonial government was instructed by Brussels to accelerate the pace of development even if it meant more aggressively undermining the traditional structures of the kingdom, as only a well-organized and efficient administrative system could guarantee investment and profit. Smaller Tutsi holders of *ibikingi* domains were pressured to liquidate their claims in favor of larger, more organized concessions for economic development. When the Rwakayihura famine struck in 1928, the Belgians used the occasion to expedite the process when Tutsi notables failed to take appropriate measures to address the suffering. Around Kigali, the administrative capital since Kandt had founded it under German auspices in 1907, the number of *ibikingi* landholdings by the Tutsi was reduced from 119 to 7. Musinga, who had seen the Belgians act against his wishes several times in the past, became ever more aware of his diminishing status, as the Tutsi chiefs most aligned with the Belgians were the very ones he detested the most. In the 1920s, many of the chiefs themselves increasingly turned to the "missionaries for support in their struggles for power." The *mwami* could do virtually nothing as Tutsi chiefs became Belgium's chiefs rather than his own.[67]

As the relationship between the Belgian administrators and their favored chiefs grew, so too did Belgian acceptance of the Tutsi's favored status. Belgian officials frequently shielded their chiefs from recalcitrant Hutu under their control, accepting in the process the Hamitic Myth of the superiority of the Tutsi and using it to justify increased demands upon the Hutu. For the Belgian colonialists, coinciding with the rise of fascist political parties in Brussels, the Tutsi were "born to rule, the Hutu to labor; the Tutsi were intelligent and decisive, the Hutu stupid and docile."[68]

Musinga, trying to protect his favored chiefs and recoup his lost authority, tried in vain to reassert his role. Rumors spread of Musinga trying to rally the Tutsi chiefs still beholden to him and expel the Belgians and White Fathers. In 1930 Charles Voisin, governor of Ruanda-Urundi and deputy governor-general of the Belgian Congo, made plans to remove Musinga from power after consulting with Vicar Léon-Paul Classe (1874–1945), who took over the newly formed Vicariate of Ruanda in 1922. Classe had originally favored minimal involvement in colonial politics and heretofore had supported the continuation of Musinga's reign. By 1927, though, Classe was undermining Musinga, denouncing him to the governor and writing in an article published in Europe that the king was the "single greatest obstacle to economic development and social progress in Rwanda." Going further, Classe accused Musinga of homosexuality and incest, writing that young Tutsi around the court "refuse to serve his shameful royal pleasures. . . . Even his sons, his daughters, are born for his pleasure. . . . We became his declared enemies!" Classe also referenced the old *kabaka* of Buganda, Mwanga, as having participated in such activities.[69]

Not surprisingly, Classe favored Voisin's plan and suggested one of Musinga's Christian-educated sons, Rudahigwa, as a replacement. On November 12, 1931, Voisin ordered Musinga to vacate the palace along with Kanjogera. The royal drum Karinga, the symbol of the *mwami*'s power, was seized and given to Rudahigwa, who was proclaimed Mwami Mutara IV, the new king of Rwanda, on November 16. To prevent a sympathetic uprising on his behalf, Musinga's life was spared. He, his wives, his children, and Kanjogera were exiled to the far southwest of Rwanda in an inaccessible area. Kanjogera died two years later. When rumors persisted of Musinga's return, he was further exiled to the Congo in 1940, where he died four years later. By effectively choosing the new *mwami*, Rudahigwa, Belgian control of Rwanda was absolute and the Christian presence secure.[70]

CHAPTER THREE

Growth, Revival, and Conflict

The Anglican Church through World War II

RUDAHIGWA'S ENTHRONEMENT SIGNIFIED a watershed moment in Rwandan history, and a seminal event for the White Fathers. On account of his Catholic education, Rudahigwa was open to Christian conversion. He was formally baptized in 1943, whereby he was proclaimed the "first Christian king" of the "first Catholic kingdom in Africa." For the Catholics, his conversion was the culmination of decades of navigating the difficult social categories of Rwandan society. Winning over the Tutsi rulers had been the Catholic aim at the beginning of the White Fathers' mission. From the outset of his own tenure as bishop in 1922, Classe had favored the Belgian policy of supporting the Tutsi and the continued rule of the *mwami*, though he ultimately turned on Musinga. Classe saw education, entrusted to the Catholic Church, as the gateway to winning over the ruling class and the avenue by which they would enter the church. After years of setbacks, special schools were created for Tutsi to learn the catechism and the French language.

The first Superior of the Mission at Save, Father Alphonse Brard (1858–1918), initially admired the Tutsi for their "intelligence, liveliness, and curiosity," and conversely harbored a disparaging view of the Hutu. But, as Ian Linden writes, "after a few months of frustrating relations with the Tutsi," and coupled with the hostility of Musinga's court, "their illusions disappeared . . . and Father Brard started to hate the Tutsi." Subsequently the Catholics turned to the Hutu, who received considerable aid from the mission stations. By 1919 the Catholics were a "Hutu Church within a Tutsi-dominated society," with few converts from among the latter.[1]

Belgian rule and Catholic schooling, however, reversed the situation. In the face of Musinga's hostility, prior to his removal, young pages from the court secretly approached the mission at Kabgayi for instruction. As the king was being progressively weakened by the mid-1920s, Tutsi elites increasingly turned to the Catholic Church as they "came to realize that conversion to Christianity was a requirement for advancement under the new system." With the very notion of kingship in crisis, they sought after the "alternate sources of ritual legitimation that Catholicism promised to provide."[2]

As discussed in chapter 1, since the time of Ndori and Rujugira, religious practices in Rwanda had always buttressed the legitimacy of the monarchy without influencing ethics or behavior. With little indication of understanding the historical dynamics of Rwanda, the White Fathers celebrated their success even while Catholicism was "accepted as a new cult rather than a religious challenge," a cult that, like the Gihanga Myth of Ndori and the Ryangombe Cult of Rujugira, added newfound legitimacy to the *mwami* and the nobility, ultimately smoothing the way toward the European racialization of the country in the colonial period. In similar fashion, the postgenocide Anglican Church of the present, with its legions of evangelical Western supporters and "Friends of the New Rwanda," has been adopted as a support mechanism to legitimize the unchallenged and less-than-democratic reign of the current government of Rwanda—an antecedent in Rwanda's precolonial history that not only survived colonialism but continues to thrive in the present day.[3]

Rudahigwa's enthronement was accompanied by accelerated conversions during a period known in Catholic history as the Tornade. In the White Fathers' annual report from 1929–30, the number of Tutsi baptisms amounted to just less than 5,000. By 1931 the number almost doubled to more than 9,000, and increased again to roughly 16,500 Tutsi by 1932. Across all social categories, the Catholics counted a bit less than 100,000 baptized Rwandans in 1930. By 1940 the number tripled to 300,000, which was less than 20 percent of the total population but still an impressive record of growth and one in which the Tutsi were represented disproportionately. Some 80 percent of the Tutsi chiefs and subchiefs were Catholic by 1936. In 1945 it was estimated that 95 percent of all Tutsi were Catholic. As Longman wrote, "Observers of the church in Rwanda in the 1930s wrote of a 'tornado' where the 'breath of the spirit' was blowing, as the churches filled with believers and thousands of Rwandans converted." Rudahigwa's baptism in 1943 was the symbolic triumph of the Tutsi Tornade.[4]

While the events of 1931 and the Tornade made Catholicism the "religion of the ruling class," the opportunity arose for Protestantism to become the religion of the oppressed. With Catholicism the veritable state religion by 1940, the Anglicans "drew upon the theologically disenchanted and politically marginalized . . . remaining a small but vigorous alternative to established Catholicism," especially among the Hutu in the north where the CMS was most active. The Ruanda Mission had also hoped at first to win over the Tutsi ruling class, especially in the 1920s when the Catholics were having difficulty doing so. In the 1930s, the *Ruanda Notes* speak glowingly of occasions when Tutsi came to the mission settlements, although the reality was that most of the Tutsi converts were "pastoralists without political clout" and not a part of the "ruling elite." While the Ruanda Mission experienced newfound growth in the 1930s, finding new mission sites became more difficult because of opposition from the mostly Catholic Tutsi chiefs, resulting in the Anglicans and other Protestant churches becoming identified as "churches of the Hutu."[5]

No mention itself was made of Rudahigwa's enthronement in 1931 by the CMS missionaries at Gahini and elsewhere, though they certainly would have been aware of the event. The only reference in the *Ruanda Notes* was in 1934 and primarily made note of how many of the old chiefs were deposed and replaced by "young men straight out of the Roman Catholic schools." Accordingly, the ongoing political concern in the 1930s for the Ruanda Mission was the continued opposition from the Catholics. The approval and allotment of land for new churches and sites had to be secured from Tutsi chiefs, most of whom were Catholic and backed by the Belgian authorities. Under pressure from the Catholic Church, the chiefs often declined their requests. On occasion, the Belgian authorities intervened on behalf of the Anglicans, but the issue was one of contention throughout the period.[6]

The most serious conflict arose in November 1933. According to Joe Church's account, a young Tutsi Christian named Margarita was residing at the Gahini Girls' School, where she had been left in the care of a missionary nurse named Theodora "Dora" Skipper (1896–1999) when her own mother died. The girl's brother, a Roman Catholic, arrived when the European staff was away to take the girl back to her family to be married to another Roman Catholic. Skipper, a pioneer missionary in Ruanda since 1926, along with Kosiya Shalita, Yosiya Kinuka, and a few others, went to the girls' home and took her back to Gahini. In the middle of the night, two White Fathers forced their way into the station and demanded the return of the girl. An altercation occurred when Skipper and the Gahini staff blocked the priests from entry; the priests then shouted obscenities, shoved Skipper several times, and threatened to bring an armed party to Gahini. The conflict was resolved when a Catholic prelate, Monsignor Verhulst, arrived in the early hours of the morning and determined the girl should stay at Gahini. Shortly thereafter, it was reported that the Catholics in the area had forbidden their parishioners from seeking medical care at Gahini even when seriously ill. Joe Church noted these were but two of many aggressions on the part of the Catholics against the Ruanda Mission.[7]

Despite the ongoing opposition from the Catholic Church and its chiefs, the letters in the *Ruanda Notes* from the early 1930s speak of progress, growth, and success for the mission. In 1931 Holmes founded a second mission at Kigeme, in south-central Rwanda, where he was joined by the Smiths in 1932. Work proceeded slowly from a lack of funds, but Smith was pleased with the progress. The area around Kigeme was densely populated and ruled by a Tutsi chief named Semugeshi, who had not yet converted to Catholicism. Smith observed as well that the Hutu in the Kigeme region were "not so slavish under the control of their Batutsi overlords as in eastern Rwanda about Gahini." In 1932 James "Jim" Brazier (1903–89) and Bert Jackson founded a third mission at Shyira, in the northwest corner of Rwanda, roughly thirty miles from Uganda and the churches in Kigezi. Shyira, with its diocesan seat at Ruhengeri, became the first Anglican Province of Rwanda. In February 1931, the Sharps opened a hospital on Bunyonyi Island, in Kigezi, Uganda, specifically for the purpose of treating leprosy. They were joined by May Langley, a trained nurse who had prior experience in the Sudan but who left the field with an illness in 1937. By the mid-1930s, the Bunyonyi Leper Hospital had grown into a full mission settlement with a church, boys' and girls' schools, and housing for the families of victims receiving treatment. At its height, more than one thousand patients resided on the island with a mixed but impressive record of success. Many years later, Leonard Sharp claimed that after four decades of treatment, aided by more advanced cures, leprosy was largely eliminated as a threat in the region.[8]

In November 1932, the Ruanda Mission received a new constitution from the CMS, making it a separate, self-governing mission in the Diocese of Uganda, the news of which was widely celebrated. Catholic opposition notwithstanding, the Ruanda Mission also garnered attention and approval from the authorities in the protectorate. Although Smith complained in 1934 that the Ruanda Medical Mission was "ill-equipped and impoverished," he, Sharp, and two others started receiving stipends as *medicins agrees* (approved physicians) from the Belgian governor, and regular monetary grants were made to the CMS hospitals, all of which offset costs for the mission. Rudahigwa visited the Bunyonyi Leper Hospital in 1932 and Gahini in 1934. Dignitaries from the protectorate often sought medical help themselves from the CMS stations. By the end of 1934, in addition to the thriving Bunyonyi Leper Settlement, the Ruanda Mission had a church, a hospital, boys' and girls' schools, and evangelists' training schools at Gahini and Kabale. Kigeme and Shyira were rapidly developing along the same lines. From the evangelists' training schools at Gahini and Kabale, CMS catechists served hundreds of village churches and claimed thousands of adherents.[9]

With the work in Rwanda well underway, Sharp and Smith were eager to move into neighboring Burundi in the south of the Belgian Protectorate of Ruanda-Urundi. In June 1934, Smith, Sharp, and a translator named Samsoni, who had helped Harold Guillebaud translate the Bible into Kinyarwanda, departed for a tour of Urundi to obtain sites for new mission settlements. Accompanying them was the king of Urundi, Mwambutsa IV (1912–77), and Kosiya Shalita, who had first traveled with Geoffrey Holmes to Gahini in 1925. Following their trek in June, the mission settled on sites at Buhiga, in eastern Urundi, and Matana, in the south. Shalita remained at Matana to begin pioneer mission work, and William Church took up residence at Buhiga.[10]

With work expanding rapidly, the bishop of Uganda, Cyril Stuart (1892–1982), appointed William Arthur Pitt-Pitts (1890–1940) as the first archdeacon of the Ruanda Mission in 1935. Pitt-Pitts was well known to the Ruanda team. He was at Cambridge with Smith and Sharp during their student days, where he had taken a leading role in the CiCCU. He went to Uganda as a missionary in 1917. In the intervening years, he was with the CMS Mission in Kenya and was made a canon in 1934. His appointment as archdeacon a year later was greeted with much enthusiasm, although he eventually fell into disfavor by the some of the missionaries over the East African Revival that was soon to grip the Ruanda Mission.[11]

Revival

In the *Ruanda Notes* of April 1934, Joe Church produced a lengthy letter describing what he called the first "Convention ever held at Gahini" on the day after Christmas, 1933. More than one thousand Rwandans attended from nearby areas, and Church noted that there was a "real movement of the Spirit in our midst." The convention lasted five days with numerous sermons and talks. Among the topics addressed were "Sin . . . the Second Birth . . . Repentance . . . the Holy Spirit . . . the Christian Walk . . . and the Second Coming." Church then recounted a conversation with a distraught Kosiya Shalita on the last day, wherein they agreed that "nothing but the Spirit could break men's hearts" and lead to "Repentance . . . the hardest thing an African can be called upon to do before God or man." Church then described what he called a "remarkable thing . . . a native Christian got up and began confessing some sin he had committed." What followed was a "wave of conviction" that lasted for more than two hours, often with several people speaking at once. According to the recounting, "Numbers of others got up and said they were convicted at these meetings, many of bad living and adultery, many of bad drinking, and in each case they promised in God's sight henceforth to step out on the new life in Christ."[12]

In September 1935, Church, Shalita, and a team from Gahini were asked to lead another convention at Kabale, as the mission there had been "praying for a revival for some time." The result, as reported in the *Ruanda Notes*, was that "many were converted, others consecrated themselves to the Lord and there has been a forsaking of sins . . . followed in many cases by restitution." The report goes on to say many African evangelists were "touring round preaching; backslidden Christians are being restored and people are standing up and asking publicly, 'What must I do to be saved?'"[13]

Thereafter, the letters from many of the missionaries routinely speak of revival taking place across the mission. Following a tour of the field, Archdeacon Pitt-Pitts noted in March 1936, "A wave of spiritual blessing seems to be spreading through the Mission." The same month, Rev. Lawrence Barham (1901–73), who along with his wife, Julia, had joined the Ruanda Mission in 1928, reported from Kabale, "You have heard from others something of the spiritual revival that is taking place in Kigezi." Barham claimed that after the convention in September, there was a wave of where the "confession of sin, restitution, [and] apologies followed. . . . Many had dreams, sometimes receiving strong impressions to read certain versus of the Bible, which led them to put away some sin, notably native beer drinking, which is such a curse to this district." Joe Church, writing from Kabale, told his readers, "The Word of God has been rushing through the station and numbers are being born again." In the summer of 1936, Church and his team from Gahini were asked by the bishop to organize another convention at Bishop Tucker College in Mukono, near Kampala. He recounted the event in similar language, describing sermons on "Sin, Repentance, and the Second Birth and the Holy Spirit."[14]

The conventions spoken of here at Gahini, Kabale, Mukono, and elsewhere form the basis of what is known in the Anglican Church and in the history of the region as the East African Revival of the 1930s. The pattern that emerged in the early years of the decade was repeated across the Ruanda Mission and in Uganda. Spirited conventions were held, also understood as revival meetings, in which European missionaries and African evangelists would sing hymns, preach, teach, and pray with large gatherings, often numbering in the thousands. Conversions occurred on a large scale, and nominal, "backslidden" Christians were frequently moved to confess and repent of past and ongoing sins. Restitutions for past grievances were encouraged. Following the conventions, "revival teams" made up of African believers would travel into the countryside, often venturing far across the region to carry the revival spirit to new congregations. As the revival movement spread, its most dedicated adherents came to be called the Balokole (or "saved ones"), or known in Kinyarwanda as the Abarokore, and they were often associated with a common anthem song and greeting known as Tukutendereza, or "Praise the Lord," in Luganda.

Writing from Kabale, Jim Brazier, a devout Revivalist missionary, summed up some of the core characteristics of the Revival fellowship. The starting point for Revival gatherings was a willingness to speak openly about one's spiritual state and make public confessions of sins. Another characteristic Brazier wrote of was a willingness to challenge the spiritual failures of others, even of those in senior positions. He referred to this as "walking in the light with others" and noted that unwillingness to do this was regarded as "fear of man" rather than of God. On this point, the Balokole were often disliked by those who were not of the same persuasion and who resented their implied criticisms. In 1941 several Balokole at Bishop Tucker College precipitated a crisis within the mission by refusing to conform to the rules of senior officials who were not, as they saw it, "walking in the light."[15]

Brazier described other hallmarks of the Revival that frequently didn't set well with those outside the fellowship. One was "exaltation of the free and extemporaneous as against the liturgical and formal." He described liturgy, a fundamental part of Anglican worship, as "a cloak for deadness," and noted that many Balokole disliked the communion rails as suggestive of a "holy place." These suggestions later led some to question whether the Balokole were Anglican at all. Also troubling for many European colonialists was the Revival's insistence on a "sense of complete spiritual equality with Africans." Lastly, Brazier maintained that Revival preaching was based on the speaker's "own experience and testimony," which was often made in a "fairly violent" style in "tempo and substance" meant to stress the doctrine of the "Blood of Christ" as necessary for "victory over sin." Some observers of the Revival criticized their method of preaching as being weak on sound instruction and theology. Others alleged that the Balokole preached so much on the blood of Christ that it had become a charm or a fetish. Brazier's commentary was written in 1945, at a time when the Revival was a subject of intense controversy that divided the Ruanda Mission within itself as well as with the church hierarchies. His tone was explanatory but unapologetic.[16]

In a spiritual sense, the Revival was generally understood as a "movement of the Holy Spirit," often described as spreading like a "wildfire" over which the mission claimed little control as it seemingly took on a life of its own. By the end of 1936, the Revival's influence was present in all the Ruanda Mission stations. Of the events at Gahini, Church wrote, "The happenings cannot easily be put into words. We cannot really explain or describe spiritual things. The medium of words is inadequate." Church later spoke of it as "essentially a Holiness movement" in which one of the central preoccupations was adherence to strict biblical orthodoxy and a fully changed life free of sin. The fully changed life is what was referred to at the conventions as the "Second Birth," which came as a result of the believer being filled with the Holy Spirit. Reminiscing in 1945 over what happened at Gahini, Church wrote, "Most of the staff, all nominal Christians, were broken down and then brought out by the Spirit of God into a life of burning zeal for God and holiness." Revivalist Christians were then called upon to maintain strict personal piety and uncompromised standards of conduct and behavior. The use of tobacco and alcohol was denounced, and polygamy was absolutely forbidden. In this area, the Revivalists were often in conflict with many traditionally accepted practices.[17]

Voluminous observations made of revival gatherings offer a generally clear picture of how the movement spread and was conducted. Less clear are its origins and definitive starting point. In the *Ruanda Notes*, the Revival is not mentioned as a definable event until 1934, when Church described the first convention at Gahini. As a result, and because of his own thorough autobiography and account of the Revival, Church and the staff at Gahini are usually credited with starting the movement. Even here, though, events are uncertain. Church wrote in a widely circulated pamphlet in 1936, titled "A Call to Prayer," that he had been at the Gahini station for about a year when he traveled to Kampala, Uganda, in September 1929. Church, suffering from the strains of the recent famine, was at a low point in his own spiritual life and needed a brief furlough. At the cathedral in Kampala, Church met with a Christian Muganda named Simeoni Nsibambi (1897–1978), with whom he prayed and read the scriptures.[18]

Nsibambi was born in 1897 to Sezi Kimwanje, a Christian chief, and was educated at CMS schools in Kampala and at King's College in Budo. When World War I began, he became a sergeant in the African Native Medical Corps, later claiming to have had his first conversion to Christianity on a ship bound for Zanzibar during his enrollment. After the war, he worked in the Ugandan colonial health department and married his wife, Eva, in 1925. One of their sons, Apolo Nsibambi, born in 1938, was the prime minister of Uganda from 1999 to 2011. In a 1952 interview with Zebuloni Kabaza, Nsibambi claimed to have experienced a "second conversion" by the Holy Spirit in 1922, a turning point in his life. By 1927 he was in a Bible class with a CMS missionary named Mabel Ensor (1878–1954). Ensor, daughter of the first CMS missionary to Japan, went to Uganda in 1915 but soon came to see the church as "backslidden" and filled with "nominal Christians." By 1927 she had started her own teaching class where she and her students prayed for revival in Uganda. According to both men's accounts, Church and Nsibambi first met in Ensor's Bible class. In 1928 Ensor broke from the Anglicans and started the Mengo Gospel Church, eventually becoming a vociferous critic of the Revival movement and its tendency to claim it was the "only way of salvation." Nsibambi stayed with the Anglicans, and the bishopric granted him permission to conduct Bible study classes at the cathedral.[19]

Church departed after their meeting in Kampala in 1929. When he returned a week later, Nsibambi had quit his government job and was evangelizing on the streets of Kampala. Church regarded his 1929 meeting as the turning point in Nsibambi's life, although this conflicts with Nsibambi's account in 1952 of having had a second conversion to the Holy Spirit in 1922. Church later claimed that the East African Revival began in 1933 at the convention in Gahini, a claim supported by the letters in the *Ruanda Notes* and endorsed again in Church's 1981 autobiographical account of the Revival, *Quest for The Highest*. Nsibambi claimed in an unpublished history of the Revival in the early 1970s that it began with his own encounter with the Holy Spirit in 1922. Despite the competing claims to the Revival's origins, Church and Nsibambi became key figures in the origins of the East African Revival.[20]

Virtually all the published histories of the Revival have been written by either participants or their associates and kin, or at least by sympathetic figures within the church. Heavily influenced by Joe Church's account, most of them endorse a standard and familiar story about its origins. According to this account, Church returned to Gahini in June 1929 after his second meeting with Nsibambi and, inspired by his example, started conducting his own daily, intensive Bible studies and prayer meetings in the evenings. Nsibambi started sending young Baganda as hospital workers to Gahini to join Church in his work. Two other men who figure prominently into the story of the Revival's origins were Yosiya Kinuka (1905–81) and Blasio Kigozi (1909–36). Both men, like Nsibambi, were Ugandan. Conventional accounts hold Rwanda as the starting place for the movement, yet Kevin Ward notes that virtually all the "chief agents of the Revival were Ugandans," a significant observation in the Anglican Church's remembrance of it presently.[21]

Yosiya Kinuka was from Ankole, a son of Hima cattle herders who became a Christian while receiving treatment for a case of yaws at the hospital in Kabale. Following his conversion under the influence of Smith and Sharp, both still at Kabale, he began working as a hospital orderly. In 1927 he met Church when he arrived at the hospital. In 1928 he and his wife went to Gahini to help start the hospital. Blasio Kigozi was the younger brother of Nsibambi, who had converted him to Christianity. After being educated as a teacher at Bishop Tucker College in Mukono, Kigozi joined the Gahini Station in 1929 to work at the Boys' School. Central to this account of the Revival, and the memory of it in present-day Rwanda, was an alleged conflict between Kigozi and Kinuka.[22]

By Kinuka's account, there were many "troubles and judgements at the hospital in those days," and he had not yet been "born again." When Kigozi arrived, the two did not like each other, and Kinuka left Gahini in 1930 for a holiday with Nsibambi. Nsibambi tried to convince Kinuka to acknowledge his wrongdoing with Kigozi and repent of his ways. According to Kinuka, his "heart was still unchanged." But on the trip back to Gahini, in a manner reminiscent of the New Testament's story of the Apostle Paul's conversion on the road to Damascus, he "yielded his heart to Christ," made peace and restitution with Kigozi, and was then "truly converted," referring to the second conversion experience the Revivalists spoke of frequently. According to Church in 1945, the Revival began with Kinuka's repentance as "most of the staff, all nominal Christians, were broken down and then brought out by the Spirit of God into a life burning with zeal for God and holiness." Kinuka and Kigozi remained key participants in Revival conventions, although Kigozi's work was cut short by his sudden death in January 1936 from tick fever. Church called him a "leader in revival," but when his death was announced in the widely read periodical the *Church Missionary Outlook*, he was called a "pioneer . . . who had been doing most valuable work in Ruanda." Owing to the controversies brewing within the mission, no mention was made of Kigozi's role in the Revival.[23]

As most of the prior histories of the Revival rely upon the reminiscences and stories of its key participants, they generally endorse these events as the definitive starting point for the movement. For the professional historian, however, the autobiographies, sympathetic histories, and testimonials about the Revival, which constitute most of the literature, must be regarded for what they were intended: accounts that were abstracted out of their political context and cast as evidence of God's work in Africa. The vocation of the historian, though, is to "disassemble Joe Church's archive, to rip the pages out of *Ruanda Notes*, and to place convert's testimonies again in the polemical world in which they were first composed." For sympathizers and believers in the Revival message, and indeed for adherents of the faith, this can seem like a disparaging and oppositional activity. Rather, the academic unpacking of a compelling story can be done without questioning the faith of those concerned, and quite often sheds new light on the significance of said events.[24]

Kevin Ward, who has written the most scholarly account of the Revival, points to a twofold origin. First, there was dissatisfaction with the spiritual state of the church in Uganda by the 1930s. He writes, "To keen Christians, the Church had sacrificed its evangelistic zeal and the quality of its Christian discipleship by its compromises with both traditional culture and the material opportunities opened up by modern society." Second, he points, as many others do, to the Ruanda Mission at Gahini as a key promoter of the Revival, most of whose Revival brethren date the start of the movement to the 1929 meeting between Church and Nsibambi. Prior to the 1934 Convention at Kabale, led by Church and his team, the Revival was confined to the staff at Gahini. This would incorrectly suggest that Church and his group were the sole originators of the movement. As Ward notes, Church was "not the originator, nor in any formal sense its director. . . . But his organizational skills . . . had a profound effect on the development of the Revival as it spread far and wide across East Africa." A close and critical reading of the letters found in the *Ruanda Notes* supports this claim, offering a more complex and nuanced picture of the conditions that led to the Revival, even while not conflicting with the supposed events at Gahini or contradicting Joe Church's role as an organizer.[25]

From the outset of their work, the missionaries were routinely troubled with the personal behaviors and social customs of their African converts. Having a decidedly pious and orthodox mindset themselves regarding what they considered proper Christian conduct, the missionaries were frustrated by the pace of change that they saw in their African parishioners. The consumption of alcohol and tobacco was a frequent complaint of those in the field. The cultural practice of taking more than one wife often continued in the face of condemnations by the missionaries, and what the missionaries regarded as the persistence of sorcery and witchcraft in the form of the Nyabingi Cult troubled them greatly. Reports of thefts and misappropriation of funds by African workers at the station are common in the letters. Their letters from the field make it clear that, by the early 1930s, African converts were not reforming their personal lives in a manner befitting what the missionaries regarded as essential evidence of true Christian conversion. As early as 1931, Lawrence Barham was complaining at Kabale of the "low spiritual standard" in Kigezi and of the "lack of missionary spirit and enthusiasm amongst our Christians." He observed that "Christian backsliding" was common. Leonard Sharp was still noting in 1933 how "fear of Nyabingi" was holding many Christians back from the mission. At Gahini in 1933, prior to the first convention held by Church, Geoffrey Holmes was urging readers to "pray for a time of real spiritual revival." In September 1933, Leonard Sharp led a revival convention at the leper colony on Bunyonyi Island months before the one Church held at Gahini the following Christmas.[26]

Working at Kabale in 1932, Jim Brazier instituted what he called "Cleanse the Church" campaigns throughout the Kigezi district notably before the

Revival supposedly began. He described the campaigns as the "public expulsion of all Christians who have gone back from their baptism vows and who refuse to repent." Polygamy, he noted, was one of the chief stumbling blocks. Writing again later in the year, he was still conducting his "Cleanse the Church" campaigns, claiming he tried to "see personally all Christians who have back-slidden" to convince them to change their ways or face what amounted to excommunication from the church. When the Revivalists and Balokole spoke, as they often did, of the need for a fully transformed life, free of sin, these were the observations of which they were speaking, "back-slidden" Christians who had not fully repented. The Revival movement embraced what they saw as the presence of the indwelling Holy Spirit, which came after a second conversion experience, as the source of power to effect this full conversion in the life of the believer. The convention at Bunyonyi and the "Cleanse the Church" campaigns, along with the accompanying observations in the *Ruanda Notes* of "backsliding," improper conduct, and of the need for revival, suggest that the field was ripe for what Church and his team are credited with starting at Gahini in December 1933, and that Church was indeed not the sole progenitor of the Revival, for which he is sometimes given a lion's share of the credit.[27]

From a theological and historical perspective, the roots of the Revival go deeper. The CMS missionaries of the Ruanda Mission were all influenced by the teachings and beliefs of the nineteenth-century Keswick Higher Life movement. The Keswick movement was a response to an earlier Higher Life movement, which emanated out of the American holiness revival of the 1830s. The Higher Life movement and its emphasis on holiness stressed the need for the believer to live a life free of sin by moving beyond his or her original conversion by being "filled with the Holy Spirit," an event sometimes referred to frequently in the *Ruanda Notes* as the "New Life." Doctrinally, the Higher Life adherents believed that a person's natural inclination, even after conversion, was toward sin and depravity. The key to overcoming this tendency and living a sin-free and effective life for the Gospel was to live under the influence and guidance of the Holy Spirit. The Higher Life movement came to England in the 1870s and was promoted at large revival meetings called Keswick Conventions. The first one was held in Keswick in 1875, led by an Anglican pastor named Thomas Harford-Battersby (1822–82). Thereafter, conventions were held regularly and continue to the present.[28]

When the Keswick movement reached Cambridge University in the 1870s, large numbers of students were drawn to its teachings. Under its influence, many Cambridge students split with the national SCM and formed the more conservative CiCCU mentioned earlier. Smith, Sharp, Church, and many others in the Ruanda Mission studied at Cambridge in these years and all belonged to the CiCCU faction. Smith's father, Stanley Smith, had been among the first Anglican missionaries to China with Hudson Taylor's China Inland Mission. Taylor was an early proponent and speaker at the Keswick Conventions, making it a certainty that the young Algernon Smith, who was born in China, was influenced at an early age by the movement's teachings. The Cambridge division was felt within the larger CMS in 1922 when Keswick-influenced conservatives formed the BCMS within the CMS. An overwhelming majority of the missionaries sent to Rwanda, as well as the members of the Ruanda Council, sympathized with the CiCCU/BCMS position and stressed the teachings of the Higher Life movement.[29]

Moreover, the Higher Life movement reached Uganda ahead of the Ruanda Mission. In 1893 a Cambridge-educated lay missionary named George Lawrence Pilkington (1865–97) arrived at Mengo, in Buganda, to translate the Bible into Luganda. After a period of "deep disillusionment" with the spiritual state of the church, Pilkington took a holiday on Kome Island, where he read a Bible tract written by a "David," a Tamil evangelist from Columbo, Sri Lanka, who had evidently "received the baptism of the Holy Spirit through contact with the Salvation Army in 1887." As a result, Pilkington claimed to have received a revelation from the Holy Spirit and became convinced of the need for revival in Uganda. Pilkington wrote to Bishop Alfred Tucker (1849–1914) of his experience, "God has enabled us to see that we have been working in our own strength and consequently there has been no power in our lives. . . . We have been brought to that command 'be filled with the Spirit.'" He started organizing prayer meetings across southern Uganda where he spoke of the need of "fullness of the Spirit" and believed a revival was taking place. James Katarikawe claims it was under the influence of the Pilkington Revival, as it is called, that Baganda missionaries started spreading across the region as evangelists.[30]

At the Kampala revival in 1936, participants read from one of Pilkington's books, as they very much saw themselves as heirs to the revival spirit he initiated. Kevin Ward writes, "Pilkington had been influenced by the Keswick spirituality of the deeper life, with its claim of victory over sin, emphases which fully accorded with the aspirations of the Ruanda Mission." Simeon Nsibambi himself was influenced by the Higher Life movement prior to his 1929 encounter with Joe Church and was impressed by his reading of a book by Charles Finney (1792–1875), *Lectures on Revival*. Prior to becoming president of Oberlin College in Ohio, Finney was a pastor and participant in the American Second Great Awakening. His teachings and revivalist-style gatherings laid much of the groundwork for the Higher Life movement.[31]

The evidence of the Higher Life holiness movement and the Keswick Conventions on the outbreak of the Revival is abundant. Church and many of the key participants remained active at Keswick Conventions in England and elsewhere throughout their lives. As the Revival was taking root across East Africa in the second half of the 1930s, Church was a guest speaker at the 1937 Keswick Convention while home in England on a furlough. There he noted how many of the supporters and members of the Ruanda Mission were "well-known on the Keswick platform" and urged the convention to continue praying for "Holy Spirit filled Christians." Worth noting too is that the revival meetings held in Uganda and Rwanda were referred to as "conventions," reflecting the influence of Keswick even if they were simply revival meetings. The early revival led by Leonard Sharp on Bunyonyi Island in September 1933 was explicitly referred to as a "Keswick Convention." As a result of the Revival, the Keswick Conventions and the Higher Life movement were at the core of the Anglican Church's founding in Rwanda and remain so down to the present. Roger Bowen wrote of the Higher Life movement, "This hunger for a deeper experience of the transforming power of God in one's life was a deep undercurrent leading to the outbreak of revival. . . . And this movement profoundly marked the Anglican Church in Rwanda at its foundation."[32]

Lastly, seen in a wider context, the East African Revival was one of many spiritual movements that emanated out of the mission churches. In the first decades of the twentieth century, African evangelists led several movements of mass conversion across the continent, most of which stressed themes familiar to the Balokole movement: repentance from sin, belief in the power of the cross, and victory over traditional practices. In 1913 William Wadé Harris (1860–1929), a Liberian evangelist with the American Episcopal Mission, baptized tens of thousands of converts after spirited messages denouncing witchcraft and the use of traditional fetishes. A charismatic religious leader in the Belgian Congo named Simon Kimbangu (1887–1951) broke with the Baptist church in 1921 and attracted a large following by claiming to have the power to heal the sick and raise the dead. The Belgian authorities, backed by the Catholic Church, quickly condemned the Kimbanguist movement as subversive and arrested him within months, though some of the Protestant churches favored a more muted response. The swift Belgian response to the Kimbanguist movement, occurring outside the control of an established church, might also have muted the political voice of the Balokole Revivalists, themselves not wishing to be labeled subversive by the authorities.[33]

Among the Luo communities in western Kenya, Christianity was first conveyed by Luo migrants who studied in Buganda, where they were exposed to the dynamic growth of the church at the turn of the century. When CMS pioneer missionaries arrived in 1906, they found Christianity already established in prayer houses and relied upon Luo catechists to spread the faith. In 1912 Ibrahim Osodu, a Luo, claimed to have a revelation from the Holy Spirit, and many of the prayer houses took on a charismatic spirit despite opposition from the CMS mission. One of his followers, Alfayo Mango, established his own prayer house and preached on the power of the Holy Spirit, prophecy, and faith healing. Mango's followers fell into conflict with the neighboring Luyia people who, backed by the Anglicans, attacked the Luo prayer houses. When Mango was immolated in his home, his followers took his death as confirmation of prophecies they claimed to have regarding his foretold demise. Many independent Luo churches broke with the CMS and founded Roho (Luo for "Holy Spirit") churches across Western Kenya.[34]

Another progenitor of an African revival movement, known to Joe Church, was Arthur Chilson. Chilson and his wife, Edna, were missionaries with the Friends African Industrial Mission, the evangelical wing of the American Quakers. Based at Kaimosi in Western Kenya, Chilson preached a message on Pentecost in 1927, after a movement of the Holy Spirit allegedly occurred. In a manner that foreshadowed the East African Revival in Rwanda and Uganda, young believers were taken with the notion of being baptized in the Holy Spirit and of the need for the public confession of sin. Starting their own semiautonomous spiritual fellowships, the Kaimosi Revivalists broke with the Friends Church in 1932, giving rise to the African Church of the Holy Spirit. The Chilsons left Kenya and founded an American Quaker mission in Burundi, where they had close contact with Joe Church and the Ruanda Mission.[35]

These movements and others across the continent, the East African Revival included, occurred at a time when the modern Western missionary movement was gaining ground even while traditional African culture was being upended by the larger colonial project. Taken together, they share similar characteristics. All of them incorporated indigenous African leadership and eventually most had a strained relationship with the formal church authorities, if not the colonial state itself. Most incorporated the revelations and inspiration of the Holy Spirit on some level, often causing some degree of angst on the part of more conservative church leaders. In some cases, the revival movements of the early twentieth century led to a complete break with their church of origin, as in the Kimbanguist movement and the Holy Spirit revivals in Western Kenya. In some cases, indigenous African revival movements, like the Church of the Bakongo and the Holy Quaternity movements, strayed far beyond biblical teachings. In all cases, the African revivalist movements were an attempt on some level to "Africanize" Christianity and called for "greater penetration of faith into society," as followers and believers sought to "define the external signs of the faith."[36]

The East African Revival belongs in this context, even while retaining a distinctive character that distinguished it from similar movements. Measured against the likes of William Wadé Harris, who promoted polygamy even while condemning witchcraft, for example, the Balokole remained thoroughly pietistic and stressed rigid adherence to literal Christian teachings regarding personal conduct. By remaining under the umbrella of the Anglican Church, unlike the Luo and Friends movements in Western Kenya, they avoided outright condemnation and being labeled subversive to the colonial order, as befell the Kimbanguists. In no small part, this is because a cohort of educated British missionaries supported and partnered with the Balokole movement, offering it guidance and leadership. However, none of this is to say that the Balokole movement was entirely free of controversy.[37]

Revival Controversies

In April 1937, the first Revival convention was held in Kenya, at Kabete. Thereafter, conventions were held regularly across what was then called the East Africa Protectorate. In June of the same year, Pitt-Pitts excused Church from his medical duties at Gahini to devote himself to preaching the Revival message. Accompanied by teams of Ugandan evangelists, Church and other Revivalist missionaries fanned out across the region and beyond. By the start of 1939, the Revival was well known across Kenya, where it remains the dominant persuasion within the Anglican Church. By 1940 "Keswick Conventions" were being held in Sudan, Congo, and Tanzania. Writing in 1975, the historian Catherine Robbins noted that the Revival movement spread into all neighboring territories and among at least twenty different language groups and several different mission bodies. Robbins wrote of the Revival, "Its characteristic hymns, greetings, teachings, and its rigid norms of dress and behavior are familiar to Roman Catholics and non-Christians as well as to the Protestants among whom the Balokole worship."[38]

In 1944 revivals were held in several major cities in South Africa. When World War II ended in 1945, revival teams, usually still led by Joe Church and Ugandan evangelists, held meetings across Europe: in Switzerland, England, and France. In the 1950s, the Revival's influence was being felt across North America. In many respects, the Anglican churches of Ruanda and Uganda remain fixated on the Revival and its impact. For both churches, the Revival occupies a central place in their history and is a source of great pride, in no small part because of its far-reaching effects across the region and the world. Yet while the personal stories and reminiscences of the Revival celebrate its

impact, heated controversies surrounded the movement almost from the outset, as the established church hierarchies in Uganda and England wrestled over
the Revival's place within the larger Anglican communion.[39]

Bishop Stuart of Uganda, under whose authority the Ruanda Mission
resided, toured the province in 1936. In his account to the "Friends of Ruanda,"
Stuart expressed "no doubt whatsoever" that God was working in Ruanda, but
he also observed "a little, though not much, of the difficult side of revival, i.e.
hysteria." Interestingly, in the same edition of the *Ruanda Notes*, Lawrence
Barham wrote of the Revival, "This is not emotionalism [i.e., "hysteria"]; it's
stern conviction of sin by the Holy Spirit." In a confidential report to the
Ruanda Council in November 1938, Pitt-Pitts, while generally sympathetic to
the Revival, wrote, "Reports come in from another station where the Revival
has gone all wrong. Not only are the Natives, but one European, has gone and
done mad things, and looking back at Gahini one can see times when it would
have gone off the lines here too." As an example, during the Revival's earliest
days in Kampala, a Balokole leader, at one point, introduced nudity as a mark
of "perfect holiness." As late as 1946, troubling reports emerged from Revival
gatherings in Eastern Congo, including several instances of Balokole women
stripping off their clothes in public gatherings and another one in which a
teacher at Mboga tried to kill his wife after her "public confession" of
adultery.[40]

Stuart, and Pitt-Pitts to a lesser degree, had harbored reservations about the
Ruanda Mission prior to the Revival. When Stuart assumed the bishopric in
1934, he wanted to integrate the Ruanda Mission more fully into the structure
of the Church of Uganda. The often stridently independent streak of the doctors and missionaries of the Ruanda Mission led him to question their commitment to the Anglican way. His appointment of Pitt-Pitts as archdeacon in
1935 was aimed at imposing more ecclesiastical regularity on the mission. Stuart and Pitt-Pitts, as Cambridge men, were known to the Ruanda missionaries, and they had their own misgivings of the two. Stuart was seen "as a representative of the liberal and modernizing wing of Evangelicalism," and while
Pitt-Pitts was initially regarded as a kindred spirit, the Ruanda Mission was
soon railing against him too as an "ecclesiastical tyrant." The problems engendered by the Revival and its Balokole adherents strained these relationships
with the larger church almost to the breaking point.[41]

As the Balokole grew in number, they demonstrated a tendency to segregate
themselves into a separate sect within the mission, often with the implication
that they were the only ones who were truly "saved." The teachings of the
Revival, the need for a "Second Birth," the rigid demand for personal piety as
evidence of salvation, and the creation of devout fellowship groups often led

many of the Balokole to adopt an aggressive and judgmental attitude toward those who were not counted among their number. Pitt-Pitts was troubled by his observation that some believers in the church seemed to "lack assurance of salvation" when confronted by revival gatherings, despite being baptized believers. Coming against the backdrop of problems caused by other spiritualist movements in Africa, concerns about the Revival emerged among members of the Ruanda Council at an early date. In a report from 1936, Pitt-Pitts acknowledged problems with the Revival, writing, "I know some of these men, who have been leaders in this movement, have made mistakes and are open to criticism, but I have warned the mission that we need to be very careful in the way we deal with this matter." Additionally, the notion that one had to follow the exclusive teachings of the Balokole to be genuinely saved produced friction within the Ruanda Mission itself.[42]

In March 1939, Pitt-Pitts convened a meeting comprising Lawrence Barham, Leonard Sharp, Stanley Smith, Joe Church, Geoffrey Holmes, and himself to discuss the various issues and divisions arising from the Revival. The meeting was prompted by an incident in which Sharp, working then at the Matana station in Urundi, had dismissed a Balokole leader and sent him back to Gahini for causing divisions and trouble. Sharp noted, in an extract included in Pitt-Pitt's letter, that the trouble had arisen from the "exclusive claims of the native Abaka [as the Balokole were sometimes known] to salvation and the tendency of some of the missionaries to form an exclusive fellowship claiming that only those in the fellowship were 'Walking in the Light' and living the 'Victorious Life,'" a belief that Sharp claimed was "at variance with God's Word." Pitt-Pitts noted of the meeting that "some held very strongly that the Abaka Movement was a Sect within the Church and that some of us had joined it."[43]

While the Revival concerns of the late 1930s were mostly private matters, known only to the leaders of the Ruanda Mission, council members in London, and the church authorities in Uganda, in 1941 a crisis over the Balokole erupted at Bishop Tucker College that exacerbated the tensions and brought the issues into the spotlight. Bishop Tucker Memorial College opened in 1913 at Mukono, near Kampala, for the training of Ugandan pastors and teachers. Two early indigenous leaders in the Revival and the Church of Uganda, Blasio Kigozi and Erica Sabiti (1903–88), the first African Archbishop of Uganda, were trained at Mukono. In 1936 Bishop Stuart had plans to launch several new missions across Uganda and invited Joe Church and his Gahini team to conduct a preparatory mission at the college to help with the training of new evangelists. In the throes of revival, Church's team ran into controversy. The warden of the college, J. S. Herbert, and the theology tutor, J. C. Jones, did not approve of the Revivalists' style and harbored "strong reservations about the emotionalism of it all." Lawrence Barham, who arrived with the Gahini team, confronted Herbert about his pipe-smoking, and Church challenged Jones on his theological views. The meeting ended unhappily, and Church left Mukono convinced that the "clericalism" of the college, its "excessive exaltation of the clerical office," and its "undue deference to authority" were stifling the spirit of Revival.[44]

Stuart, still trying to recruit young men into the ministry, admitted a Balokole leader from Gahini named William Nagenda (1912–73), who accepted the offer in January 1940. Nagenda was an educated Muganda who had worked for the colonial office before his conversion to Christianity in 1936 by Nsibambi, whose wife was the sister of Nagenda's wife. When Blasio Kigozi died, Nagenda took his place at Gahini, where he became a prominent member of the Balokole and one of Church's main partners in spreading the Revival beyond Rwanda. According to Kevin Ward, Stuart's hope was that Mukono would have a "restraining influence" on the energetic Nagenda. When the "Mukono Crisis," as it was known, erupted in 1941, it was evident that Nagenda had not in any sense been restrained.[45]

From the start, Nagenda gathered other Balokole around him and, true to the Revivalist style, started daily prayer and praise meetings in the mornings. J. C. Jones, now warden of Mukono, was a staunch Anglican traditionalist in style but an evangelical liberal in theology. He disapproved of the Balokole and their daily meetings from the start, threatening at one point in 1940 to ban them. Nagenda's meetings continued unabated until Easter 1941, at which point the Balokole became more outspoken. They denounced the "various sins they saw in life at the college" and took a more militant stance toward Jones, refusing to take notes in his Bible class because of his "modernist views." Nagenda wrote to Stuart and suggested the college was "holding up revival in Uganda." Stuart's reply was less than gracious.[46]

In October 1941, the confrontation boiled into a crisis. The Balokole added preaching to their morning devotions, often denouncing non-Balokole students for their sins at a time when they were supposed to be working in their rooms. Church defended their preaching by adding that the Balokole, unlike other students, were never allowed to preach in the chapel. Jones banned the daily prayer meetings and preaching, and had the dormitory locked during lecture hours to prohibit private meetings. When Nagenda and the Balokole informed Jones of their intention to disobey, he expelled twenty-six of them from the college, some of whom had but one year until they graduated. Nagenda wrote of his willful disobedience to the new rules, "I had the assurance I had obeyed God. . . . The Warden rebuked us for the Gospel we preached."[47]

When the expulsions occurred, Stuart was in Zanzibar. Church maintained Jones made his move at just such a time to prevent the bishop from intervening. Upon his return, however, Stuart supported Jones's actions but offered the Balokole one final chance to repent of their disobedience and return to school, so long as they obeyed the rules. None of them did.[48]

At the heart of the Mukono Crisis was the insistence by Joe Church and the Balokole that they were not rebels, and that the church authorities in Uganda were trying to stifle the Gospel and the Revival message. Stuart always maintained that it was simply a question of obeying the rules of authority figures placed in position by God. In 1942 a Commission of Inquiry was convened to investigate the crisis and arrive at a solution for integrating the Balokole more fully into the Church of Uganda. The commissions' report in April 1943 did little to heal the rift between the church and the Balokole, and for that matter between the Ugandan church and the Ruanda Mission. Very few students from either Kigezi, a hot bed of Revival in Uganda, or Ruanda attended the college until the 1950s, not doing so in any appreciable way until Jones resigned. From 1946 until the 1960s, Nagenda traveled widely with Joe Church as a lay preacher. He died in 1973.[49]

In the immediate fallout from the Mukono Crisis, Stuart suspended Church in 1942 from preaching in Uganda, though he was free to continue in Ruanda. According to Stuart, in February 1942, Church organized a convention in Kampala to which Nagenda summoned all the Balokole groups. Stuart insisted that he had instructed them to wait until the "Mukono business had been forgotten," but they went behind his back and called the convention anyway. When Stuart found out, he sought a compromise, despite his irritation, and agreed to a more limited leaders' convention. When he attended one of the meetings, he maintained that "the whole theme was 'how evil the church of Uganda was and how good they were.'" When Church requested permission to hold two conventions in Uganda in 1943 along "Keswick lines," Stuart declined the request, retorting that he and the Uganda mission was already on "Keswick lines." In one of his sharpest criticisms of the Balokole, Stuart wrote to the Ruanda Council, "It is Joe Church and his crowd who have left Keswick lines and are running a mission party . . . partly on weird imaginings of their own." When Stuart learned of Church going behind his back again by booking a hotel for a convention, Stuart suspended him. Following this, in October 1942 the CMS issued a circular to their missionaries that sought to better define the "interrelation of the organized church and the Revival movement."[50]

Foreshadowing divisions soon to emerge among the Ruanda missionaries themselves, Leonard Sharp followed the letter with one of his own, wherein he supported Stuart's actions. The Sharps and Kosiya Shalita, then based in

Urundi, had always kept their distance from the Balokole movement. Shalita, who had been instrumental in founding the Gahini station, was never counted among their number. By the 1940s, as evidenced by his letter, Sharp had become a more vociferous critic. He agreed with Stuart's accusations, writing in October 1942, "These Conventions which Joe and his friends undertake are not really right on Keswick lines, but on Group lines. . . . The members of the Group do not really fully cooperate with the missionaries and native church leaders of the places to which they go. Also the people who are helped by the mission are organized as new members of the Balokole rather than becoming keener Christians of the church . . . as if they were the only people who are preaching the true Gospel, and the only people who are really saved." Sharp concluded, "This deplorable situation of distrust on both sides can only be overcome by the Balokole acquiring a more charitable attitude towards other servants of the Lord. I feel that our mission is going through a very critical time which may affect its whole future."[51]

Some of the Sharps' disagreements with the Revival movement may have been of a personal nature. Writing from her home at the Lake Bunyonyi Leper Colony, Esther Sharp claimed in a confidential letter to her friend Dorothy that Joe Church was "blinded on a good many points," noting that he frequently, when addressing African gatherings, spoke critically of other missionaries "behind their backs." She further alleged that she had heard "Joe speak in such a way of the Bishop to a whole roomful of Africans that they sniggered." She reiterated her husband's concerns about the Balokole's claim and asserted that she had heard it said many times that there "are no Christians in Uganda except Balokole," the same criticism Mabel Ensor had made of the Revival from early on. Sharp concluded that it was dishonest and hypocritical of Church and the Balokole to "repeatedly shelter under the CMS and Church of England and yet spend their time declaiming and trying to destroy both these institutions." In this, Esther Sharp revealed a private but growing concern among many in the CMS that Joe Church and his like-minded Revivalists were seeking to split from the Anglican Communion itself.[52]

The October 1942 circular, which addressed the "inter-relation of the organized church and the Revival movement," warned that the "movement must do all it can to keep within the Churches in which it is at work." The circular reminded its readers, "No great revival ever sought to break away from the Church" and take on the character of a "sect." The tensions continued to grow. In 1943 Stanley Smith threatened to resign from being Secretary of the Mission over "the increasing party spirit among the missionaries of the Balokole Persuasion and their attitude of ostracism toward others." Leonard Sharp wrote in response a few months later, in January 1944, that Smith was "guided right in his threat to resign" but expressed hope that his threat would serve as a warning to the Council "to take some action" to express its confidence in Smith and to insist that all the missionaries "render honest and loyal cooperation" to "him, the Bishop, the Ruanda Council, and the CMS." He warned that many missionaries had been "skating on very thin ice in regard to their loyalty."[53]

A year later, in 1945, Stanley Smith was asked to provide the Ruanda Council with answers to several questions concerning the situation in the field with the Ruanda Mission and the Revival. When asked if the churchmanship of the mission was "loyal to the Church of England," he replied that it was loyal on all essential matters and "had no desire to separate from it." He admitted there had been an "anticlerical trend among some" but cast the issue in terms of the African context, arguing that the Ruanda Mission was "faced by the twin forces of paganism and Romanism, both of which . . . have a priesthood claiming magical powers." This, he argued, was a "constant and subtle temptation to our clergy," and "without constant vigilance and practical demonstrations to the contrary, the African Church would readily give their clergy superstitious reverence, which is one of the greatest dangers in the ministry."[54]

A month later, Bishop Stuart responded to Stanley Smith's effort at peacemaking by claiming to the Ruanda Council that Smith was not getting to the "root problem[,] which is 'what authority does the Ruanda Mission recognize?'" He claimed that the Balokole "do not admit the authorities of the Church." Stuart even questioned the integrity of the Revivalists in asserting that they will often "admit there have been mistakes in the past but never the present." He went further, writing, "I have been appalled at Confessions made by them in which they admit to sins to which they have been tied up to a few months ago—though they have been Abalokole for years and I am left with the impression that next year they will have a few more to confess." Over the next few years, the crisis simmered. In 1946 the mission was rebuffed when Lawrence Barham was nominated to be the bishop of Ruanda-Urundi but rejected by Bishop Stuart over his involvement in the Revival. A Ruanda missionary evidently sympathetic to the Revival, K. L. Cooper, wrote, "For years there have been efforts at reconciliation, and everybody has gone away happy, only to be disappointed after a few weeks or days." He concluded that it seemed to him "there was no hope for the mission except a painful split."[55]

By 1949 the tensions settled down, and a split was avoided. In May 1948, the Ruanda Council issued a statement strongly arguing for unity in the mission and a resolution of differences in the face of new postwar challenges. In the aftermath of World War II, the CMS was lacking in funding and feared the advance of Catholicism, noting the "Roman Catholics are prepared and anxious to have the monopoly of this field. We too have our plans laid and if they are in line with God's will, they only lack His seal of funds to put them into action and save the youth of the country. . . . We must be united on this matter." Bishop Stuart replied in support of unity, suggesting that the Ruanda missionaries publicly pledge loyalty to the Church of England and the CMS, and he and the Ruanda Council would pledge loyalty to the Revival, "in so far as it is compatible." In this way, he concluded, "the dark cloud over our Mission will be lifted." A year later, the CMS Regional Secretary for East Africa, G. C. Grimshaw, toured the Ruanda Mission and reported that the majority of the Revival leaders wanted to "keep within the Anglican Communion" and had come to feel "strongly that the Lord could keep spiritual revival ablaze" only if they were holding positions of responsibility within the organization of the Church."[56]

The Anglicans under Belgian Colonialism

The Higher Life Movement and the East African Revival also impacted the church politically within Rwanda and continues, in a fashion, to the present. From its beginning and throughout, the CMS missionaries were keenly aware of the political maneuverings of the Belgian government and the Catholic Church. They were aware too of the deep social cleavage in Rwandan society between Hutu and Tutsi. Many missionaries were influenced by social Darwinism and the scientific racism of the time. The Ruanda missionaries remarked on these matters frequently in their early letters, even endorsing the Hamitic view of the Tutsi being of a separate race. Yet one of the hallmarks of the Revival message was Christian unity, unity between Hutu and Tutsi and between Africans and Europeans. As such, commentaries and remarks about Tutsi racial superiority become noticeably absent in their letters from the 1930s onward. Often, the missionaries still made note of what they considered important, key conversions by upper-class Tutsi. But on a deeper level, the Revival message spoke against these divisions. In Bible studies, public confessions, and collective prayer, the Revival saw the ground "level at the foot of the cross," and a "new fellowship of forgiven sinners—African and European—was formed, who knew they had been made brothers and sisters in Christ." However, while unity and equality may have characterized the Anglican mission stations, Rwanda was politically and socially more divided than ever.[57]

When control of Ruanda-Urundi passed to Belgium in 1919, it did so under the Mandate System of the newly formed League of Nations. Under Article 23 of the League of Nation's charter, Belgium was legally obligated as a trustee to provide for the fair treatment of the native inhabitants and maintain humane working conditions, in addition to other stipulations. Almost from the start, however, Belgium adhered to few of these requirements in Ruanda or Burundi.

Starting in the 1920s, Rwandans were obligated to pay an annual tax to the colonial state, which increased year after year. Although the Belgians formally abolished domestic slavery in 1923, Rwandans were still made to work as unpaid laborers on various projects for either European enterprises or on the land of the chiefs under whose control they resided. Following the Rwakayi-hura famine of 1928, farmers were compelled to build anti-erosion ditches and plant more famine-resistant crops. The weight of these hardships and requirements fell upon both Hutu and Tutsi alike, but Tutsi were "usually in a better position than Hutu to secure channels of escape" and were more likely to "receive supervisory roles that Hutu."[58]

The traditional *ubureetwa* clientship system, whereby a Tutsi land chief could requisition labor from the Hutu cultivators under his authority, was made more onerous and exacting by Belgian policy. Prior to colonial rule, *ubureetwa* demanded two unpaid workdays out of five from each family. In 1916 the German colonial state adjusted the system to two or three days out of every six. The Belgians changed it again via an edict in 1927 to one workday per seven-day week for each Hutu adult male. The 1927 edict was looked upon by the colonial state as a significant liberalization of the system. Understood in context, however, individual males were called upon "more frequently and more regularly to perform *ubureetwa*," whereas previously, under the precolonial system, a single individual could fulfill the kin groups' corporate obligation. The new Belgian system diminished the ability of corporate kin groups to resist exploitation by the Tutsi chiefs and "brought thousands of people into direct contact with political authority through an extractive relationship." The changes wrought by the Belgian government in the 1920s—increased taxation, more labor requirements, and the further extension of *ubureetwa* obligations—were viewed more onerously in the areas more recently brought under the control of the Tutsi monarchy, backed by the Belgian authorities. The growing sense of class-consciousness and exploitation emerging among the Hutu masses against the Tutsi chiefs and Belgian administrators was thus more pronounced in these regions.[59]

Alongside harsher economic realities for the Hutu farmers, the power and prerogatives of the Tutsi chiefs were significantly augmented by Belgian's adoption of the British colonial practice known as "indirect rule." Under indirect rule, the precolonial power structures were preserved and used for carrying out colonial policies through the existing apparatus. This naturally predisposed the colonial authorities to favor the largest of the Tutsi chiefs. Wanting to give the impression that they "understood Rwandan society, colonial authorities imagined it according to a European 'feudal' model composed of *Signeurs* Tutsi and *Serviteurs* Hutu." While only 5 percent of the Tutsi in Rwanda had any real political power in 1900, the effect of Belgian rule was to intensify the "existing process of hierarchization with a form of indirect rule that devolved new forms of power and wealth accumulation to the chiefs, accelerating the crystallization of the Hutu-Tutsi social distinction begun under Rwabugiri."[60]

Accordingly, in 1926 colonial governor Georges Mortehan (1883–1955) introduced the Mortehan Reforms, which undertook a territorial reorganization, significantly reducing the number of Hutu chiefs, and recruited collaborators and officials from the ranks of the most important Tutsi families, especially young men trained in the Catholic schools. While the precolonial monarchy included many Hutu leaders and chiefs, in spite of the hardening of social lines between the two groups in the nineteenth century, Hutu were dismissed from all public offices and, according to Ian Linden, "what was formerly a fluid ethnic border, which the Hutu who wanted could easily cross, became under Belgian administration an insurmountable barrier between castes which delimited access to public office." All positions of authority formerly held by Hutu were removed by this process of "Tutsification." In 1936 Native Tribunals, headed by Tutsi chiefs, were introduced. Abuses by the chiefs were overlooked, and many Rwandans came to see Belgian rule as "the time of the whip."[61]

The undergirding ideology of Belgium's indirect rule and its concomitant policies was the Hamitic Myth, which posited the Tutsi as a superior race. As such, European ethnologists in the 1920s tried to identify a distinct physiology for each group. What followed was the measuring of heights, facial features, skull profiles, and analyses of skin and hair types to determine the extent of the Tutsi's supposed "Caucasoid" origins. The culmination of this process was the census of 1933–34. Partly to maintain administrative clarity, every Rwandan was issued an identification card specifying him or her as either Tutsi (15 percent of the total), Hutu (84 percent), or Twa (1 percent). Following patrilineal custom, children inherited the identity of their father. What began as a distinct social and political dichotomy under the precolonial Nyiginya Dynasty reached its apogee under Belgian rule, a legal codification between the two groups and the emergence among Rwandans themselves, even after colonial rule ended, of the false narrative of Hutu and Tutsi being two separate races. This was the divisive pressure cooker that boiled over numerous times before and after independence in 1959, until finally exploding in genocide in 1994.[62]

When the CMS missionaries began work in Rwanda, their early observations from the field reveal an acceptance of the Hamitic Myth of the racial separateness of the Tutsi, and even a belief in their higher, more advanced status. The mission intentionally sought out and celebrated conversions from among them and their chiefs, as the Catholics themselves had done. They also decried the abuses inflicted on the Hutu and expressed a hope for eventual change in Rwandan society. At its foundation, the CMS was committed to the notion of social reform and the eradication of exploitive practices. Accordingly, when the Revival began, the missionaries spoke frequently of reconciliation and unity between the two groups. Laurent Mbanda, in his critical study of the Catholic Church in colonial Rwanda, praised the stance of the CMS missionaries on the ethnicity question. Mbanda wrote of the issue, "The time came when Protestant (and especially the Anglican British) missionaries decided to take a strong stand on social and political issues, motivated by the identity card based on ethnicity. . . . And the CMS is said to have addressed the problem and given their views against the card. It passed into use despite the CMS's uncompromising expression of what they believed."[63]

Mbanda's work is not sourced by primary evidence, but if he is correct, CMS opposition must have been private and somewhat apolitical. In his diary of the East African Revival, Joe Church makes no mention of the missions' opposition to the identification cards and the ensuing Belgian practices. Nor is mention made in the letters published in the *Ruanda Notes* or in other accounts of the Revival. Based on the primary sources available, the mission remained publicly silent in the face of Belgian policies in the 1930s, policies that served to perpetuate the elite status of the Tutsi over the Hutu majority. If one can assume the CMS missionaries were aware of the full extent of Belgian practices, as they certainly were, the public silence of the mission must be explored if one is to assess the role of the Anglican Church in what followed in Rwanda's postcolonial history.

Access to Rwanda by the British missionaries had always been contingent upon the goodwill of Belgium. Generally viewed with suspicion by the White Fathers, the CMS missionaries walked a fine line in the protectorate and could easily have been expelled. The enthronement of Rudahigwa in 1931 formally confirmed the primacy of the Catholic Church in Rwanda, which always had the primary support of the Belgian colonialists. One can assume, then, that the missionaries had no desire to provoke the authorities in Belgium or the protectorate. As Mbanda also wrote, "If the CMS missionaries had political convictions as to how Rwandan society should look, they suspended them for the sake of a Christian witness and the unity of the community around them," pointing to a deeper theological tendency among the CMS and one that persists in the church presently: a reluctance to challenge political authority.[64]

In writing of the influence of the Pilkington Revival and the Keswick movement, Kevin Ward notes that from early on the Ruanda missionaries asserted the "spiritual over the political and social in the life of the church." Roger Bowen concurred, noting how the Ruanda Mission's more conservative attitude toward scripture led to an "emphasis on evangelism rather than any engagement with the public life of the nation or critique of the sociopolitical context" and that the missionaries were "dependent on the goodwill of the colonial administration and sought to be apolitical." John Taylor notes that the Revival helped forge this tendency, as the Balokole showed "an introverted tendency to withdraw from . . . questions of politics and social responsibility." Several historians of the church in Rwanda, mostly writing of the Catholics, have equated the apolitical stance of the CMS missionaries with tacit support for colonial policies. In this regard, the Anglicans became implicated from the start in the Rwandan genocide, with the assertion that "most Protestant missionaries did not differ substantially from the White Fathers in their attitudes toward political power and ethnicity."[65]

During this period, however, the Ruanda Mission's public disengagement with colonial politics did not per se mean that they supported Belgian policies, unlike the Catholics who "continued to support the centrality of ethnicity to Rwandan politics" while "individuals within the church continued to use their political power to influence the selection of political leaders," the most notable example being Classe's support for the enthronement of Rudahigwa. Privately, the CMS missionaries harbored considerable animus toward the Catholic Church and its practices, even as they measured their words about the colonial state itself. Additionally, the political disengagement of the men and women of the Ruanda Mission was born of more than a simple, evangelistic commitment to conversion alone. Virtually all of them were premillennialists who believed in a literal and imminent "Second Coming" of Christ, which rendered earthly politics as unworthy of much concern.[66]

Premillennialism is a belief among orthodox Christians that Christ will return in physical form to inaugurate a thousand-year reign on Earth among the believers. Drawn from a literal reading of the New Testament book of the Revelation and supported by select passages from the Old and New Testaments, the "Second Coming" signals the end of time and the fulfillment of the Christian narrative. Dating back to at least the seventeenth century, premillennialism gained modern popularity among numerous groups of orthodox Christians with the 1907 Scofield Reference Bible, an annotated version of the King James Bible edited and published by Cyrus Scofield (1843–1921), an American theologian. Scofield was a proponent of dispensationalism, which views history as unfolding in several distinct Christian periods, or dispensations. The dispensationalist view maintains that the book of the Revelation was not an account of past events but a vision of the future wherein Christ would return to inaugurate the Christian millennium. Coming as it did in the first years of the twentieth century, Scofield's editing suggested to dispensationalists and premillennialists, who pessimistically saw much of the modern era as materialistic, sinful, and corrupt, that Christ's return was imminent. As such, the politics of the modern world were viewed with a sense of inevitability and disdain. Scofield himself, in Philadelphia in 1918, stated there was "no hope for humanity except in the personal return of the Lord in glory."[67]

The Scofield was the Bible of choice among the missionaries of the Ruanda Mission. Church recorded that he always prepared his studies and teachings with the "Scofield Bible chain references." When Church met with Nsibambi in Kampala in 1929, he wrote to his CiCCU supporters at Cambridge that he and Nsibambi went over "Scofield's notes on the Holy Spirit." Throughout the letters on the Revival Conventions in the *Ruanda Notes*, references are made to teaching sessions on topics such as the "Second Coming" and "Christ's Return." Most of the histories of the church in Rwanda either downplay or ignore the abundant evidence of the impact of Scofield's premillennial teachings on the nature and stance of the Anglican Church. Taken literally as it was by the orthodox missionaries of the CMS and their converts, premillennialism played a significant role in crafting the apolitical character of the church, a characteristic that initially led to a withdrawal from the public life of the nation, or arguably in the case of the present-day Anglican Church in Rwanda, a naive and uncritical support for those in power.[68]

The result was a church ill-prepared and believers ill-equipped to confront the racialization of Rwanda happening in their very midst, with disastrous consequences for the future. The church they bequeathed to their spiritual descendants after the 1959 revolution bore the same restraints. Bowen argued that the church's teaching style "encouraged little reflection, avoided the crucial issues troubling society, inculcated uncritical obedience to government authorities, and failed to teach Christians that situations can be so dire that 'we must obey God rather than man.'" Throughout the events surrounding the genocide in 1994, most of the Anglican hierarchy was not only silent but complicit, partly because the "revival doctrine of sin underestimates the power and depth of evil, and by focusing on personal/private morality was quite inadequate to tackle the hideous strength of structural evil and corporate sin manifested in an act of genocide." One can hope that the present generation of Anglicans in postgenocide Rwanda are better prepared if the current government breaks, but the evidence is not promising.[69]

CHAPTER FOUR

The Unraveling

The Ruanda Mission and Independence

THE END OF World War II in 1945 left the European colonial powers in disarray. Effectively bankrupt and with a shattered infrastructure at home, the former "great powers" of France and Great Britain found themselves responding to new pressures and new realities at home and abroad. Belgium, with its fewer colonial territories in the Congo, Rwanda, and Burundi, was no exception. While most observers foresaw the coming of independence for the African territories at some point in the future, the future turned out to be less distant than policy makers could have imagined in 1945. The global war against totalitarianism and fascism had raised expectations across the colonized world for freedom and self-government. A pan-African movement for independence and democracy swept over the continent, forcing the European powers to consider and renegotiate their position on multiple fronts and in multiple colonies.

As the events leading to independence unfolded in Rwanda after the war, the Anglican community had little choice but to respond. Both churches found themselves in a strong position after the war in terms of numbers and growth. For the Catholics, however, the ranks of the priesthood came to be dominated after the war by Flemish priests who, with a more working-class worldview, found more solidarity with the Hutu masses and who equated the "Tutsi with arrogant Walloons who had historically dominated Belgium." As a result, independence was aided by the Catholic Church by a switch in support from the Tutsi elites to the Hutu masses. The switch in support to the Hutu also meant support not only for independence but for majority rule, yet the Catholic's revised political stance did little to mitigate the violence and postindependence oppression of the Tutsi minority.[1]

The Anglicans responded to the politics of the postwar years in much the same fashion as they had always responded to the politics of Rwanda. They remained disengaged for as long as they could, trying to continue their work under the radar of the events that swirled around their mission stations in the 1950s and early 1960s; much of the same can be observed of the Anglican Church in contemporary Rwanda. On the surface, the Anglican response took on the veneer of neutrality, which presumably would have left them and their congregants without complicity. Yet, infatuated as they were with the monarchy, the Ruanda Mission never overcame its complicit, and sometimes overt, support for the Tutsi rulers, leaving them on the wrong side of history and with a price to be paid. For both churches, their involvement, or lack thereof, in the events leading to the First Republic of Rwanda in 1961 left them unprepared to play a constructive role in the years and decades after independence, ultimately leaving both churches with considerable victimhood in 1994.

In no small part because of its greater numbers, the Catholic Church in Rwanda played a much larger role in the events leading to the revolution. The East African Revival of the 1930s was shadowed in the Catholic Churches by the Tornade, a term first used in 1936 in reference to a wave of conversions among the masses and noted earlier. In addition to being less charismatic and pietistic than the Anglican Revival, the Tornade was, at its foundation, the result of psychological and political pressures. Like the Anglicans, the Catholics had from the beginning prioritized the conversion of the Tutsi elites as the quickest path to mass conversion. The enthronement of Rudahigwa in 1931, accompanied by the requirement that Catholic baptism was necessary for holding the position of chief, was the culmination of this process. By 1936, 80 percent of the chiefs and subchiefs identified as Catholic; four years later, the number was estimated at 95 percent. Moreover, the White Fathers requested that chiefs who wished to be baptized should present a goodly number of postulants under their authority for catechism training. For the chiefs then, it "became in fact both a duty and a question of political survival to push the population to conversion," accounting for roughly three hundred thousand Catholics by 1939.[2]

The result was a supposedly mass Catholic conversion movement, but it was the result of downward pressure and with dubious authenticity. While celebrated as the "Tornado" in Catholic missionary literature, the movement was known in Kinyarwanda as *Irivuze umwami* (what the king has said you must follow). The king never issued a conversion order, but the Catholic missionaries allowed the misperception to persist to reap the numerical benefit, and the numbers materialized: between 1933 and 1939, the number of baptized Catholics roughly quintupled. Tharcisse Gatwa described the conversions as "an artificial phenomenon. The numbers were exaggerated, and quality was missing, whilst the clergy slipped into triumphant attitudes and laziness.

Hence little effort was made to bridge the gap between professing Christian faith and the people's practices." When the Catholic Church began the postwar years with a ceremony on October 27, 1946, with the "consecration of Rwanda and its people to the Virgin Mary and Christ the King," it did so ill-equipped to confront and mitigate the violence soon to unfold.[3]

Politically, in postwar Rwanda, the demand for independence rose among both Tutsi and Hutu. The Tutsi elites saw quick independence as the safest means of preserving the monarchy in the face of Hutu demands for self-government and majority rule. For the Hutu, the demand for independence was coupled with a demand for equality and an end to their historic servitude to the Tutsi elites. As the Belgian colonial government took steps after the war to prepare Rwanda for eventual self-government, it found itself having to resolve the political divide between the two groups, a schism its earlier practices and policies had entrenched more deeply than ever.

From an international legal standpoint, following World War I, Ruanda-Urundi was handed to Belgium in 1919 by the League of Nations as a Mandate Territory, wherein the colonial power in question was entrusted with stewardship and development. With the dissolution of the League in 1946, the Mandates were transferred to the newly created United Nations (UN) as "trust territories," overseen by the Trusteeship Council, wherein the colonial powers were to develop their territories in preparation for independence and self-government. The treaty confirming Belgium's Trusteeship was ratified by the UN on April 25, 1949. Regardless of its original timetable and plans for independence, Belgium was quickly overwhelmed by the conflicts and demands plaguing Rwanda's social groups—conflicts exacerbated, ironically, by its very attempts to reform colonial society in accordance with its trusteeship.[4]

Prior to its Trusteeship role, Belgium took steps to modernize the economy and eradicate the most abusive practices in Rwanda. Compulsory coffee production was introduced in 1931 as a profitable export commodity. In 1946 a Coffee Stabilization Fund was established to provide equipment and technical training. Coffee remained a primary export throughout the postcolonial era. Ironically, it was the collapse of worldwide coffee prices in the 1980s that plunged Rwanda into an economic crisis that in part created the conditions leading the genocide in 1994. In 1946 the administration abolished whipping by the Tutsi chiefs and subchiefs of those who had violated the law. Five years later, in accordance with the UN Trusteeship Council's insistence, corporal punishment carried out by indigenous courts was eradicated.[5]

In 1949, with Hutu discontent growing, the colonial government took what appeared to be steps to reform Rwanda's social structure. *Ubureetwa* labor requirements were abolished in favor of a monetary payment system. The authorities hesitated, however, to abolish *ubuhake* cattle clientship so as not to undermine the Tutsi chiefs entirely. But by 1951, in response to pressure from the Trusteeship Council, Belgium announced plans to end *ubuhake* as well, the institution upon which the chief's authority rested. The phase out of *ubuhake* began in 1954 with a decree from the king providing for the distribution of cows to former Hutu clients. The elimination of both institutions was undertaken in part to prepare Rwanda for its place in the emerging global economy, as both *ubureetwa* and *ubuhake* were viewed as outdated institutions more suited to an agrarian society.[6]

The eradication of these precolonial institutions was meant to undercut the two main sources of discontent and protest from the Hutu. On this point, many of the Tutsi chiefs favored the policies. They could do so without undermining their authority because the elimination of *ubuhake* failed to address pasturage rights. The chiefs still controlled the land. Thus, while former Hutu clients acquired ownership of cattle, they still depended on their former Tutsi patrons for access to pasture. Quite often the patrons demanded a form of *ubureetwa* service in exchange for access. The result was a de facto preservation of both systems that continued into the late 1950s with political tensions continuing to simmer. The primary aim for the colonial state was to "abolish the most evident symbols of exploitation under Tutsi colonialism," even while leaving "the essential structure of the exploitation intact. Power remained in the hands of Tutsi chiefs." Moreover, for younger Tutsi, the colonial administration had provided new avenues for power and social dominance through privileged access to education, bureaucratic jobs in the colonial apparatus, and in the church.[7]

As the administration took more concrete steps toward eventual self-government, Tutsi privilege continued. On July 14, 1952, four types of advisory councils and memberships were established with advisory power to territorial officials: sub-chiefdoms, chiefdoms, district councils, and a High Council of State. Members of the sub-chiefdom councils were selected by a group of notables, who in turn were selected from a list compiled by the sub-chiefs in accordance with the preferences of local inhabitants. The other councils consisted of chiefs or sub-chiefs, ex officio members, and co-opted members. The formation of the councils was similar in a fashion to the legislative councils established throughout British Africa in the years after World War II. European colonial thinking held that Africans needed a preparatory period far in advance of independence, and African-only councils were aimed to provide tutelage for the legislative process and the exercise of self-government. In Rwanda's case, the councils merely continued Tutsi dominance, as Tutsi controlled the process of selecting and naming the authorities at every level. In the

first sub-chiefdom council elections of 1953, Tutsi were in the majority everywhere except in Ruhengeri in the north. Hutu had approximately 25 percent
representation in all other districts and provinces and ended up with only
three of the fifteen seats available. By constructing the membership process
around "selections" by the chiefly caste, rather than by "elections," Hutu were
effectively shut out. Even when Hutu were included in the councils, they were
merely the *abagaragu* (clients) of the Tutsi chiefs, leading to a "diffusion of
power but principally among the group which already possessed it, that is to
say the Tutsi caste."[8]

The de facto effect of the reforms, the preservation of Tutsi prerogatives,
was not lost on educated Hutu leaders. As a result, more pronounced political
activity ensued. In 1956 Aloys Munyangaju published a newspaper titled *Soma*
("to read," in Kinyarwanda) that criticized the power of the Tutsi chiefs and
discrimination in Rwandan society. In 1958 Munyangaju became editor of the
Temps Nouveaux d'Afrique, a similarly pro-Hutu periodical published by the
Catholic Church in Burundi. The publication of *Soma* was followed in March
1957 by a ten-page text addressed to the vice governor-general of Rwanda but
meant for an upcoming visit by the UN Trusteeship Council. Written by nine
Hutu intellectuals, the document was titled *Notes on the Social Aspect of the
Racial Native Problem in Rwanda*, generally known as the "Bahutu Manifesto."
The document criticized the monopoly on power held by the Tutsi and the
social and cultural inferiority of the Hutu enforced by decades of colonial
policy. The document further contended that without liberation from both
the Belgian colonialists *and* the Tutsi elites, Hutu suppression would continue
even after independence. The most alarming and divisive aspect for Rwanda's
future, evident from the title itself, was the way independence was being cast
in racial terms.[9]

The Bahutu Manifesto demonstrated how the original Hamitic Myth, originating with the European colonialists and endorsed by the church, of the
Tutsi being a separate race of outside invaders, had become the underlying
assumption among many Rwandans themselves. As late as 1994, during the
genocide, Léon Mugesera, a Hutu Power fanatic on Radio des Mille Collines,
was urging Hutu to "send the Tutsi back to Ethiopia from whence they came."
Surprisingly at the time, but not so much in hindsight, the Manifesto advo-
cated maintaining ethnic distinctions on identity papers. Doctors were even
called upon to settle cases of "cross-breeding." In a response that further inflamed the increasingly heated racial rhetoric, Tutsi notables at the court issued their own response in May 1958, in which they denied all kinship with
the Hutu and proclaimed the Tutsi as the sole founders of Rwanda. Nonetheless, the intent of the Hutu Manifesto was to establish a "Quota Democ-

racy," which became the law of the land in independent Rwanda, providing for a reversal of both the precolonial and colonial order that had privileged the Tutsi. Concomitantly, maintaining ethnic distinctions led to the oppression of the Tutsi minority at the hands of the Hutu in the years after independence.[10]

With protests rising both in Rwanda and across the continent, political parties formed in the late 1950s. The first, in June 1957, was the Mouvement Social Muhutu (MSM, Hutu Social Movement), formed and led by Grégoire Kayibanda (1924–76). One of the nine signatories to the Bahutu Manifesto and later the first president of Rwanda, Kayibanda was born on May 21, 1924. Educated at the Catholic Petit Seminaire and Grand Seminaire, he was a teacher at the Institute Classe in Kigali until 1952. While there, he became involved in a Rwandan cultural association known as the Amitiés Belgo-Congalais and wrote several articles for the monthly periodical *L'Ami*, published by the Catholic seminary at Kabgayi. By 1953 he was a secretary for the Education Inspection Division in Kabgayi. By 1955 Kayibanda was working as personal secretary to Monsignor André Perraudin and editing a church newspaper, *Kinyameteka*.[11]

Published since the 1930s by the Catholic press, in the 1940s *Kinyameteka* started publishing anti-Tutsi articles especially critical of the inequality in land ownership. In 1957, however, the editorials took on a more "resolutely critical and denunciatory tone," and was "transformed into a list of grievances" to denounce "social inequalities, forced labor, corrupt judges and chiefs, the unequal distribution of land, the head tax, the bridge price and corruption of magistrates." *Kinyameteka* became the most widely read paper in Rwanda, with its readership reaching an estimated twenty thousand by the late 1950s. The articles published in *Kinyameteka*, as well as in Munyangaju's *Temps Nouveaux d'Afrique*, "gave voice to attitudes and discussions occurring at the grassroots level in many areas of the country."[12]

In 1957 Kayibanda was chairing the board of directors for a coffee cooperative called TRAFIPRO (translated as "Work, Fidelity, Progress"). Kayibanda's work with *Kinyameteka* and TRAFIPRO, both supported by the Catholics, exposed him to the growing pro-Hutu Christian Socialist movement within the church. He came to believe educated Hutu elites had to work harder to identify themselves with the struggles and oppression of the rural masses. Only by seeking an understanding of the hardships faced by the peasantry at the hands of the Belgians and the Tutsi rulers could future Hutu leaders hope to succeed. He argued that the ideal leader "spends time with people on the hills, chats with them often, knows their aspirations better, their distress, their complaints, and sees better the injustices of which they are the victims."

Consequently, he entered the political arena directly with the founding of the MSM "to defend the 'humble folk' or the 'masses' (that is, the Hutu) against the abuses of the 'feudals'" (understood to be the Tutsi).[13]

Two years later, with the MSM gaining little traction, Kayibanda transformed it into the Parti du Mouvement de l'Emancipation Hutu (PARMEHUTU, Party of the Movement of Emancipation of the Bahutu). At nearly the same time, in 1958, Joseph Gitera founded the Association pour la promotion sociale de la masse (APROSOMA, Association for the Social Promotion of the Masses), of which Munyangaju was vice president and later president. Both men were also signatories to the Manifesto. Gitera was a Hutu businessman and brick foundry owner from the south with a reputation for populist rabble-rousing and demagoguery. Like other leading Hutu intellectuals, he published his own periodical, *Voice of the Little People*, which made scathing attacks on the monarchy. In October 1958, he asked Perraudin to get rid of the sacred drum of kingship, Karinga, against which the Tutsi court protested strongly. Decorated as it was with the testicles of Hutu chiefs, Karinga could hardly suffice as a symbol of national unity, he argued. With further forebodings for Rwanda's future unity, APROSOMA, owing to Gitera's background, was mostly a southern-based party, while PARMEHUTU appealed to northerners in the Ruhengeri region. Initially, Hutu leaders still favored a more prolonged approach to full independence, viewing the "poorly prepared masses" as unready for universal suffrage, but when Mwami Mutara died suddenly from a brain aneurism while under a doctor's care in July 1959, events accelerated.[14]

With suspicions running high at the court that the *mwami* had been poisoned by Hutu militants, royalist Tutsi created their own party in August, the Union Nationale Rwandaise (UNAR, Rwandan National Union), for the preservation of the monarchy, and enthroned Kigeri V Ndahindurwa, another son of Musinga, as his successor. Tutsi aspirations for preserving the monarchy were driven in part by the fear of living under Hutu majority rule but also by the emergence of a "revivalist [not to be confused with the East African Revival] movement fascinated with traditional culture." At the onset of the 1950s, a "cultural renaissance movement" coalesced around the *mwami* and chiefs with the support of prominent Tutsi priests in the Catholic Church, most notably Abbé Alexis Kagame (1912–81). In 1957 this movement, in part, "led to demands for political sovereignty."[15]

While not all Tutsi supported it, UNAR was openly hostile to the Belgians and wanted immediate independence. Against expectations, the colonial government was not consulted in the choice of Ndahindurwa, accelerating the process of the Belgians breaking with the monarchy. Coming as it did in the

Cold War context of the 1950s, which saw the Soviet Union undermining the Western powers across the colonial world, UNAR "was stigmatized as an ally of the communists" for receiving money and support from the communist-bloc countries on the UN Trusteeship Council, which served to "deepen the antagonism between the Tutsi and the Belgian authorities." By then, Vice Governor-General Jean-Paul Harroy (1909–95) noted, "the unspoken agreement which the administration had made in the 1920s with the Tutsi ruling caste in order to further economic development was allowed to collapse," although as Newbury points out, Harroy's comment notwithstanding, the creation of UNAR and the enthronement of Ndahindurwa illustrated the degree to which the Belgians were losing control of the unfolding situation. Harroy's comment also belies the depth of his antipathy toward the Tutsi. Later, when ordinary Tutsi were being persecuted across the countryside, Harroy acknowledged in his memoirs, "The great mass of victims were the simple Tutsi . . . who deserved to be spared." But, he noted, "that was the price to pay."[16]

With the "winds of change" blowing fast, the Belgians made one final attempt to seek an accommodation. In September 1959, the colonial authorities released from custody a Tutsi chief known as Prosper Bwanakweri, who, five years earlier, had represented a group of young, progressive-minded Tutsi seeking to liberalize social relations. Mutara and the court conservatives cast him as a subversive troublemaker and asked the colonial government to deport him, a reminder that powerful factions in the Tutsi central court threatened a unified position. Bwanakweri was arrested and detained in Rwanda until his release in September. His release was the occasion for him and his, albeit small, number of supporters to create a counterparty to UNAR, the Rassemblement Démocratique du Rwanda (RADER, Rwandese Democratic Union). RADER formed an alliance with the Hutu parties, themselves divided in their response, and called for a constitutional monarchy, democratization of the political structures, and progressive social reforms. Seen as a Belgian ploy to delay independence, RADER was openly opposed by conservative, monarchist Tutsi, and with many Hutu mistrusting its intentions, the party stood little chance of success and remained on the sidelines. Before the year was over, violence began.[17]

With various political parties vying for support and with ethnic tensions running high, it's important to avoid falling for what David Newbury calls one of the "myths of recent historiography" about Rwanda. The leaders on both sides who spoke for their parties and negotiated with the colonial government represented the educated elites who each shared in their own way the colonial vision of a Rwanda determined by its racial origins. Both Hutu and Tutsi elites were educated in the colonial schools and seminaries where each group absorbed the Hamitic Myth of the Tutsi being Nilotic invaders from outside the region. In short, when speaking of their aims and intentions, both sides "were speaking to colonial power in the colonial discourses of the day. To be taken seriously by those in power . . . they had to present their case within the parameters of colonial perceptions; therefore, both sides adopted the racial language of European ideology." Tutsi leaders defended the monarchy and their privileged status based on "right of conquest" as outside invaders who possessed an innate capacity to rule. Hutu leaders premised their demands upon a rejection of conquest and their own right of earlier settlement and prior occupation. The "myth" is in the assumption that Hutu and Tutsi elites spoke for the masses. No discernible evidence exists to support such an assumption. As Newbury concludes about the racial discourse adopted by the party leaders, "To those who were not schooled, those arguments made little sense: what they experienced was the result of colonial oppression," having almost nothing to do with Rwanda's distant past and origins.[18]

Yet, since the genocide, many historians have failed to take account of this colonial nuance and have assumed, without evidence, that the leaders on both sides represented the views of nonelites, both Hutu and Tutsi. The silencing of moderate political voices after independence, such as those in RADER, compounded this view. By not taking account of this, postgenocide historians have, inadvertently perhaps, projected Rwanda's racial divide into the past to a degree not supported by dispassionate analysis. Casual observers of present-day Rwanda have, in turn, adopted this oversimplified, dichotomous vision of the nations' supposed racial past. In a more troubling way, Rwanda's own spokespersons in the Anglican church and state have absorbed and propounded the assumption. The often-made assertion of the killings being directed against "Tutsi and *moderate* Hutu," as well as a considerable body of postgenocide laws, has the tendency to cast all *nonmoderate* Hutu as potential killers and all Tutsi as victims.[19]

When Western missionaries, aid workers, and visitors to Rwanda are regaled by the Anglican Church and others to the canard of there no longer being Hutu and Tutsi, only Rwandans, the implication is that the country's so-called racial problem has been healed. The effect is to obfuscate the observation that for many among the masses at independence, the problem was one not so much of *racism* but rather of *oppression* at the hands of the colonial state. In turn, outsiders assume Rwandan leaders, with opposition voices stifled, speak for everyone and are led to believe that all is now well, when the original issue, political oppression, is still rampant. In this sense, the overstated Hamitic Myth of yesteryear is as dangerous now as it was then.

The Coming of the First Republic

On November 1, 1959, Dominique Mbonyumutwa (1921–86), a PARME-HUTU activist, was attacked and beaten by a group of Tutsi who belonged to UNAR. Following false reports of Mbonyumutwa's death, reprisal attacks occurred across the country. PARMEHUTU directed killings and house burnings of Tutsi regardless of their social standing or political stance. UNAR ordered the assassination of Hutu leaders and organized commando-style units to attack both APROSOMA and PARMEHUTU activists. Confusion was rampant, and many of the killings were spontaneous. To restore order, the administration brought in Belgian paratroopers from the Congo under Colonel Guy Logiest (1912–91) and imposed a military regime. From the start, Logiest and the Belgians were sympathetic to the Hutu, and the killings continued. On occasion, Logiest's troops did not intervene when Tutsi houses were being torched. Peace finally ensued by mid-November, but not before hundreds of Tutsi were dead and thousands of homes destroyed. More than one thousand from both sides were arrested. The *Muyaga*, a Kinyarwanda word generally thought of as a "tempest," a "strong but variable wind with unpredictable consequences," was underway.[20]

In Chrétien's words, a "de-UNARization" of the country followed. More than half the Tutsi chiefs and three hundred out of five hundred sub-chiefs were dismissed by the colonial authorities, all replaced by Hutu chiefs and sub-chiefs. The government organized preliminary elections for July, which returned a large majority, more than two out of every three seats, for PARME-HUTU. On January 28, 1961, with the support of Logiest, Rwanda was declared a Republic, and the Tutsi monarchy was abolished. Ndahindurwa fled to Congo and eventually to the West, dying in 2016 in Washington, DC. A second round of legislative elections followed in September, which ratified the regime change and returned another overwhelming majority for PARME-HUTU. Independence was formally proclaimed on July 1, 1962, with Kayibanda as the president of the First Republic of Rwanda.[21]

Foreshadowing much of the country's future, PARMEHUTU's ideology, premised on a continuation of racial divisionism, was apparent from the start. The party declared it had "restored the country to its owners" and invited the Tutsi to return to Ethiopia. So extreme was the party's rhetoric that it was denounced by RADER and APROSOMA. The persecution of ordinary Tutsi continued on the hills of Rwanda under the newly established Hutu chiefs. Hundreds more were killed by 1963 and thousands of homes were burned. In the years between 1959 and 1963, as many as 150,000 Tutsi fled as refugees to neighboring countries. Some went to Congo or Tanzania, but most fled to camps in southern Uganda, where they shared cultural commonality with the

Hima pastoralists of Ankole. Their descendants, decades later, formed the core of the Rwandan Patriotic Front.[22]

In his chapter on the events leading to independence in Rwanda, Ian Linden described this period as one of "Freedom *for* Oppression," for what followed was a reversal of the precolonial, and colonial, social and political order. Tutsi left behind in Rwanda lived under a system of Hutu oppression under two consecutive presidents. A UN Trusteeship report from March 1961 observed, "The developments of these last eighteen months have brought about the racial dictatorship of one party. . . . An oppressive system has been replaced by another one." The report added ominously, "It is quite possible that some day we will witness violent reactions on the part of the Tutsi," although its prediction was already being born out. With the radical monarchists now settled in neighboring countries, they "made declarations . . . indicating they were preparing for war so as to reclaim the power they lost during the revolution." Throughout the early 1960s, Tutsi guerillas, referred to as *inyenzi* (cockroaches), routinely made attacks across the border from Uganda and Burundi. By the end of 1963, an estimated five thousand to eight thousand Tutsi who remained in Rwanda had been killed in retaliation as a result of incursions that made "all Tutsi who remained in the country targets of suspicion." These attacks and counterattacks foreshadow the armed invasion of Rwanda in 1990 by Paul Kagame's forces, for whom the term *inyenzi* was resurrected for use by many of the Tutsi militants themselves. This invasion explicitly set into motion the events leading to the genocide three years later and that, as in 1960, led to reprisal attacks against "interior Tutsi" who remained in Rwanda. Guy Logiest did not see these events in the same way, calling the revolution, which was an ethnic reversal of power, "a total and definitive victory for the Rwandese people."[23]

Those who thought they knew Rwanda best in 1961, and who claimed a supposedly new nation was born in the aftermath of such violence, echo the many voices in Rwanda who presently maintain that a new and inclusive social order was founded in the aftermath of 1994. As it was in 1961, those with the closest relationships to postgenocide Rwanda, generally missionaries and aid workers from Western churches, choose to see a new nation in which progress and development are taking place under the auspices of a benign president, wherein the distinction between Hutu and Tutsi has been relegated to the past. They listen to lofty pronouncements from church figures and accept without question the RPF's version of history and politics.

Those who see Rwanda differently and who make critiques of the present political situation in the country—usually academics, historians, policy makers, and area experts on the region—are often labeled "outsiders" who lack sympathy with Rwanda's plight. On occasion, they have been labeled "geno-cide deniers," and some have been barred entry into the country. Like observ-ers at the UN in 1961, it is often, ironically, those furthest away who are best positioned to make unbiased critiques of the reigning political order, an order in Rwanda that is still unwell and far from inclusive and democratic. When sympathetic Westerners parrot what they hear from within the country and disregard those who differ, they fulfill Prunier's declaration that Logiest was "unfortunately not the last foreigner to voice such deadly certainties about the complex realities" of Rwanda.[24]

The Anglicans in the Muyaga

The postwar years for the Ruanda Mission began on February 24, 1946, with the celebration of its Silver Jubilee and more. By 1946 the CMS claimed eight mission stations across Rwanda and Burundi. Nearly 1,200 churches were being staffed by almost fifty European missionaries and many more African laypersons and clergy, but with the accumulation of losses as well during the war years and immediately afterward. Cecil Verity, who went to Kabale in 1928 as a pioneer missionary, left the field in 1939 to serve as an Air Force chaplain at Cardington, dying in 1995. William Orpwood, along with Margaret, left in 1940, also to serve as an Air Force chaplain. Dr. Jack "Chris" Symonds, who, along with wife Sonia had gone to Kabale as pioneer missionaries in 1935, left the field in 1940 to serve in the war as an army doctor. William Pitt-Pitts, the first archdeacon of the Ruanda Mission, died of a blood infection in Nairobi in 1940. Harold Guillebaud, one of the first pioneer missionaries in the field in 1926, was Pitt-Pitt's replacement, only to die himself a little more than a year later in 1941 from a respiratory ailment. Jim Brazier replaced him as the next archdeacon. Harold's wife, Margaret, remained behind until poor health took her back to England in 1956. Several of their children and a grandson took up the call to be missionaries in Rwanda and Burundi. Two more of the original pioneer missionaries left the field in these years: Bert Jackson returned to England to be a vicar in 1946. He died in 1970. Geoffrey Holmes, another of the pioneer missionaries, retired to Surrey, England, where he lived until his death in 1964.[25]

The celebration of its jubilee also brought good financial news for the mis-sion. In February 1946, the minister of the Belgian colonies announced that the government had decided "to place all the Christian missions . . . on the same level, and with equal guarantees, regarding the granting of state subsidies in education, as well as other areas." Thereafter the mission started receiving hospital and school subsidies from the colonial government on an equal foot-ing with the Catholics. With the achievement of this long-sought aim, the

Anglicans enjoyed a further upswing in church attendance. The European missionaries and staff remained focused on schools and education, health care and medical development, and church growth. The letters sent home to the Ruanda Council spoke frequently of revival, but without the controversies of the 1940s. The acquisition of financial support from the colonial government, coupled with the ongoing work of the mission, paid dividends. According to J. J. Carney, "By 1958, nearly 100,000 Rwandans and Burundians professed the Anglican faith."[26]

Financial parity, though, was not the only reason more Rwandans turned to the Anglican mission in the 1950s. By the late 1940s, many Tutsi were aware of the Catholic Church's newfound embrace of the Hutu masses and became suspicious of the White Fathers' intentions. As a result, after the war, increasing numbers of Tutsi turned to the Ruanda Mission, whose affinity for seeing the Tutsi as the natural rulers of the country was long-standing and enduring. Ian Linden observed, "From 1943 onwards a number of Tutsi from poorer families, followed by a few nobles, began to take an interest in the CMS, asking for their schools and some actually converting." By the mid-1950s, Mwami Rudahigwa started making frequent visits to the CMS mission stations and became a close friend of Joe Church at Gahini.[27]

The Ruanda Mission had, from its inception, sought converts from the Tutsi ruling class and from every indication welcomed this turn of events. The 1957–58 *Ruanda Notes* proudly reported to its readers of the traditional "King's Day" being celebrated at Gahini. The *mwami* himself attended with his *intore* dance troop, and it was noted that the celebrations "were organized by the Gahini church, as a demonstration of their loyalty to their *Umwami*." The king was presented with a monogrammed Bible, and he sent a special message of Thanksgiving to Stanley Smith for his translation work. If the mission had any awareness that the *mwami* was merely seeking allies in the face of rising Hutu class consciousness, and that their dalliance with him was going to embroil them in the Muyaga, no indication of such is apparent from the sources. As a result, like the Catholics, the Anglicans were ill-equipped to play a constructive and meaningful role in the preindependence politics of the 1950s. Thus, when the leaders of the Ruanda Mission finally recognized that its association with the Tutsi ruling class was going to have unfortunate repercussions, it was too little, too late.[28]

None of this is to say that the mission was entirely unaware of the political stirrings in Rwanda. They were very much cognizant of the nationalist sentiments growing around them. As early as 1950, the mission was seeing the impact of Belgium's efforts to reform Rwanda's social structures. In a letter to the Friends of Ruanda, Archdeacon Jim Brazier informed his readers that "there has been a rapid rise in African standards of living due to the increasing prices they receive for their products, such as coffee, hides and foodstuffs, and for their labour also." The mission was aware that instead of "so many days of labour each month . . . an annual payment is now allowed" and that the "old system of corporal punishment has been largely superseded by a system of fines." In typical fashion, the mission was either unaware or unwilling to acknowledge that, throughout these years, the Tutsi chiefs still controlled the land, one of the main sources of Hutu nationalism and discontent. In 1954 Jim Brazier naively and incredulously asked, "Why is there so much discontent everywhere when material possessions are increasing?"[29]

Down to independence, the mission continued in its support for the monarchy, even as they were aware of both the Belgian efforts to reform Rwanda in preparation for independence and rising Hutu nationalism in the country. When Ndahindurwa was enthroned by the royalists against Belgian wishes in 1959, the *Ruanda Notes* urgently asked its readers to "pray for the new *mwami* and his advisors that they may lead the country forward into peace." Even after the monarchy was abolished and independence declared, the mission at Gahini still projected a decidedly muted response. During one of Mwami Musinga's earlier visits, he presented the Gahini station with the sacred drum Rwamu, which was played only at Christmas or during one of the king's visits. In the early 1960s, when Kayibanda visited Gahini, Joe Church refused to allow the drum to be played in his honor, rationalizing that "since the drum was to be used to play for Christ, the king of all nations . . . it could not be played for a ruler who discriminated against people because of their ethnicity as did Kayibanda." Despite his excuse, Rwamu, like the sacred drum Karinga, was a symbol of Tutsi dominance, one of the main foci of Hutu nationalism.[30]

Nationalism for the Ruanda Mission, rather, was viewed in different ways. The mission noted that the modernizing changes were "producing a new sense of independence and an awareness of the possibilities of new freedoms to be gained." Peter Guillebaud (1914–96), son of Harold Guillebaud, noted in 1949 that the mission was challenged in doing its work because of the demands of the government on the schools and the "tremendous surge forward of the Africans these days towards freedom, culture, social advancement and education." At times, though, nationalism was processed by the mission in almost apocalyptic terms. Rattled by violent events in Kenya, Harold Adeney (1914–2010), a pioneer missionary to Burundi with his wife, Isobel, who were then serving in Rwanda, wrote in 1952, "Looking to the east the storm clouds of Mau Mau can be seen on the Kenya horizon. Here all is peaceful at present, but there are not lacking signs of rising nationalistic aspirations. God's work continues to go forward but there is a feeling of battle as Satan amasses his forces for what may perhaps be the final great struggle for world domination."[31]

Adeney's "great struggle for world domination" may refer to the mission's sense of dread that nationalism would lead to communism. An editorial in the *Ruanda Notes* from 1949 noted that the ideals of the African may be right, but soon he may find "an enticing path bearing the name communism, and many are being side-tracked in this direction." As a British mission during the emerging Cold War, some of this is not surprising. Lawrence Barham proclaimed in 1950, "Communism is just around the corner and God has revived his church as the answer." Barham's proclamation, that a "revived church" was the answer to communism, coupled with the mildly approving but anxious feelings toward nationalism, reveals the depth of the Rwanda missions' unwillingness to engage constructively and informatively with the times.[32]

From its start in Rwanda, the mission avoided informed political engagement, focusing solely as they did on evangelism and church work. Laurent Mbanda noted that often during their history, "if the CMS missionaries had political convictions as to how Rwandan society should look, they suspended them for the sake of a Christian witness." Writing of the Anglicans in the years after World War II, Tharcissee Gatwa stated, "The dynamics of political and social change in the 1950s did not awaken the Protestants from their political apathy. Except for a few initiatives of humanitarian assistance, Protestants remained outside the political debate." As a result, when the politics of the Muyaga could no longer be avoided, the Anglicans were woefully unprepared to respond in a meaningful and productive way.[33]

Roger Bowen and other Anglican apologists have argued this was mostly the result of the CMS's theological orientation, which prioritized individual Gospel conversion above political and social reform; meaningful and progressive changes for society started first in the hearts and minds of the believers. Harboring such views led the Anglicans into complacency and disengagement regarding divisive political issues. This not only delayed a more constructive and informed response but also, being focused as they were on revival among individual converts in their mission stations, led to a myopic view of what was unfolding and an arguably tragic misreading of what was happening on the ground outside their mission stations. The CMS Regional Secretary for East Africa reported in 1950, "Another very real result of spiritual revival is the breaking down of age-old hatreds and divisions between the people of Urundi and Ruanda, and between the Batutsi, Bahutu, and Batwa tribes. I saw reconciliations which had every semblance of being genuine, taking place at meetings." However much this may have been true in the Anglican mission stations, within ten years nothing could have been further from the truth in Rwanda at large.[34]

In the aftermath of the revolution, another defense made of the CMS's seeming disengagement from politics was that the CMS was staffed with doctors, nurses, pastors, and educational professionals, none of whom were positioned to train up African leaders or provide direction to the mission when the hostilities unfolded. H. H. ("Herbert") Osborn, legal representative to the Ruanda Mission, wrote after the fact, "There was not . . . a public condemnation of ethnic discrimination and violence by Rwandan church leaders. Part of the explanation may be that the leadership of the church was still in missionary hands. There was not, therefore, any Protestant Christian Africans in sufficiently senior positions to be able to speak in the name of the church to African authorities." In 1986, as Rwanda was unraveling economically under Habyarimana and the Hutu Power movement was beginning, the mission was still processing the growing troubles as "spiritual warfare" and blaming the problems on Rwandans' "deep fear and superstition arising from witchcraft and other occult practices." The article admitted, in confirmation of Osborn's analysis, to a lack of "mature, committed Christians who can nurture and disciple new Christians."[35]

These defenses of the CMS in the years leading up to the revolution belie a more troubling observation of the mission. The fact remained true throughout the 1950s that the leaders of the Ruanda Mission harbored a deep and abiding admiration for the Tutsi, viewing them as they had from the very beginning as the natural-born rulers of the country. Ian Linden writes, "As late as 1959 the CMS could conceive of no other future for Rwanda than a Tutsi-dominated one." To make the case, he quoted the *Ruanda Notes* from 1959: "They [the Tutsi] have an innate capacity to rule born of centuries of experience." Linden's frequent criticism of the CMS on this point was that the Anglicans were political conservatives who, with their "Cambridge and army backgrounds leant naturally towards the Tutsi aristocracy, personality, and culture."[36]

Linden went further, noting that Joe Church's ancestor, Samuel Church, served as a boson on Charles II's yacht, and both Stanley Smith and Leonard Sharp had served in the East African Rifles. Geoffrey Holmes, a pioneer participant in the Ruanda Mission, had been an international ice hockey player who, according to Linden, naturally admired the Tutsi *ntore* [dancers] as fine athletes and highjumpers." While Linden's observations regarding the background of the Ruanda Mission's leaders and their personal inclinations are purely speculative on his part, his suggestion that they were inclined toward a pro-Tutsi and monarchical point of view has merit.[37]

One could also argue that, in the context of the 1920s, when the Ruanda Mission began, their racially oriented attitudes about the Hutu and Tutsi merely reflected common European assumptions at the time. Nonetheless, decades passed between the 1920s and 1950s. By the late 1950s, the colonial world was undergoing proto-democratic transitions. The modern civil rights movement was emerging. Fascism and Nazi-inspired racism had been confronted and defeated across the world by the Western powers. In consideration of the Ruanda Mission specifically, Smith, Sharp, and Church were Cambridge-educated doctors, as were others in the field. Being among some of the best-educated medical minds of their day, one must wonder why they were unable to espouse and articulate, even as political lay persons and non-participants, a more enlightened and sophisticated view of Rwanda's social classes and divisions. That so many in the Ruanda Mission still saw the Tutsi, as late as 1959, as having an *innate* capacity to rule and a more advanced culture is troubling and begs explanation. Even in December 1959, Jim Brazier was asking readers to "pray for the young Mwami Kigeri V, because he can still be the unifying influence needed to counteract the evils of tribal and party strife."[38]

The close relationship between the Tutsi and the Anglicans dated back to the start of the mission. From the beginning, the mission attracted both groups, and Hutu Anglicans were always in the majority, but pioneers of the mission were especially eager to attract Tutsi chiefs, seeing this as a "Constantinian" route to mass conversion. The conversion of Tutsi chiefs was always celebrated in the *Ruanda Notes*, and this relationship accelerated over the course of the 1940s. According to Timothy Longman, "As early as the 1940s, as their anger with the White Fathers and Belgian colonial rule increased, Tutsi royalists turned increasingly to the Anglican Church. With their upper-class backgrounds, CMS missionaries were more comfortable with Tutsi aristocrats and uncomfortable with popular rebellion." While Tutsi converts were welcomed from the start, by 1959, as the revolution accelerated, members of the mission started feeling the effects of their association with the monarchy and involved themselves in the conflict, to the consternation of the CMS in London.[39]

In December 1959, the general secretary of the CMS, Max Warren (1904–77), sent a "personal and urgent" memo to CMS president Kenneth Grubb (1900–1980) apprising him of troubling actions on the part of Joe Church and Harold Adeney. Warren's first concern was the appearance of an article in the *Sunday Times* alleging that the CMS was accusing the Belgian colonial government of favoring the "violently tribalist APROSOMA party." Warren maintained the accusations were wrong. The article, which Warren attached, stemmed from a letter Harold Adeney smuggled out of Rwanda to Uganda in November 1959, in which he explicitly accused the colonial government of such actions. The issue resulted in a statement to Governor Harroy, signed by Bishop Jim Brazier and H. H. Osborn, affirming the mission did not associate itself with "any political party, and assures the Governor of the Society's earnest desire to cooperate with the Government in restoring peace in Ruanda."[40]

Along with Adeney's letter, Joe Church also smuggled out his own observations. He noted the unfolding violence and had met with Governor Harroy to seek his protection for the mission centers. In what no doubt alarmed Warren, Church told of how the leading Protestant chiefs, upon learning the "rioters were coming to Gahini," stated that they did not want the protection of the Belgian soldiers and that they would defend the mission themselves. When Church cautioned them against this, they proclaimed, "Gahini is *our* hospital. We will protect the mission." In light of these observations, Warren stated that the Ruanda Mission had no "conception of the extent to which they were playing with fire" and that the "strongest presentations have now been made to them that all information coming in about disturbances in Ruanda and the sequels to what has now appeared in the press should be communicated to us at Salisbury Square immediately." Additionally, he noted that Lawrence Barham and Talbot Hindley should press upon Church and Adeney to exercise the "greatest wisdom and caution" in the manner in which they "deal with these matters." He finished by adding, "It would do no harm if they were to be thoroughly frightened!"[41]

On November 21, 1959, the missionaries Alan and Catherine Lindsay reported from their station at Shyira that many "houses belonging to our workers who live off the station have been destroyed." Incredulously, their letter expressed hope that this "may be the Lord's way of breaking the tremendous power of the Roman Catholic Church in this country." Clearly, the anti-Catholicism of the Ruanda Mission ran deep. Throughout 1960, the missionaries continued to report outbreaks of violence against Tutsi in all parts of the country. They were very much aware of the house burnings, cattle killings, and physical attacks. Harold Adeney wrote in May 1960 that ever since November of the prior year, "when the Bahutu rose against the Batutsi . . . their houses were burned, and they had to flee for refuge to the Mission or Government centres," leaving very few Tutsi in northwest Rwanda. Naturally, the mission took pity on the plight of the Tutsi. As Peter Guillebaud wrote in October 1960, "It is tragic to see the plight of these thousands of folks, who, rightly or wrongly, have been the leaders of the country's life, now in exile, in captivity in refugee camps, or just wandering from pillar to post. Many of them are our own friends, some are our fellow workers and brethren in Christ."

During the turmoil, the mission found a new purpose in taking in the refugees, who sometimes numbered in the thousands clustered around the
churches and schools.[42]

In part because of their reputation for being a haven for the Tutsi refugees,
and no doubt because of their past support, the missions themselves were
often targets of suspicion and violence, despite their best intentions. A memorandum from 1959 reported that Tutsi were taking refuge at CMS centers,
giving rise to the "belief that the Mission favors the Tutsi." While proclaiming
that "our missionaries would shelter *any* refugees fleeing for their lives," Tutsi
or otherwise, the die had already been cast. On January 14, 1960, the mission
school at Byumba was set on fire. The following month, a Belgian administra-
tor visited the Byumba station to investigate reports of seditious songs being
sung at the school despite the burning. Amid these events, in January 1961,
Ndahindurwa, chosen *without* Belgian approval, visited Gahini, where he was
received with "hymns and patriotic songs" despite the CMS's prior commitment to cooperate with the government. Astonishingly, in the face of such
theatrics, at a 1959 meeting of the CMS Africa Committee, it was reported
that the mission had "become *unwittingly* associated with and culturally integrated" (emphasis added) with the Tutsi. Rather, the mission *invited* suspicion
and hostilities, and reaped what it had sown.[43]

By January 1961, when Rwanda became a republic and the monarchy was
abolished, the mission was aware of the gravity of events on the ground, and
its stance was becoming more circumspect. In a formal report to the Ruanda
Council at the end of 1961, it was noted that "a tribal conflict has become a
fierce political struggle by the majority PARMEHUTU party against the royalists who want the king back." Writing from Kigeme in December 1961, near
the seat of the king's former court, Peter Guillebaud explained, "It would be
out of place here to describe how the situation changed and how, by invasion
from outside and subversion from within, the royalists, though locally greatly
in the majority, found themselves harassed, beaten up and their houses and
property destroyed." In writing of "invasion from outside," presumably Guillebaud was speaking of the Tutsi-led *inyenzi* invasions of the early 1960s. Jim
Brazier, then bishop of Ruanda-Urundi, was more direct in early 1962, writing, "Since the New Year there have been occasional terrorist raids by small
groups of armed men directed against . . . Bahutu leaders. The result is an
atmosphere of strain and fear which has accentuated the hostility between
Batutsi and Bahutu, and has turned the country into an armed camp." In the
same essay, he concluded, "There is no sign of tribal reconciliation," a far cry
indeed from ten years prior when the mission declared that "age-old hatreds
and divisions were breaking down."[44]

With the violence growing around them, the missionaries were evidently aware of how the *inyenzi* invasions resulted in retaliations against innocent Tutsi. Yet the mission was unable to shake off its association with the ruling class, an association that became more fraught with consequences at Gahini in 1961, home to the Church family. In 1960 the *mugabekazi* (queen mother) arrived at Gahini for medical treatment after her home, property, and cattle were destroyed. Joe Church escorted her into Uganda for protection and refuge, with Belgium's consent. In June 1961, the missionaries at Gahini watched with binoculars as villages burned across the lake, prompting "thirty or forty" to come to the mission for treatment. Although Church protested that he acted on his "neutrality as a doctor and as a preacher of the Gospel," his actions on this and many other instances had "drawn the fire on Gahini and on [him] personally." As a result, in August 1961, the British Consul advised Church to leave the country, as his safety could no longer be guaranteed. He and Decie left Gahini for Uganda after thirty-three years of service. After eleven years of work in Uganda, they retired to Cambridge in 1972. Joe Church died in 1989, and Decie followed in 1991.[45]

Many other of the Ruanda missionaries mentioned in this work left the field in these years. William Church, Joe Church's brother, a tropical medicine specialist and pioneer missionary at Buhiga, retired to Cambridge in 1957 and died in 1979. Dora Skipper retired in 1958, as did Lawrence Barham, who went on to become general secretary of the Ruanda Mission. Constance Hornby, who joined the Smiths and Sharps in Kabale in 1923, retired from the field in 1965. She was buried at the Anglican Cathedral in Kabale in 1972. Her tomb is still visible and well cared for on the hill in front of the cathedral. Stanley and Zoe Smith had retired from Rwanda in 1956 and resided at Mbarara, Uganda, where they continued with translation work. When the violence began in 1959, they worked on outreach among Tutsi refugees who settled in a camp in the Orukinga Valley not far from the border. They left Uganda in 1977 and spent their last few years in England. Stanley Smith died in 1978. Zoe followed in 1980. Leonard and Esther Sharp left active service the same year as the Smiths. They lived for six years in their home on what is still called Sharp's Island, across the water from the leper colony they founded on Lake Bunyonyi. Presently, their home has been converted into a boutique resort. In 1962, they retired to Mombasa, Kenya, where they spent their final years. Esther Sharp died a year later in 1963. Leonard Sharp lived thirteen more years, dying in 1976. Jack Symonds, who had left the field in 1940, returned briefly in 1967 for two years of medical work in Uganda. He died in 1993. In May 1964, Jim Brazier retired as bishop of Ruanda-Urundi after thirty-four years and returned to England, where he died in 1989. His departure marked the last of the original pioneer missionaries to leave Rwanda. Harold and Isobel Adeney, not pioneers to Ruanda but deeply involved nonetheless, retired in 1982. H. H. Osborn, who went to the Ruanda Mission in 1951, left in 1968 to become chairman of the mission, a position he held until 1981.[46]

Throughout 1961, the mission stations witnessed the violence firsthand, and felt its effects directly. Harold Adeney reported in December that a Rwandan Anglican pastor at Shyira Diocese was murdered. Refugees continued to pour into the mission stations. The troubles at Gahini, an area especially associated with Tutsi monarchists, continued after Joe Church's exit as well. In September 1961, his son, Dr. John Church, left in charge at the station, forced a PARMEHUTU gang out of the hospital ward after they rushed in to capture a Tutsi sub-chief seeking refuge at Gahini. He reported afterward, "We have first-hand information that the gang have said that if they see any of us missionaries off the Mission, helping UNAR, they will kill us." As it happened, none of the British missionaries themselves suffered any personal violence. In the following number of the *Ruanda Notes*, Harold Adeney noted the independence celebrations in May 1962 with little commentary. In October, Jim Brazier reported that the mission stations had been "at peace" and "tribal feeling had cooled off," with the armed invasions of the royalists having "fizzled out."[47]

The Second Republic of Habyarimana

Grégoire Kayibanda's presidency and Rwanda's First Republic lasted eleven years, from 1962 until his overthrow in 1973. From the outset, he sought to embody Hutu solidarity in much the same way as the "*mwami* once symbolized Tutsi supremacy." To observers in the 1960s, he seemed to represent the incarnation of Rwandan moral values, with an overt, quasi-religious authority to issue special prerogatives. He was often referred to as the "idol of the people," a form of deference once reserved for the king. In such a context, the presidency was not subject to political competition and challenge. In Lemarchand's words, "The whole purpose of presidential elections [was] not to provide opportunities for replacing the incumbent but, rather, to affirm his permanence in office." By 1964, with the threat from the Tutsi exiles and the *inyenzi* neutralized, Kayibanda consolidated power internally and quickly moved toward eliminating any political competition. Like Kagame today, he believed that "political opposition distracted Rwandese from the work of development."[48]

In the reelection campaign of 1965, he and PARMEHUTU candidates ran unchallenged. Kayibanda received more than 90 percent of the vote, mirroring the vote totals received by Paul Kagame in his so-called elections since

1994. Kayibanda made virtually all political appointments and nominations, even down to the lowest levels. By doing so, he marginalized what remained of the other pre-independence political parties, ultimately pushing them aside to make way for one-party rule under PARMEHUTU. APROSOMA disappeared from the scene and was banned, along with UNAR and RADER. By 1966 Rwanda was a one-party dictatorship. Insulating himself even further, between 1964 and 1967, Kayibanda's government came to be dominated by PARMEHUTU members from central Rwanda, primarily from Gitarama and Butare, transforming Rwanda's ethnic divisions into sectional ones. The regional factionalism he engendered across the country ultimately precipitated his downfall.[49]

Despite the openly Hutu orientation of his government and following the initial rounds of ethnic violence and the flight of many from the country, Kayibanda did not entirely dispossess the Tutsi. Tutsi representation, "both as teachers and students in high schools and postsecondary institutions, and in the ranks of salaried workers, remained significantly higher than their percentage in the population." Nonetheless, resentment of the Tutsi flared again in 1972 as a result of Hutu massacres by the Tutsi government in neighboring Burundi. In February 1973, anti-Tutsi sentiment in Rwanda blossomed again into violence. Tutsi were attacked, fired from jobs, and expelled from schools, and their homes were burned. Another wave of Tutsi fled the country as refugees to the north. Nor were they the only victims. Owing to pent-up sectional resentments under Kayibanda, many southern and central Hutu were attacked by northern Hutu. Hutu shopkeepers saw their stores looted, and several PARMEHUTU politicians were killed. Many escaped as refugees to the east in Tanzania, where Burundian Hutu had fled from Tutsi dominance in Burundi. As Reyntjens observed, the violence "clearly went beyond the level of ethnic struggle and became more a conflict between classes and regions, in which the north openly opposed the central and southern portions of the country."[50]

As a result, on July 5, 1973, Major General Juvénal Habyarimana (1937–94) led a successful coup against Kayibanda. Habyarimana was born to a prosperous Hutu-Bakiga family from the north in Bushiru, near Gisenyi. Following his education in Zaire, he became an aid to the Belgian commander of the colonial forces in Rwanda. Two years later, he was named head of the Rwanda National Guard. In 1965 he was promoted to head the Ministry of the National Guard and Police, a cabinet-level position that made him the most powerful figure in the Rwandan military. Though he supported Kayibanda at first, by 1972 he viewed him as having done little to alleviate poverty in Rwanda or develop the country economically. With ethnic and regional violence continuing into the summer of 1973, Habyarimana launched a bloodless coup, although numerous members of the previous government were executed later. Kayibanda was placed under house arrest and died three years later. In a style almost identical to both Kayibanda's earlier regime and the RPF presently, what followed was a consolidation of power with a "primary objective to reestablish state authority through a system of parallel control: party representatives would combine administrative and political functions, thus ensuring a firm hold over populations left rudderless by shattered political structures."[51]

Habyarimana's seizure of power continued the regional dimension of Rwandan politics. While Kayibanda's regime had been dominated by Hutu from the southern and central regions of the country, Habyarimana and his wife, Agathe Habyarimana (1942–94), represented northern Hutu who had experienced discrimination under Kayibanda's government. Even the educational system was skewed with administrators and children from the northwest. Children from the northwest needed a test score of only a 50 to be admitted into secondary school, while children from the rest of the country needed an 80 or 90. Most of the military and political associates who joined Habyarimana in the coup were northerners as well, who continued their dominance of the new regime. The army, for instance, was composed to a large extent of recruits from the president's northwest region of Gisenyi. Not surprisingly, then, in the aftermath of the genocide, many observers and journalists fell victim to RPF propaganda regarding the so-called *akazu* (Kinyarwanda for "little house"), a supposed command structure of Habyarimana's northern in-laws, headed by his wife, who were alleged to have organized a "Zero Network" of presidential death squads to eliminate Tutsi.[52]

Organized massacres of Tutsi did indeed occur in the immediate years before the genocide, but they were organized by "other people and at different levels of the state apparatus." The *akazu* and "Zero Network" allegations, first propagated by Christophe Mfizi, a defector from the pregenocide regime, was meant to validate the RPF narrative of the genocide being methodically calculated by Habyarimana's northern relatives. The episode provides one of the first illustrations of the masterful way in which the RPF manages and manipulates information for the outside world. After resigning in 1996 as the RPF's first ambassador to Paris, Mfizi obtained political asylum in France, after which he repudiated the term *akazu* before the ICTR.[53]

When Habyarimana came to power, he claimed he was establishing a "moral revolution" built upon the political revolution of 1959–62, which "promoted restoration of national unity and reestablishment of order." As he consolidated power, the country became more stable and made economic progress. Ethnic violence decreased and there was little social differentiation between Hutu and Tutsi farmers. Rwanda became a darling of the Western donor community. For fifteen years, the country prospered and "became a favorite recipient of foreign aid from overseas donors."[54]

In per capita terms, Rwanda became one of the largest recipients of Official Development Assistance in Africa. Life expectancies were rising by 1978 and death rates were falling. Food production rose and the government "developed an effective nation-wide system of services reflected in rising literacy rates, a high vaccination rate of children, and perhaps the densest paved road network on the continent." In terms of "electricity supplies, clean drinking water, clinics, schools, and good roads, Rwandans were well provided for, even compared with wealthier neighboring countries." Teachers, nurses, and other government employees "received salaries that, although not generous, allowed them to live decent lives." At the foundation of Habyarimana's seemingly successful Second Republic was a strong farming sector.[55]

In his rhetoric and speeches, Habyarimana wanted Rwanda to be an agricultural society. From researching the language used in his presidential speeches, Philip Verwimp concluded, "He glorified the peasantry and pictured himself a peasant. In his ideology of rural romanticism, only the Hutu were the real peasants of Rwanda; the Tutsi were a feudal class closely associated with colonialist occupation." Accordingly, by 1980, 93 percent of the population was engaged in farming. To accommodate a robust population growth, the government pursued a policy to further increase the farming sector by means of "developing new land and decreasing fallow with the result that growth in agriculture" came "overwhelmingly from extension (clearing forests and draining marshes)." Moreover, vast tracts of land in the eastern regions were freed up for planting when Tutsi refugees fled the country; however, "since these newly vacated lands were previously used for pasturage, they were not actually well suited to agriculture." As a result of such policies, nearly all available lands, minus roughly 20 percent set aside for national parks, were under cultivation by the mid-1980s.[56]

The developmental successes enjoyed by the new regime provided an excuse for the outside world to look the other way in the face of Habyarimana's authoritarianism, in much the same way that Kagame and the RPF's current progress in Rwanda allow for critics to be sidelined and their human rights abuses to be overlooked. Achievements like the ones noted above under Habyarimana are often extolled as proof of the RPF's progress, yet other, less admirable, similarities exist. When Habyarimana achieved power, Kayibanda's PARMEHUTU party was abolished. A new party was created, the Mouvement Révolutionnaire National pour le Développement (MRND, National Revolutionary Movement for Development), to which it was declared all Rwandans

belonged by virtue of birth. Its stated goal was the "fostering of unity and cooperation among ethnic groups and regions and mobilizing the population for
development." The party claimed to encourage "responsible democracy, meaning the free expression of ideas on condition that they are seen as useful to the
collectivity." In practice, "responsible democracy" meant Habyarimana, following the promulgation of a new Constitution in 1978, was "reelected" three
times with vote tallies exceeding 95 percent. For those familiar with contemporary Rwanda, such vote totals are routine when Kagame stands for "reelection"
and the "free expression of ideas" are allowed in as long as they do not question
the RPA's narrative of Rwanda's history and present political order. To do so
runs the risk of being accused of being a "genocide sympathizer."[57]

Despite the expansion of the agriculture sector and the receipt of vast
amounts of foreign aid, Habyarimana's agrarian paradise was falling apart by
the mid-1980s. Drought and an accumulation of environmental problems
owing to aggressive land extension—including deforestation, soil erosion, and
a decline in soil fertility—started damaging crop production. As the population grew, the country continued with traditional farming methods and failed
to modernize (relying on handheld hoes, picks, and machetes). No effort was
made to introduce more productive and efficient crop varieties available on
the world market. The regime did implement family planning in 1981 through
the Office National de la Population (ONAPO, National Office of Population) but never expanded crop production. Thus, by 1990, per capita food
production had fallen 25 percent since 1984. Famines and hunger began to
resurface by the late 1980s. In 1989 an unusually severe drought compounded
the suffering. Habyarimana's regime failed to respond to these early warnings
in the face of widespread crop failures.[58]

Rwanda's export economy struggled as well. The price of coffee, Rwanda's
most valuable product, declined sharply on the world market over the course
of the decade. Coffee export receipts fell from $144 million in 1985 to $30 million in 1993. By 1989 the Rwandan franc had fallen by 40 percent. When
Rwanda's balance of payments fell behind, the IMF / World Bank imple-
mented a structural adjustment program, including austerity measures, which
further reduced incomes. Budgetary shortages and higher import costs eroded
health care services. Maternal and infant mortality rates rose sharply. By 1990
the country experienced, on top of severe food shortages, a sharp rise in
malaria. In the same year, about one out of six people in urban areas lived
below the poverty line, while in rural areas this applied to more than 50 percent of the population.[59]

In mid-1989 *Kinyamateka* started publicizing information about the famines, corruption, and rampant land accumulation by government officials.

Riots erupted among university students and unemployed graduates in several cities. One student was killed and many were wounded when the Rwandan security services responded. The regime silenced the press and brought legal action against its growing number of critics, with political "opposition coming mainly from the South and center as most positions of power in the regime were held by those from the president's district in the North." Responding to these internal pressures for reform and worried about his international reputation among donors, Habyarimana reluctantly agreed to a series of constitutional changes in 1990. Freedoms of the press and political associations were restored as quickly as they had been curtailed. A constitutional amendment in June 1991 legalized a multiparty system, which led to the creation of new parties like the Mouvement démocratique républicain (MRD, Republican Democratic Movement), the Social Democratic Party, and the Liberal Party, which welcomed Tutsi participation. Coalition governments were formed following elections in 1992.[60]

Habyarimana's reforms had far less than universal support. Long-entrenched politicians in the ruling MRND, with many at the root of the corruption in Rwanda, saw much to lose in the president's new course and had no wish to share power with opposition parties who were gaining support among the masses, although such power-sharing would have released World Bank dollars. Moreover, the president himself was surrounded by senior military and civilian cronies from the north. Later, although somewhat erroneously known as the *akazu*, they centered around the powerful northern clan of his wife, Madame Agathe. Blaming Rwanda's troubles on the meddlesome Tutsi exile community, extremist "Hutu Power" politicians from within the MRND and the military, with the support of some "powerful business and media interests . . . set their faces towards 'genocide' as the final solution to their problems."[61]

Here again, in a familiar pattern, a revision and "rewriting of Rwandan history" occurred, with the assistance of the Hutu Power advocate and university history professor Ferdinand Nahimana, one of Habyarimana's northern relatives. Nahimana undertook and popularized politically motivated studies on precolonial Bantu kingships in the northwest of Rwanda. He erroneously claimed, for instance, that Mwami Rujugira had made planned invasions to conquer the Hutu in western Rwanda in the mid-nineteenth century in order to remind the masses that the Tutsi were invaders intent on reconquering Rwanda. He founded the Radio Télévision Libre des Mille Collines to broadcast his claims to a wider audience. His rewriting of Rwandan history provided the "intellectual respectability and historical legitimacy that the *akazu* craved, by supporting their claims of Bantu purity."[62]

The Anglicans under Habyarimana

From the time Kayibanda's First Republic began until publication ceased in 1971, the *Ruanda Notes* makes virtually no observations of politics and offers no commentary on the social situation in Rwanda. "Hutu" and "Tutsi" never appear, nor are tribal conflicts noted. Kayibanda's name is rarely even mentioned. Interestingly, although Keswick Conventions continued to be held, the East African Revival is not specifically noted either. The same apolitical pattern continued through the Habyarimana years and afterward. The mission magazine *Partners Together*, which replaced the *Ruanda Notes* in 1971, was in circulation until 1999. Prior to the shooting down of his plane in 1994, only two references are ever made to Habyarimana, wherein he was praised for being present at the consecration of the new bishop of Butare in 1976 and for attending the opening of the new clinic at Shyira in 1977. "Hutu" and "Tutsi" appear only once in reference to a prayer request for the "Hutu to love the Tutsi, the Black to love the White."[63]

Rather, *Partners Together*, followed by *Mid-Africa Ministry News* in 1999, are focused on continued development and the need for more funds, workers, and missionaries. Church growth slowly continued, and schools and clinics continued to be built. In 1978 a much-celebrated physiotherapy clinic, the first of its kind in Rwanda, was opened at Gahini. Despite the continued concern for health care, the famine and hardships caused by the drought and collapse of coffee prices starting in the mid-1980s are mentioned only in passing, noting a "reduced harvest . . . rising cattle stock prices . . . and people coming to the missions for food." One can only assume that to delve further into the issues and causes would put the mission on political ground, a position clearly avoided after the events of the Muyaga.[64]

Structurally, in 1961 Ruanda-Urundi became a separate diocese under Bishop Jim Brazier. In 1965 the CMS relinquished control of the churches to indigenous leadership. Rwanda became a separate province altogether, along with Uganda, Burundi, and Boga-Zaire, under Erica Sabiti as first archbishop in 1966. When Sabiti retired in 1974, he was replaced by Janani Luwum (1922–77). *Partners Together* noted Luwum's ascension but also declared that the Ruanda Mission was satisfied that they had received guarantees from the CMS that the mission would continue on "Keswick lines." Straying from the apolitical tendencies of the church, Luwum became an outspoken critic of the Idi Amin (1925–2003) regime in Uganda and was murdered in 1977. His death announcement in *Partners Together* made no mention of the circumstances. Otherwise, supporters of the mission continued to send aid and missionaries down to the present, staying informed of events through the pages of *Partners Together* and *Mid-Africa Ministry News*. For the missionaries in the field, one surmises that they tried to maintain a low profile, even as the church's increasingly Hutu leadership partnered with the state and events careened in hindsight toward the genocide.[65]

In accordance with his proclamation of a "moral revolution," Habyarimana's regime promised reconciliation between Hutu and Tutsi, with the hope of a reduction in ethnic tensions. The considerable development that occurred seemed to offer promise as well. For the Catholics and Anglicans, the "moral revolution" of the new regime marked the beginning of a complete church-state symbiosis. Health care and education were left to the church yet subject to political control, such as the maintenance of an ethnic quota system in clerical promotions. Vincent Nsengiyumva (1936–94), archbishop of the Catholic Church, was a member of Habyarimana's inner circle and occupied a seat on the committee of the MRND. Leaders of the Anglican, Presbyterian, and Baptist Churches were also closely aligned with the regime, and local pastors and priests were allied with local burgomasters and councilors.[66]

Expectedly, then, in the late 1980s, as the socioeconomic forces that led to the genocide unfolded, church leaders were largely silent. No reaction followed in 1990, for instance, when Sylvio Sindambiwe, a writer for *Kinyameteka*, was murdered for speaking out against corruption. Several Tutsi priests were arrested in the aftermath as well. Hoyweghen argues that the church was "mute" during these years and did not question "the political structures in which it comfortably operated." While several church organizations were in fact critical of Habyarimana, the senior clergy, allied with the regime, "had no eye for social justice nor the oppression of its own Tutsi clergy." The same can be observed of the Anglicans.[67]

Numerous pregenocide Anglican bishops and pastors were vocal in their support of Habyarimana's regime and supported the genocide. Archbishop Augustin Nshamihigo and Bishop Jonathan Ruhumuliza acted as spokespersons for the Hutu Power regime even during the killings, although the Diocese of Worchester in England later found no evidence of guilt for Ruhumuliza's role in the genocide. Nshamihigo remains in exile with unknown whereabouts. The former Anglican bishop of Shyogwe Diocese Samuel Musabyimana was indicted by the International Criminal Tribunal for Rwanda (ICTR) for betraying Tutsi parishioners who came to him for protection from the militias. Many other Hutu Anglican priests were found culpable as well, although one would know none of this from the pages of *Partners Together* and *Mid-Africa Ministry News*.

The Genocide of the Tutsi

The Hutu Power movement, which took seed under Habyarimana's reforms, was further inflamed when the Rwandan Patriotic Army (RPA), the military

arm of the RPF, invaded northeast Rwanda on October 1, 1990. Led by Fred
Rwigyema (1957–1990) and Paul Kagame, the RPA was composed overwhelmingly of Tutsi exiles, many of whom had lived most if not all their lives in
Uganda. When hundreds of thousands of Tutsi refugees fled Rwanda after
1959, and in subsequent waves, most of them settled in refugee camps in
southern Uganda. They and their descendants formed a Tutsi Diaspora who,
from the 1960s and until the RPA invaded, longed to return to what they saw
as their homeland, although many have speculated that the RPF invasion was
timed to derail Habyarimana's democratic reforms, which would have relegiti-
mized his presidency and removed the justification for a Tutsi resumption of
power. André Guichaoua agrees, contending that the invasion was intended to
"short-circuit the negotiations that were underway." These negotiations, conducted by the United Nations High Commission for Refugees (HCR), were
ultimately intended to facilitate a "voluntary return of all Rwandan refugees."
Yet RPF leaders "had little interest in plans to resettle Tutsi refugees. . . . Heavy
pressure was brought to bear on candidates for repatriation to dissuade them
from going along with HCR repatriation plan." RPF leaders popularized the
slogan "We left together, we will return together."[68]

Despite this, much of the postgenocide propaganda emanating out of
Rwanda, embraced and promoted by the Anglican Church, supports the image
of the Tutsi returnees as suffering refugees seeking only to return home and
obscures both the RPF's overriding single objective of returning to Rwanda to
assume power and the complex role played by the exiles in Uganda's own turbulent political history. Such has not always been the case, even in the Anglican's own earlier literature. In 1991 the invading RPA was described as "rebels
entering the country from Uganda." During the civil war, *Partners Together*
reported to the church's supporters in England that "rebelling Ugandan army
officials initiated the conflict." Throughout Milton Obote's first presidency
(1966–71) and Idi Amin's subsequent dictatorship (1971–79), the "59ers" were
frequently viewed as meddlesome outsiders who had overstayed their welcome.
Initially, the Tutsi refugees were tolerated, but when it seemed they would
remain in the country indefinitely, "hospitality fatigue set in and generosity
turned into hostility." In 1980, when Obote gained power a second time, Tutsi
refugees joined Yoweri Museveni (1944–present) and his guerilla army, the
National Resistance Army (NRA), in their struggle against Obote, comprising
up to three thousand of the NRA's fourteen thousand rebel forces. Many of
them joined the NRA following "state-sanctioned pogroms" against Tutsi in
Rwanda in 1982.[69]

With Museveni's victory in 1986, after considerable loss of life in Uganda,
Tutsi leaders, among them Rwigyema and Kagame, formed the RPF/RPA in

1987 as a paramilitary unit of the NRA to assist in putting down counterinsurgencies in eastern and northern Uganda, which left more than one hundred thousand dead. While participation in the NRA's struggle allowed the RPF to recruit many more refugees and perfect their military skills, the effect on Museveni's alliance with the "59ers" was to greatly heighten anti-Tutsi feelings among the Ugandan populace. By 1989 Rwigyema was second only to Museveni in the military hierarchy of the NRA, and many other Tutsi had obtained key political, military, and economic posts. The increased presence of the Tutsi refugees confirmed the claim of many that the NRA itself was a "Tutsi organization"; and Museveni's political opponents frequently mocked him as a "Rwandese refugee."[70]

By 1990 the large Tutsi presence in Uganda had "become an embarrassing political issue" for Museveni and created a significant citizenship crisis. When Museveni gained power, the NRA's opponents demanded that only indigenous Ugandans receive priority in the new state. To resolve the question of who was indigenous or not, and thus who was or was not a citizen, the NRA made a distinction between residents and nonresidents. Museveni, after initially promising that any Rwandan who was a resident for ten or more years would be entitled to citizenship, clarified that only indigenous Ugandans would enjoy citizenship, to the exclusion of the Tutsi refugees. With this change of course in 1990, the refugee community, realizing that they would have neither land nor political power in Uganda, concluded that they would have no future unless they returned to Rwanda. Prior to Museveni's clarification, evidence suggests that most of the rank-and-file refugees were content to become naturalized Ugandans. The majority had never set foot in their parent's homeland. Rwanda existed for them as a nearly mythological "land of milk and honey." Nonetheless, Museveni absolved himself of the Tutsi problem by providing logistical support to the 1990 invasion, culminating in the genocide.[71]

The history and complexities of the RPF's involvement in Uganda's citizenship crisis are not spoken of by Anglicans, and their Western supporters remain largely oblivious to these and other issues as well. For instance, a narrative persists, neither refuted nor challenged by the Anglican Church, that Kagame and the RPF invaded Rwanda *only* to stop the genocide and *rebuild* the country. However, Alan Kuperman's research among former RPA officers demonstrates that the rebels "expected their challenge to provoke genocidal retaliation but viewed this as an acceptable cost of achieving their goal of attaining power in Rwanda." Ignorance of such counterarguments allows many of Rwanda's supporters to picture themselves as coming along behind a benevolent RPF to rescue the country from its underdevelopment and help in its recovery without having to face the RPF's history or the larger political issues at stake for Rwanda and the region.[72]

Lost to casual and unstudied outsiders, with no remedy offered from any present voices from within Rwanda or the Anglican Church, is the degree of violence Kagame and the RPA engaged in with the NRA during its counter-insurgency operations in northern Uganda in the late 1980s. A Catholic priest in Gulu, in the northern Acholi district, reported that the RPA would "herd women, children, and old people into houses and set the houses on fire." Violence against their own took place as well among extremist members of the RPF. Fred Rwigyema, for instance, was a Muhindiro Tutsi from the "purist royal lineage of the Nyinginya dynasty," whereas Kagame was from the lesser Bega clan. When Rwigyema was killed on the second day of the invasion, many former members of the RPF "remain persuaded that [his] murder was a carefully contrived plot to eliminate a brilliant man whose combination of royal legitimacy and revolutionary charisma made him a probable future national leader." According to Susan Thomson, two officers, Chris Bunyenyezi and Peter Bayingana, allegedly killed Rwigyema under Kagame's orders. Both were subsequently arrested, tried for treason, and executed, again under Kagame's orders, to pave the way for him to take full command. Many friends of Rwigyema now live in exile. Although "these events are still vividly in the minds of most Rwandese today," his death, and the extent of RPA atrocities in northern Uganda, have never been accounted for or investigated. Nor are they spoken of in Rwanda by figures in the Anglican Church or otherwise.[73]

The RPA's October invasion was quickly halted and pushed back by the Rwandan army, the Forces Armées Rwandaise (FAR), backed by French, Belgian, and Zairian units. With Ryigyema dead, Kagame returned from military training at Fort Leavenworth, Kansas, and took control of the forces at the front. With an RPA guerilla war underway and with the FAR unable to fully dislodge them back to Uganda, Habyarimana played two lines. He gained foreign support as a result of his ongoing democratic reforms, even agreeing that Rwandan exiles who wished to return would be allowed to do so. But he also turned to ethnic propaganda against the "feudal Tutsi," even staging a fake attack on Kigali on October 4 as a pretext for arresting eight thousand Tutsi suspected of pro-RPF sympathies. Virulent Hutu-Tutsi cultural nationalism soared on both sides. Thousands of Tutsi exiles from around the region, driven by the oppression of the "interior Tutsi," reinforced Kagame's RPA units from Uganda. The Hutu Power faction within Rwanda intensified its extremist rhetoric. In January 1991, Kagame raided the northern city of Ruhengeri and liberated Tutsi political prisoners, killing many Hutu civilians in the process.

Over the next few years, as the war ground to a stalemate, ethnicity became "the tool of power for the elite, as it had been for the last thirty years."[74]

With a stalemate in the north between the two factions, a small UN force under Canadian general Romeo Dallaire was inserted in 1992 to enforce a truce. Under pressure from the UN to engage in talks with the RPF, Habyarimana agreed to negotiations in Arusha, Tanzania. As the talks proceeded, the Hutu Power movement grew, and further killings of the Tutsi took place inside Rwanda. Hutu extremists, aided by violent hate speech from the notorious Radio des Mille Collines, encouraged hostile anti-Tutsi feelings among the populace, reviving old beliefs that the Tutsi were foreigners bent on reasserting the monarchy and oppressing the Hutu. Hutu Power proponents organized a paramilitary militia called the Interahamwe (Those who stand together), mostly unemployed Hutu youths plied with alcohol and drugs, and encouraged them to prepare for the extermination of the Tutsi, dehumanized as "snakes" and *inyenzi* (cockroaches).[75]

When a power-sharing agreement was reached with the RPF in August 1993, Hutu Power fanatics believed Habyarimana had capitulated to the Tutsi. On April 6, 1994, he was returning to Kigali from Dar es Salaam following further negotiations with Burundi and Tanzania. As his plane approached the airport, a rocket was fired from the presidential guard's Kanombe barracks, destroying the aircraft, and killing all on board, including Habyarimana and Burundian president Cyprien Ntaryamira (1955–94). The genocide commenced in the immediate hours after the assassination. Culpability for Habyarimana's assassination became the subject of argument for several years, with mostly French officials alleging RPF agents downed the airplane to spark the genocide as a pretext for Kagame's renewed invasion in April, with the intent to assume power. Diplomatic ties between Paris and Kigali were severed over the investigation and Kagame's frequent assertion that French soldiers were involved in the genocide. An official French investigation into the allegation was dropped in December 2018 over lack of evidence. Relations between the two countries have resumed but remain tense.[76]

The gruesome specifics of the genocide have been recounted elsewhere and bear no repeating in detail here. Suffice it to say that the violence shocked the world in its ferocity and thoroughness. Over the course of nearly one hundred days, more than 800,000 people were massacred, though some estimates place the number over one million when the RPF's killings are included. In addition to hundreds of thousands of Tutsi, many Hutu sympathizers were also killed. Family members, longtime friends, and neighbors turned each other in to the *genocidaires*. Thousands were killed in their churches after being welcomed by priests and pastors and then betrayed. Sexual assault was rampant. Victims were piled en masse on roadsides or tossed into rivers and lakes, resulting in a further catastrophe wherein East Africans were unable to eat fish from Lake Victoria for several years as it was assumed the fish were feeding on dead bodies. The genocide unfolded so rapidly that the world was caught off guard and, with little knowledge of what was then seen as an obscure Central African country, the violence was blamed on "ancient tribal hatreds," which stymied efforts to respond. Well documented now was that diplomatic wrangling at the UN, coupled with the Clinton administration's unwillingness to see intervention as being in America's national interest, prevented a meaningful response to stop the killings, allowing the RPF to leverage Western guilt over the genocide and gain a carte blanche for its autocratic actions in the years afterward.[77]

The churches of Rwanda bore their own share of guilt. When the genocide began, most of the Christian churches—Catholic, Anglican, Seventh-day Adventists, and others—remained silent and even cooperative in the face of the killings. Worth noting, however, is that there were "no mass killings" of Tutsi in mosques, and "no Muslim leaders were implicated" in the violence. Not surprisingly in retrospect, African Rights reported that more Rwandans died in churches than anywhere else. One of the first places attacked was the Centre Christus in Kigali, where the Hutu priests and laity were spared while the Tutsi priests were killed, along with a group of visiting Tutsi schoolgirls. Reports abounded from across Rwanda of both Catholic and Anglican clergy who stepped aside to allow the Interahamwe to massacre their Tutsi parishioners hiding in the churches, in many cases hiding there because they were invited in by the priests and pastors. When the genocide was over, the Catholic Church had lost, in addition to its credibility, roughly half of its priests. By the summer of 1995, only two hundred or so priests were left in Rwanda out of a total of nearly four hundred; the rest were either dead or hiding in refugee camps. In June 1994, Catholic archbishop Vincent Nsengiyumva, two bishops, and ten priests, all Hutu, were killed by the RPF in retribution for the genocide. Hoyweghen described the postgenocide Catholic Church as "de facto beheaded" and "in a state of shock." Owning to the actions of Nshamihigo, Ruhumuliza, Musabyimana, and many others, the Anglican Church was in no better of a position.[78]

The genocide ended in July 1994 when the RPF, who recommenced their invasion southward in April, captured Kigali and instituted a new regime under Kagame. The coming to power of the RPF, following Habyarimana's death and the ousting of the Hutu Power regime, marks the beginning of the current phase of Rwanda's history. What followed was a period of stabilization and an effort to reconstruct a new civil society, supposedly inclusive of all Rwandans.

Ethnic identity cards were abolished and the RPF affirmed its commitment to the Arusha Accords and a multiethnic government based on power-sharing. Foreign aid began flowing, and numerous dignitaries made pilgrimages to Rwanda to apologize for not doing more to stop the genocide.[79]

Within a few years, more than half a million former ("old case load") Tutsi refugees returned to Rwanda after decades in Uganda and elsewhere abroad. A substantial number of them are Anglican and see themselves as heirs to the East African Revival, committed to the reconciliation and rebuilding of a new Rwanda. Many in the West, including numerous aid organizations, nonprofit NGOs, and American churches, "driven by an acute guilt syndrome," saw the RPF as the "good guys" and joined in the ranks of the "Friends of the New Rwanda," as they are often called. The narrative of Kagame and the Tutsi-dominated RPF being the "good guys" persists, aided and abetted in its pronouncements and actions by the hierarchy of the Province de l'Eglise Anglicane au Rwanda (PEAR, Province of the Anglican Church of Rwanda). Much like the older "Friends of Ruanda," who supported the colonial Anglican Church and the Tutsi monarchy without question, the present-day "Friends of the New Rwanda" support Kagame's regime and the RPF with a blind eye toward the true nature of the regime and a willful ignorance of history.[80]

CHAPTER FIVE

Revival and Reconciliation

The Anglican Church in Postgenocide Rwanda

W HEN PAUL KAGAME came to power in 1994, he was seen as a forthright and visionary leader. As the new government took office on July 19, the RPF affirmed its commitment to the terms and spirit of the 1993 Arusha Accords, known as the Fundamental Law, and the logic of power-sharing it contained. While the MRND and the CDR party of the extremist Hutu was banned, other political parties took seats in the new parliament. Kagame offered positions to former Hutu who opposed the Habyarimana regime. Faustin Twagiramungu, a Hutu from the MDR, became the first prime minister. Others among their number were Pasteur Bizimungu, first president of the transitional government; Pierre-Célestin Rwigyema, second prime minister; and Seth Sendashonga (1951–98), first minister of the interior.[1]

Following such actions by the new government, the most "common discourse" to emerge in postgenocide Rwanda, for both the church and the state, was and "remains that of reconciliation." Following his assumption of power, Kagame's government promoted a "National Politics of Reconciliation" platform and created the National Unity and Reconciliation Commission (NURC), currently headed by former Anglican bishop John Rucyahana, which develops reconciliation projects around the country. In a top-down approach to reconciliation by fiat, the use of the terms "Hutu," "Tutsi," and "Twa" were banned by law, to be replaced with the often-heard national mantra "We are all Rwandans." Unlike in the Western context, churches in Rwanda are positioned to "assume a crucial role in all processes affecting Rwandan society," affording them a "high significance in the country's reconciliation process." As such, the churches have been "partnering with the government in the national process of reconciliation, supplementing the government's top-down strategy with bottom-up approaches."[2]

The RPF's efforts at seeking a reconciled society also held forth great hope and seemed to mirror the efforts at national forgiveness being promoted by PEAR. When the RPF consolidated control of Rwanda, it found itself with an unprecedented problem. Nearly one million lay dead and a million more were IDPs (internally displaced persons). The social fabric of the country was in tatters as neighbors and even family members had committed acts of violence against one another. Lawlessness was epidemic, the economy was in shambles, and thousands suspected of acts of genocide and related crimes still roamed free. In most cases, the crimes associated with the genocide, ranging from mass killings to property theft, occurred in rural communities with little evidence apart from eyewitness testimonies. With the pregenocide legal system and courts virtually nonexistent, Rwanda's prisons soon contained more than one hundred thousand suspects. Providing fair trials for so many suspects would have been a crushing caseload for the court system, requiring decades for full resolution. To alleviate the burden, in 2000 Kagame's government instituted a precolonial justice system based on reconciliation and forgiveness known as *gacaca*, or "courts on the grass," in Kinyarwanda.[3]

The *gacaca* system was meant not only to expedite the legal proceedings of those formally accused but also to promote community healing and reconciliation, and economic stability and recovery, as well as to provide a forum for the airing of truth for the survivors, victims, and their families. As the system unfolded, local judges were selected by community elections, the names of those killed and the crimes committed in the community were enumerated, and lists of the accused were drawn up. The most serious cases were referred to the national courts, but trials for lesser crimes were conducted in the villages. Those accused were urged to fully confess their actions in exchange for lessened sentences.[4]

Many observers initially applauded the success of *gacaca* as more than ten thousand courts were held, trying more than a million accused perpetrators. Tens of thousands were brought to justice who otherwise would not have been. Proponents of the system credited it with bringing healing and stability to a decidedly traumatized nation. However, problems quickly became apparent. The government eventually had to require participation, as many Rwandans feared for their safety when it came to confronting suspects, especially when reports emerged of retributions against those who testified. The reintegration of former criminals into society, however much they may have repented, created a climate of suspicion and unease in many cases. Research by Jennie Burnet affirms that *gacaca* deepened the cleavages between Hutu and Tutsi, making even some Tutsi genocide survivors "increasingly mistrustful of the current government and of the RPF."[5]

For many observers, the *gacaca* courts provided no justice for those victimized by Tutsi crimes against Hutu and numerous acts of violence and massacres by the RPF forces during their invasion and subsequent stabilization of the country. Many Hutu who protected Tutsi during the genocide feared that for their acts of heroism they would be deemed accomplices. Many feared retribution and discrimination from Hutu who supported the genocidal regime. One Hutu exile reported to Burnet that Hutu who sheltered survivors were often told by other Hutu, "We told you they [the Tutsi] would subjugate the Hutu as they did under the monarchy."[6]

The Revival Returns

In 1996, following the flight and discrediting of its pregenocide leadership, the Anglican Consultative Council ordained new Anglican bishops. Following this, numerous Anglican clergymen returned from exile, primarily from Uganda, to rebuild the church and join the effort in promoting recovery and reconciliation. Field research and interviews confirm many of the priests and Tutsi returnees were attracted to Anglicanism, as opposed to the Catholicism practiced by most Rwandans, largely because the exile community mistrusted the pro-Hutu Catholic Church before 1994 and held it complicit in the genocide, even though many in the Anglican hierarchy were guilty as well.[7]

Following the council's actions, Emmanuel Kolini became bishop of Kigali Diocese and archbishop of the Anglican Church of Rwanda (PEAR). Kolini, who has extensive contacts in the United States, was born Tutsi in the former Zaire (Democratic Republic of the Congo). He was educated in Uganda, where he attended seminary and served as priest and headmaster of several refugee schools for the Tutsi exiles. When the genocide began, he was serving in Zaire. Along with Kolini, most of the initial wave of bishops and clergy in PEAR were Tutsi who returned from Uganda after the RPF seized power. A similar pattern characterizes the trajectory of virtually all the Anglican bishops in Rwanda, as well as those of most of its priests and officers.[8]

Second only to Kolini in his prominence among the "Friends of the New Rwanda" is Bishop John Rucyahana. A Tutsi exile from 1959, Rucyahana grew up in Uganda, where he served as a priest until 1997 when he was appointed bishop of the Shyira Diocese. They, and nearly all the Anglican pastors I spoke with over the course of two field research visits to Rwanda, were Tutsi refugees who returned in the wake of the genocide. Educated in Uganda, they speak English as a primary language and Kinyarwanda as a second language, if at all. Hardly any of them are fluent in French. Even as late as 2005, the new provincial secretary for the Anglican Church, Emmanuel Gatera, left his post at Mukono University in Uganda to assume his position in Rwanda. Many have become prominent spokespersons to a wider audience outside Rwanda and have downplayed their origins and Tutsi identity as they contribute to the rebuilding of the church and the promotion of reconciliation in postgenocide Rwanda.[9]

While the new Anglican leadership is making genuine efforts to promote reconciliation, bringing many resources and much outside attention to the country, their close association with and support of the RPF, dating back to their own origins in Uganda, have made them a politicized church along the same lines as the Catholic and Protestant churches both during the colonial period and under both Kayibanda and Habyarimana. They support the post-genocide narrative proffered by the RPF and have been enlisted in the campaign to rewrite Rwanda's history. Several of the more prominent leaders in PEAR have garnered outside attention by publishing mainstream memoirs in which they hold to the RPF's narrative of Rwanda's history and the genocide. They are, to use Longman's description, "repatriated intellectuals—including government officials, professors, and other intellectuals, such as priests . . . [who] work on revising Rwanda's formal history." As such, they have become complicit in presenting the RPF's version of Rwanda's history and contribute to Kagame's less-than-democratic hold on the reins of power, to the endangerment of the nation's future and efforts at long-term stability.[10]

Outsiders and Western church supporters of PEAR often accept the "We are all Rwandan" mantra at face value and remain unaware of the history of the Hutu-Tutsi relationship and the politics behind the RPF's effort to erase ethnicity by mere fiat. Nor are they aware that such an effort has been unsuccessfully tried before in the region. From 1976 to 1987 in Burundi, under the Tutsi military dictatorship of Jean-Baptiste Bagaza (1946–2016), ethnic identification was forbidden, and ethnicity was erased from identity cards. In the years since 1987, however, Burundi has been wracked by periods of civil strife and violence that always falls squarely along ethnic lines, demonstrating that "top-down prohibition of ethnic alignment does not work."[11]

For its part, the Anglican hierarchy has attempted in its rhetoric to promote unity and reconciliation under the banner of Christianity, among its now both Hutu and Tutsi congregants. To this end, the Anglicans frequently recall the spirit, practices, and memory of the East African Revival, which originated from the Ruanda Mission and to which they see themselves as direct heirs and present participants. All the pastors and bishops whom I interviewed insist that the Revival has returned to Rwanda and remains the principal dynamic within the church. Effectively, new Balokole now occupy the highest levels of Anglican leadership in Rwanda. As such, the Revival and its history have been incorporated and retold as an organizing framework for making sense of the past and explaining the present. Specifically, the Revival is used to explain both what happened in Rwanda in the years leading up to the genocide and to encourage reconciliation and healing in the postgenocide state.[12]

Central to the theology of the new Revival movement is the belief that only the Holy Spirit can move people's hearts to repentance, reform, and ultimately a reconstructed society. For the new Balokole, the Revival movement comes and goes with the Holy Spirit, which, as they explain it, left Rwanda in 1959 with the Tutsi refugees but returned with them and their descendants after the genocide. A retired headmaster of a school in Shyogwe during the 1950s, who left for Uganda after the 1959 Revolution but who now lives in Gahini, claimed there was "no Holy Spirit in Rwanda during the 1960s, but [the Spirit] was in Uganda," presumably with the Tutsi Diaspora. This belief, that the troubles that beset Rwanda from 1959 until the genocide was over occurred because of the parting of the Revival spirit with the Tutsi Balokole, is widespread and endorsed from the highest levels of PEAR.[13]

Archbishop Emmanuel Kolini explained to me that when the Tutsi left Rwanda for the refugee camps, the Spirit left as well. He attributed their survival in the camps to an "outpouring of the Holy Spirit" and a renewal of the Revival among the refugees. Kolini noted how Western churches and aid workers often tell him "one cannot worship God on an empty stomach." He denied this and said of the Revival in the camps in the 1960s, with an air of sincerity: "We were living in hell. Children were dying young and the people had no food or medicine, but when the Spirit came, we were praising God and He preserved us." Catherine Robbins's work lends credibility to his claim about the revival among the refugees, noting a renewal of the Balokole Movement in the early 1960s in the Kigezi District of Uganda, which had long been a stronghold of the East African Revival and where many Tutsi refugees resided. Zablon Nthamburi concurred, claiming Kigezi was a stronghold of the Balokole movement. The diocesan office in Kabale maintains an archive of Revival literature. Moreover, during my field research in Kabale, Uganda, numerous Anglican figures confirmed the persistence of the Revival among the refugees who fled northward to Kigezi. Kolini further maintains the Revival has returned and will bring healing to Rwanda from the genocide. The same sentiment was also expressed to me by many pastors and officials across the dioceses in Rwanda.[14]

As I frequently observed at Anglican church gatherings in Rwanda, the fundamental practices of the Revival, like the ones described throughout the *Ruanda Notes* by the CMS missionaries and observed by Robbins in 1975, are still evident. Anglican services and "Revival meetings" are energetic and spirited, with pastors often giving personal testimonials and calling people to seek a "transformed life" in the Holy Spirit, as espoused by the Keswick Movement. Singing often erupts sporadically and sometimes, as evidence of the Ugandan heritage of many Rwandan Anglicans, in Luganda, as was observed by me at the St. Pierre Remera church in Kigali. The historical anthem song of the Revival, "Tukutendereza" (meaning "Praise the Lord" in Luganda), can frequently be heard throughout the country.[15]

The Revival's newfound impact on postgenocide Anglicans is evident outside church gatherings as well. In accordance with Revival orthodoxy, the use of alcohol and tobacco products and gambling is strictly prohibited, and formal Western dress codes are adhered to closely, especially by men. Monogamy is encouraged and expected. On the occasions in which I spoke to and greeted Anglican gatherings, it was suggested that the introduction begin with "I am the husband of one wife." Many young men and women, usually workers at the Anglican guesthouses, gather on their own to pray and study long into the night, much like at the start of the Revival in the 1930s. While some of this may be ascribed to conservative church practices common to many denominations, they are exactly as the reports from the *Ruanda Notes* described at the start of the Revival.[16]

Additionally, the Holiness Movement teachings of the East African Revival permeate the Anglican Church. While there is no specific doctrine regarding what are called the "sign gifts" of the Holy Spirit, the practices take place, such as a belief in supernatural miracles, praying in tongues, prophecy, and divine healings. Such was communicated to me by then diocesan secretary Nathan Amooti, currently bishop of Kigali. A pastor in Kibungo Diocese claimed to me that a man had recently been raised from the dead in his parish after an all-night prayer session. Many parishioners in Gahini Diocese believe a structural problem in the diocesan office walls was miraculously saved by divine intervention, which may be a selective memory reference to a rare hurricane that struck Gahini in December 1986, over which CMS missionaries Paul and Jean Daltry declared, "Miraculous . . . God brought the trees down in exactly the right places." Like many other African Pentecostal churches, the Anglicans in Rwanda believe in the literal persona and power of the Holy Spirit as well as the sign gifts practiced by the New Testament church. In that sense, the revivalist tradition in Rwanda resembles what Jesse Zink labeled, in writing of the so-called new generation churches in Nigeria, as "Anglocostal," which themselves were inspired by a revival in the 1960s.[17]

Central to this is the biblical, and widespread African, belief in prophecy. In July 2004, I attended a five-day Revival Crusade in Ruhengeri, sponsored by the Shyira Diocese. The culmination of the crusade was the dedication of a newly constructed cathedral, for which Paul Kagame himself came out to offer his remarks before a crowd of roughly five thousand. Most of the speeches were given in English and translated into Kinyarwanda by Amooti and others, as the present Anglican hierarchy was then fluent only in the former, while most of their Hutu parishioners spoke French or the latter. At the crusade, the church claimed a divinely inspired prophecy had been issued for Rwanda, asserting that the country will be "a model of reconciliation and recovery, and that the wider world will look in awe upon the ability of Rwandans to heal from the genocide."[18]

The prophecy, printed in the program guide, further claimed that "Rwanda will become the source of a 'Spiritual Renaissance' for the world. The revelation to His [God's] servants was that Rwanda would be united and reconciled to such an extent that the whole world would marvel. This has inspired them to search after the God of the impossible." The crusade literature also expressed the hope that fulfillment of the "Divine Prophecy" would be realized and claimed that Rwanda's destiny was "Pardon for sins for those who confess" [presumably genocide perpetrators] and to gain "protection against curses, plagues, poverty and famine."[19]

The program cited the biblical prophet Zechariah as its authority, specifically chapter 8, verses 22–23, which read, "Many peoples and strong nations shall come to seek the Lord of hosts in Jerusalem, and to entreat the favor of the Lord. Thus, says the Lord of hosts: In those days ten men from the nations of every tongue shall take hold of the robe of a Jew, saying, 'Let us go with you, for we have heard that God is with you.'" Symbolically, for evangelical Christians, the "Jew" spoken of in the passage is a reference to Christ himself, in whom forgiveness and reconciliation can be found. When the passage speaks of "men from every tongue" taking hold of Christ, the implicit message is that only Christ can overcome the divisions wrought by the genocide. The very theme of the crusade was "We Wish to See Jesus."[20]

Considering the history of northeastern Rwanda as the starting point for the East African Revival, divine prophecy has deep cultural roots and elicits attention from Rwandan Christians. Moreover, the synthesis of biblical teachings with pre-Christian African traditions, as in the co-opting of the early twentieth-century Nyabingi cult by the CMS missionaries, reinforces belief in the prophetic, despite the Revival's efforts at distancing itself from what it considered to be the "work of the devil." Given the crusades' location in Ruhengeri, the prophecy, with its divine exhortation for reconciliation, carried additional weight. The 1959–63 violence against Tutsi was especially widespread in the north, and Habyarimana himself was from the north, as was the establishment largely responsible for the genocide. Large-scale massacres also took place in the region from 1990 to 1993. Thus, the area was home to many genocide perpetrators, and it was communicated to me that there were many former *génocidaires* in attendance at the crusade.[21]

In all its practices, from its acceptance of a Holiness-inspired interpretation of the Bible to its espousal of prophecy, the present Revival practices of the Anglican Church bear stark similarity to Pentecostal traditions, although the Balokole founders would have denied any formal connection to Pentecostalism itself. In part this reflects somewhat of a divergence from the original Revival movement by its present practitioners. Nor is the charismatic nature and miraculous claims of the Revival movement confined to the Anglicans. Pentecostal and independent charismatic churches have mushroomed since the genocide and now constitute the largest group among the Protestants, although one should note that when speaking of charismatic, Pentecostal churches in Africa, "a limited . . . understanding of 'Pentecostal' fails to recognize the great variety of different Pentecostal movements in most of the rest of the world, many of which arose quite independently of Western Pentecostalism and even of Azusa Street." Concomitant with the rise of Pentecostal practices is a wider belief in miraculous healings and divine visions and interventions, a belief to which the Anglicans adhere.[22]

Interestingly, coming alongside the return of the new revival movement in the Anglican Church, most of the other new charismatic churches have been started by Tutsi returnees as well, who mistrusted the pregenocide churches and who are also fluent only in English. Anne Kubai has written on the proliferation of new churches in postgenocide Rwanda, noting, "Rwanda is experiencing what has been termed 'Gospel explosion,' as evangelists from different parts of the world conduct large interdenominational 'Revival Conferences' and 'Crusades.'" While the Anglican churches are not new per se, many of her insights are applicable owing to the nature of their Revival practices. Kubai writes, "The term 'new' is being used here to refer to churches which were not present in Rwanda prior to the genocide . . . that have now been imported into Rwanda by the returnees." In practice and effect, the coming to prominence of the Revival-inspired Anglican Church in Rwanda represents one of the "new churches" of which she speaks.[23]

The importation of the Revival movement into Rwanda by the Tutsi returnees, as they see it, and the dominant role they now play in the Anglican Church at large, also provide for the same need Kubai speaks of when she writes of Pentecostal churches: they "offer people a purpose to live and a strong sense of identity—the purpose to live for survivors and returnees and a sense of identity—which are crucial for the creation of a newly reconciled society." She could well be writing of the Anglican churches when she says, "They encourage their members to participate in the national reconciliation and political process. They preach forgiveness and impress on its importance as a religious imperative."[24]

In this light, by exhorting Rwandans to find their identification in Christ, the church tries to offer a powerful, constructionist mechanism for rebuilding society and overcoming the deep divisions that still plague the country. In the language of political science, the constructionist approach to nation building is explained as being that "of offering individuals a sense of identity . . . constructed largely unconsciously or intuitively as a category of understanding. This suggests institutional arrangements which an individual inhabits may become the defining categories of political understanding concerning their identity, interests, and goals." This approach suggests that the church in Rwanda is positioned to play a constructive role in recovering from the genocide by defining a new of national identity rooted in Christianity. Nonetheless, this is problematic when the Anglicans, as they often do, accept without challenge the various platforms and policies of the RPF.[25]

The "Chosen Ones"

Apart from church practices, the Revival also provides the Tutsi returnees with a mechanism to process and explain both their own history and plight in the refugee camps in Uganda and a means by which to cope with and heal themselves and Rwanda from the traumas of the recent past. As René Lemarchand writes, "Genocide leaves a profound imprint on the processes by which people write, or rewrite history, on what is being remembered and what is being forgotten." In seeking to promote a new, and supposedly ethnically harmonious, nation inclusive of themselves as newcomers in a Hutu majority populace, the Anglicans have constructed a revised historical narrative that places the East African Revival at the center of their personal and collective history.[26]

In such a spirit, the Revival has been remembered and reconstructed in such a way as to remind not just the Hutu majority but more specifically the Tutsi returnees themselves of the paramount importance of reconciliation between the two groups, not just for Rwanda's future but for their own. In 1995 Liisa Malkki produced a study of how a cosmological history was constructed by Hutu exiles from Burundi in the camps in Tanzania in the 1970s. She notes that the past, among a dispossessed population of refugees, not only explains aspects of the present but also contributes to structuring social action in the future.[27]

As argued here, the memory of the Revival is being put to the same use in postgenocide Rwanda by the Tutsi returnees. According to a diocesan official in Gahini, the Baganda catechists credited with starting the Revival were initially disliked, "not because they were from Uganda," as much of the present

Anglican hierarchy is, but because they were "harsh in their dealings with the Rwandan students." And "when they repented of their harsh ways, they were accepted." In this, one detects hope among the returnees that they can find healing for themselves and postgenocide Rwanda if they, also de facto catechists from Uganda, repent of their past as Tutsi elites and work for reconciliation and justice.[28]

The son of the first Rwandan pastor at Gahini Diocese, a returnee now living at Gahini, told me: "Gahini is a chosen place and we are a chosen people." In this, he echoed a sentiment common to many of the Balokole Tutsi in Rwanda: they are a "chosen people," whose history was ordained by God. Their past history, as heirs to the Revival spirit, as sufferers in the Ugandan refugee camps, and now as returnees in postgenocide Rwanda, was part of a divine plan, leading and preparing them to rebuild a new Rwanda, based on inclusion and reconciliation, chosen to fulfill the prophecy at Ruhengeri that Rwanda would be the source of a "spiritual renaissance" for the wider world. Moreover, this belief identifies the Tutsi refugees with the suffering of the Jewish diaspora, the original "chosen people" of the Bible, fulfilling God's divine plan during their suffering. Many are the Tutsi returnees in Rwanda who compare their return to Rwanda after 1994 to the Exodus of the Hebrews out of Egypt to the Promised Land as recounted in the Old Testament.[29]

The discourse of the Tutsi being "chosen people," comparable to the plight of the Jewish diaspora, exists beyond the Anglican Church and finds affirmation in several ways. Virtually every significant publication on the genocide after 1994 invokes the Nazi Holocaust of the Jews. Relations between the RPF and Israel have been close, and the Simon Wiesenthal Center has been active in assisting survivor treatment and national healing programs. In this sense, many have come to see the Tutsi as "post-Shoah Jews." In January 2000, a Tutsi ultranationalist named Jean Bwejeri presented an address in Brussels wherein he went so far as to suggest the Tutsi were "Falasha Jews from the White Nile" of Ethiopia, implying the Tutsi may even have Semitic roots. Disturbingly, one fears in this sort of rhetoric a resurrection of the now-discredited and divisive Hamitic Myth of earlier times, especially when one considers that Ethiopia, according the nineteenth-century theory, was the supposed homeland of the Nilo-Hamites.[30]

In her own study on the development of extremist Hutu ideology among the Burundian exiles in Tanzania, Malkki suggests life in isolated refugee camps creates conditions in which cosmological histories are created as a means of survival. Arguing that a number of its constitutive features had the effect of historicizing and collectivizing the lives of its inhabitants, the camps, she writes, "ended up verifying that its inhabitants were not just a chance assortment of individuals but a well-defined, recognized collectivity worthy of the power exercised over them. . . . This situation made the camp a fertile ground for the elaboration and production of a mythico-history." Ironically, the Hutu refugees also constructed biblical analogies of themselves as Israelites wandering in the wilderness. For the Tutsi refugees, I argue that the same process occurred in the pregenocide camps of Uganda. A mythico-history of themselves as a "chosen people" was constructed and remains an organizing narrative in the postgenocide Anglican Church.[31]

The Anglican Mission in the Americas and the Evangelical Embrace

Concomitant with its Revival-inspired message of reconciliation and unity, PEAR has reaped great largesse for itself and Rwanda by its embrace of American evangelicals, especially dissatisfied Episcopalians. Among those in attendance at the 2004 crusade in Ruhengeri were four priests of an alternative Episcopalian province then known as the Anglican Mission in the Americas (AMIA), welcomed as special guests of Kolini. The presence of the AMIA pastors, honored participants throughout the crusade, was the culmination of Kolini's efforts to promote postgenocide recovery in Rwanda by welding together PEAR with evangelical, orthodox Americans who have severed their communion with the Episcopal Church of the United States (ECUSA).[32]

On various occasions, the AMIA pastors were invited to address the crowd and lead workshops on various topics for the Rwandan parishioners. In his closing address at the dedication of the cathedral, Kolini declared the AMIA attendees "part and parcel of the Church of Rwanda, his spiritual children, indeed Rwandese living in America as missionaries." During the dedication, the most senior of the AMIA clergymen was invited into the cathedral, along with Kagame, to take part in the prayers of consecration. The existence of AMIA is but one example of how PEAR has demonstrated keen political skills in forging an international alliance with American church congregants who know little or nothing of Rwanda's history or the genocide.[33]

Soon after their ordination as bishops, Kolini and Rucyahana attended the 1998 Lambeth Conference of the worldwide Anglican Communion, held every ten years to address matters of faith and doctrine in the church. At the conference, they joined with other Primates from Africa and Asia who were increasingly angered at what they saw as the growing liberalism of western Anglicanism. Specifically, by the late 1990s, the issue of same-sex marriage and the ordination of openly gay priests was becoming a major point of contention between orthodox Anglicans and church liberals. Liberals, led by the bishop of ECUSA, Frank Griswold, endorsed a more open acceptance of homosexual practices. The traditionalists, represented strongly by churches in

Africa and Asia, condemn homosexuality, and its acceptance, as incompatible with the authority and teachings of the Bible. At Lambeth, bishops from Africa and Asia formed most of the votes in the passage of a statement condemning the "evils of homosexuality and the impossibility of reconciling homosexual conduct with Christian ministry." Prior to the August 5 vote, Kolini joined with eight other archbishops from Africa, Australia, Asia, and South America in an open letter to the conference urging support for the statement. Its subsequent passage was sternly condemned by the North American church hierarchies. Griswold labeled it "dangerous fundamentalism."[34]

For his part, Kolini first drew attention in 1996 when he published a brief article in *Christianity Today*, a leading evangelical periodical. In "Cheap Evangelism," Kolini endorsed the Anglican commitment to evangelism but took issue with what he called "wrongful understandings concerning the teaching that the gospel is for all people, regardless of their sinfulness." He claimed to observe "a weakening in the Christian commitment to God's call to transformation, particularly when it comes to sinful expressions of sexuality and harmful lifestyle choices." In that spirit, Kolini's role in the Lambeth controversy was born.[35]

Nor is he alone in his condemnation of homosexual lifestyles. In November 2003, the consecration of Gene Robinson as the first openly gay bishop elicited howls of criticism from Anglican leaders across South America and Africa. The *New York Times* noted that opposition to homosexuality is the most vociferous in Africa, where "gays remain closeted and popular sentiment regards same-sex relationships as a vice exported from the West." Following Robinson's consecration, Benjamin Nzimbi, Anglican archbishop of Kenya, declared, "The Devil has clearly entered our church." Peter Akinola, former Archbishop of Nigeria, home to the largest Anglican population in the world, equated homosexuals with "pigs and dogs."[36]

Homophobic statements by church leaders across Africa often echo the voices of political leaders who frequently scapegoat homosexuals to distract from their own shortcomings. In January 2006, former Nigerian president Olusegun Obasanjo told a conference of Nigerian bishops, "Such a tendency [homosexuality] is clearly un-Biblical, unnatural and definitely un-African." Prior to his ouster from power in 2017 and subsequent death, Robert Mugabe (1924–2019), the longtime dictator of Zimbabwe, was well known for condemning homosexuals and blaming them for his and Zimbabwe's problems. In 2019 Uganda considered, but retracted, a law that would have punished homosexual acts with death. Most recently, in August 2020, the embattled president of Burundi blamed homosexuals for the COVID-19 pandemic. One can speculate that PEAR's outspoken condemnation of homosexual lifestyles has distracted Western evangelicals from the church's support for Rwanda's own dictatorial regime.[37]

Shrewdly, perhaps, Kolini made his message more palatable to American evangelicals by avoiding bombastic public statements, such as those of Nzimbi and Akinola. In interviews and press statements, Kolini emphasized the issue as being one of scripture, rather than sexuality. In September 2003, Kolini claimed, "We denounce and declare that the Episcopal Church USA has departed from the doctrine, discipline and worship of Christ." In August 2004, Kolini noted that the Episcopal Church's argument was that "it's about interpretation of the Bible. We think its culture. You can't impose your culture onto other people. To be Christian, there are some fundamentals, some basics to our faith. The question is 'is homosexuality a sin or not?' If the Scripture calls it a sin, then it's a sin."[38]

Statements and declarations such as these often lead Western evangelicals to believe that African society is either inherently antigay or that African Christians are admirably literalistic in their interpretation of the Bible. However, African views on same-sex relations must be understood against the historical backdrop of African sexuality. Same-sex sexuality was known in premodern Africa, yet homosexuality "as an identity or an exclusive life choice did not exist when the pressures to have sex for reproduction were so over-determined by material, political, spiritual or other cultural considerations." Regarding the perception that contemporary Africans are exceptionally hostile to gays, Marc Epprecht argues that "revulsion against same-sex behaviors, acts, relationships, and thoughts (that is, homophobia) was introduced into the region by European colonialists and preachers" and that Africans "were encouraged through these discourses to equate homophobic constructions of sexuality, sensuality, and gender with civilization and progress."[39]

Despite the historical and sociological issues with this narrative, the denunciation of homosexuality was welcomed by many conservative, rank-and-file Episcopalians in America who increasingly found themselves at odds with their more liberal overseers. Many were the former Episcopalians who were spiritually titillated by the wrongheaded notion that homosexuality was unknown in east-central Africa. Church visitors to Rwanda are generally not aware that homosexual practices routinely occurred in the Nyiginya monarchy. Numerous kings had male lovers, for "homosexuality was admitted at court and quite commonplace in military circles."[40]

Nonetheless, on January 29, 2000, Kolini became a lead figure in the controversy when he joined with then archbishop Moses Tay of Southeast Asia in ordaining two American bishops, Charles Murphy and John Rodgers, to serve as "missionary bishops," charged with ministering to orthodox congregations who felt "isolated or repressed by liberal leaders" of ECUSA. While Anglican tradition holds that an archbishop is free to ordain anyone he chooses, the bold move was condemned by the archbishop of Canterbury, and head of the worldwide Anglican Communion, George Carey, who refused to recognize Murphy and Rogers's ordination. The archbishop of Canada, Michael Peers, declared: "Bishops are not intercontinental ballistic missiles, manufactured on one continent and fired into another."[41]

Despite the opposition, Kolini ordained four more American bishops in 2001 to preside over what became AMIA, a "virtual province" of the Anglican Church of Rwanda residing in America, with Emmanuel Kolini as its archbishop. Jenkins described AMIA's purpose as being a "missionary province," charged with the task of leading the Episcopal Church "back to its Biblical foundations and restoring traditional teachings" on issues like the ordination of gay clergy and the blessing of same-sex marriages. At the heart of Kolini's mission is the claim that what happened in Rwanda in 1994 is comparable to the current state of the Episcopalian Church.[42]

Kolini and his bishops often declare that what is happening in the American church is tantamount to "a spiritual genocide of the truth." As early as 1997, Kolini expressed his belief that "there is not one, but two genocides—a physical genocide and a spiritual genocide. Spiritual genocide refers to the presence of sin in people's hearts." In January 2005, Kolini's former provincial secretary, and bishop of Kibungo Diocese, Josias Sendegeya, claimed, "The Rwandan people know what it is to suffer. We experienced genocide and the horror that no one in the world came to help us. What has happened in the Episcopal Church feels like genocide, too. But it is spiritual rather that physical." In effect, the Anglicans in Rwanda have cast their mission as one of rescue. In one of his remarks about AMIA at the dedication of the Ruhengeri cathedral, Kolini declared: "Ten years ago, when Rwanda cried out to the world for help, no one answered. When we heard the American church crying out for help, we decided to answer," hence the prophecy espoused by the church that Rwanda will be a source of spiritual renewal for the world, complete with a reminder of Western guilt for not stopping the genocide.[43]

The AMIA movement grew rapidly as the formal North American churches continued in their perceived liberalism, culminating in Robinson's 2003 consecration. Kolini's message, and the actions of the church in Rwanda, resounded loudly with AMIA parishioners, and the association between Rwanda and AMIA has paid large dividends for the country. Following Kolini's retirement in 2011, Archbishop Onesphore Rwaje presided over a "missionary province" in the United States that claimed close to twenty thousand members and more than one hundred congregations. These "Rwandese Anglicans living in the United

States," as Kolini called them, also saw themselves as beneficiaries of the East African Revival. The AMIA's website and literature frequently claimed it had inherited Rwanda's "revival DNA" as they, with PEAR's leadership, promote a revival of church orthodoxy in America. At AMIA's annual Winter Conference in 2005, John Rucyahana, bishop of Shyira Diocese, delivered a speech on the East African Revival to the American attendees, but with little historical context.[44]

My research in Rwanda, and at the AMIA Winter Conference in 2005, confirms that the majority of AMIA parishioners, as well as many other evangelicals in America, see the Anglican Church's work in Rwanda as utterly genuine and along biblical principles. Many of them saw Kolini's adoption of their churches as a rescue from theological heresy, and they returned the favor, even while remaining largely unaware of the complexities of Rwanda's history and politics. Numerous AMIA congregations gave, and some continue to give, money for development in Rwanda, in addition to the substantial ecclesiastical contributions AMIA churches made to their new home province. AMIA congregations, and many former congregations, routinely undertake mission trips to Rwanda to take part in development projects. The cathedral at Ruhengeri and the new Kigali Episcopal Theological College are two such examples. The financial contributions to Rwanda have amounted to millions of dollars.[45]

In December 2011, however, the formal ties between PEAR and AMIA were dissolved due to internal disagreements between Rwaje and Murphy over issues ranging from financial accountability to disagreements over church direction. Still, many former AMIA parishes remain deeply involved in Rwanda. Kolini and numerous Anglican clergy from Africa have remained actively involved as well, traveling frequently in the United States to meet with supportive congregations.[46]

The support for Rwanda went well beyond AMIA and various other Anglican splinter groups. In no small measure because of Kolini, Rucyahana, and their AMIA supporters, Rwanda has drawn the attention of numerous evangelical megachurches in America. Most notable among their number is Rick Warren, founder and pastor of Saddleback Church in California and author of the best-selling *The Purpose Driven Church* and *The Purpose Driven Life*. Warren, whose books have sold more than twenty-six million copies since 2003, is one of the most recognized figures among American evangelicals. In the summer of 2005, Warren, by then a member of Kagame's Presidential Advisory Council, and several other megachurch pastors traveled to Rwanda and met with Kagame and Rwandan church leaders to outline their plan to mobilize American churches to address the problems of poverty and disease in Africa. At a gathering of nine thousand Rwandan Christians, Warren pledged to make Rwanda the first "purpose driven nation," an initiative to "harness business-people, politicians and pastors against the nation's biggest social problems." He remains deeply involved. The website of Saddleback Church is replete with references to Rwanda and the church's many programs and aid initiatives.[47]

Toward Dictatorship

In less than a decade after taking power, the RPF's initial embrace of ethnic and political plurality in government was soon revealed as a facade. With power in Rwanda consolidated, the new government introduced a series of amendments to the Fundamental Law, which modified the political regime. It introduced a stronger executive presidency, imposed the dominance of the RPF in the government, and redrew the composition of parliament. The amended Fundamental Law "was a subtle piece of constitutional engineering which attempted to mask the consolidation of the RPF's hold on political power" into the foreseeable future. Regarding opponents and dissenters who threatened his power, Kagame once said, "A barrel can be emptied with a coffee spoon." In 2000 Kagame took the spoon to the opposition.[48]

Bizimungu, along with former transportation minister Charles Ntakiu-tinka, was placed under house arrest and accused of rekindling ethnic hatred for creating his own political party, Ubuyanja (Renewal). He was sentenced to a fifteen-year jail term in 2005 but has since been pardoned. He has lived a secluded life since and makes no public appearances or statements. Other members of Ubuyanja were either jailed or assassinated, as in the case of Gra-tien Munyarubuga, or simply disappeared, such as Frank Bizimungu (no relation to Pasteur Bizimungu). Within a year of the RPF's crackdown on Unu-yanja, Rwigyema was in exile and Sendashonga had been assassinated in Nairobi. Fearing arrest, Twagiramungu, the first prime minister, fled Rwanda for Belgium after the 2003 election. Alphonse Mbayire, an RPA officer who was working at the Rwandan embassy in Kenya when Sendashonga was killed, was murdered by "unknown persons" in Kigali a few days after his name was mentioned in the Nairobi murder trial. Even Joseph Sebarenzi, Speaker of the Rwanda Parliament from 1997 to 2000, and an outspoken voice for the Tutsi survivor community, was exiled.[49]

Most recently, the RPF started turning on its own. The chief of staff of the army, General Kayumba Nyamwasa, survived an assassination attempt in 2010. In January 2014, Patrick Karegeya, RPF member and former head of Rwandan intelligence, was assassinated in South Africa for opposing Kagame's dictatorship. Reports of other political killings abound in Rwanda. As Marco Jowell claimed, "Assassinations and extra-judicial killings are understood to be an accepted method of dealing with dissidents, especially from within the military."[50]

The same tactics were meted to any who threatened to provide damning information to international bodies concerning the RPA's extrajudicial killings of civilians in Rwanda in 1994 and in Congo (a topic discussed in detail later in the chapter). To cover up these crimes, the RPF "never hesitated to rely upon all means of blackmail and pressure, up to and including physical elimination, against witnesses who risked divulging its 'secrets.'" Dozens lost their lives because of the regime's attempts to conceal or suppress incriminating evidence. Guichaoua documents the killing even of foreigners who were eyewitness to its massacres, including Canadian clerics Claude Simard and Guy Pinard, four Spanish Marist priests who were in a refugee camp in South Kivu, three Spanish aid workers with Médecins du Monde, and Croatian priest Curic Vjekoslav. This list is not exhaustive.[51]

Not surprisingly, the RPF has since stifled political opposition, curtailed the press, and governs as a virtual dictatorship, unopposed by the Rwandan church community or any other civic body. As early as 1995, "38 international NGOs had been expelled and the activities of 18 others suspended" by the RPF. In 1998 "two leaders of the human rights associations Cladho and Liprodhor went into exile." Ibuka, a Tutsi survivors' association often critical of the government, was silenced after its leaders were either exiled or assassinated. André Sibomana (1954–98), appointed Catholic bishop of Kabgayi after 1994 and chair of the Rwandan Association for Human Rights and Public Freedoms (ADL), was harassed and intimidated over his advocacy of human rights and prison reforms, a stance he held under the Habyarimana regime as well. In 1998 his health "fell into decline," and he died after the RPF denied him the right to leave Rwanda for treatment in Belgium. In 2010 two Rwandan newspapers, *Umuseso* and *Umuvugizi*, were banned from covering the election of that year, the election in which Kagame said, "Rwanda was not ready for democracy." When several opposition parties registered to participate in the August election, they were met with "swift and radical repression." The leaders were arrested and sentenced to long prison terms. The vice president of the Democratic Green Party was "found beheaded." The editor of *Umuvugizi* fled to Kampala, while his coeditor was killed in Kigali for publishing a story on the "regime's hit squads." Charles Ingabire, editor of the *Inyenyeri News*, which was critical of the RPF regime, was shot and killed in Kampala, Uganda, after receiving death threats "warning him to stop writing articles critical of the Rwanda government."[52]

With political opposition and civil society neutralized, "the manipulation of elections allowed [Kagame] to confer a layer of democratic legitimacy on what was in reality the closing off of political space." Kagame and the RPF remain firmly in power as of this writing, winning "reelections" with vote tallies above 90 percent. Filip Reyntjens, one the most astute observers of Rwandan politics, accused the international community of naivete after the 2001 elections and referred to the 2003 elections as a "cosmetic operation for international consumption." In the 2008 legislative elections, described as "fake elections" by Reyntjens, the RPF received an implausible 98 percent of the vote but reduced its official total to 78.76 percent to make the election more credible to European Union observers. Expectedly, in 2015, at Kagame's behest, the constitution was changed again to allow him to run for a third term in 2017. On August 4, 2017, he was reelected with more than 98 percent of the vote to a seven-year term. Those who dare to challenge these results face jail, exile, or worse.[53]

The Misrepresentation of Politics and the Revision of History

However laudable PEAR's efforts may appear on the surface, and regardless of the sincerity of their personal beliefs, the Anglican hierarchy has played an active role in the misrepresentation of Rwanda's history and present political climate, and of their own past. A politicized and misleading narrative of Rwanda, supported by PEAR, has led many outsiders, including the former AMIA, into embracing a country with many social and political barriers to overcome. Moreover, the church's relationship to Kagame's regime has disturbing parallels to the church's relationship to the pregenocide government. Just as both the Anglican and Catholic Churches were closely aligned with and supportive of the previous Hutu governments under Kayibanda and Habyarimana, the Anglicans presently are deeply aligned with Kagame and the RPF, never challenging the reigning political order.

Mahmood Mamdani confirms even moderate opponents of the RPF complain that not only were the structures of power in Rwanda "Tutsified" but even civic bodies such as the media, the churches, and other nongovernmental organizations were cleansed of any but a nominal Hutu presence. My observations on the Tutsi background of the Anglican hierarchy suggests PEAR is no exception. In a process reminiscent of "Tutsification" under Belgian rule, Longman observed that in postgenocide Rwanda, "the RPF-dominated government has been careful to prevent an independent civil society from reemerging. The government has actively sought to place its allies in charge of most important social organizations, including the selection of church leaders." Reyntjens confirms that the churches were "considered a potential challenge to the RPF's hegemonic project" and forced them to select leaders "acceptable to the regime." In 1995 a meeting of the Free Methodist Church was surrounded by RPF troops until they selected the regime's preferred candidate for leadership. Both the Episcopal and Pentecostal Churches saw their bank accounts frozen by the RPF until they agreed to leadership changes. In such circumstances, the RPF understandably exercises considerable political sway over the actions and pronouncements from the highest levels of the Anglican Church, and the church responds in kind.[54]

As a point of confirmation, in 2007 a controversy erupted at All Souls Anglican Church, an AMIA congregation in Wheaton, Illinois, over Paul Rusesabagina. Rusesabagina, the subject of the popular 2004 award-winning film *Hotel Rwanda*, was invited by All Souls to speak at a fundraiser the church was holding to build a school in Gashirabwoba. Upon the film's release, the movie was well received in Kigali, and Kagame and his minsters were present at a packed stadium when it premiered. But after Rusesabagina publicly criticized the RPF and Kagame's regime, claiming the country was being ruled for the benefit of an elite group of Tutsi, he was accused of being a genocide sympathizer and became the victim of "character assassination." He was subsequently barred entry into the country. In 2007, at a forum in Chicago organized by Rev. Jesse Jackson and attended by several former U.S. ambassadors to Rwanda and Burundi, Rusesabagina was publicly accused by James Kimonyo, Rwandan ambassador to the United States, of being involved in "arms trafficking with a view to attacking Rwanda."[55]

When word of Rusesabagina's speaking engagement reached Kigali, Kolini was directed to intervene as archbishop and insist Rusesabagina be disinvited from the church. Apart from the incredulousness that a head of state in Africa could direct the activities of an American congregation, the episode illustrates the close alignment between PEAR and the RPF. Moreover, Kagame's knowledge of the church's invitation to Rusesabagina in the first place bespeaks to the degree to which the RPF can monitor and police the actions of its perceived opponents, even abroad. Rusesabagina confirmed as much to me during a 2010 visit to Longwood University, as well as answering other questions. As of this writing, on July 7, 2021, Rusesabagina, a Belgian citizen, was under arrest in Rwanda on charges of "terrorism, arson, and murder"; according to Rusesabagina, he has suffered torture at the hands of the Rwanda Investigation Bureau. By the Rwandan government's own admission, Rusesabagina was duped by a Burundian pastor named Constantin Niyomwungere into boarding a plane he believed was bound for Bujumbura but in reality took him to Kigali for detention.[56]

At other times, bishops within PEAR have been vocal in their support for Kagame's persistence as president. Susan Thomson noted in 2018 that John Rucyahana "sets the tone for church-government interactions, acting as a cheerleader rather than a counterweight to government policy." Unsurprisingly, in 2017 Rucyahana voiced support for Kagame's third term, in a country the *Economist* described as a "thinly-disguised autocracy, where dissidents, who are usually accused of genocidal tendencies, live in fear, or exile, or both" and where serious domestic opposition or free speech is not tolerated.[57]

Apart from its political support for Kagame's ongoing monopolization of power, now one of Africa's longest-serving presidents, the pastors and bishops of PEAR endorse the RPF's version of Rwanda's history. The most routine way in which they do this is in their insistence that the distinction between Hutu and Tutsi was a European invention that is no longer relevant. In a refrain familiar to any who interact with the country, they claim that there are no longer any Hutu or Tutsi, only Rwandans, a practice mandated by the government in Kigali and observed by me elsewhere among contemporary Rwandans. Only after I pressed the issue did PEAR clergymen admit to being "former Tutsi." Nathan Amooti echoed the official, RPF-endorsed version of history when he explained that the classification system was a false European construct. He claimed that, apart from the old Belgian identification system, "Rwandans don't know who is Hutu or Tutsi until they talk about their fathers and grandfathers." Similar false statements are routinely made to outsiders.[58]

The Kizito Mihigo affair illustrates the dangers faced even by prominent Christians if they refute the RPF's preferred line. Mihigo, an internationally acclaimed Catholic Gospel singer and genocide survivor, was arrested in April 2014 and sentenced to ten years in prison for uploading a "new song on You-Tube that allegedly disputed the official narrative of the genocide." His arrest sent "shockwaves" through the country and made it clear "no one was immune from the grasp of the RPF." The Catholic Church shamefully distanced itself from Mihigo after his arrest and remained silent throughout. In 2018 Mihigo was released, only to be rearrested in February 2020. He died in police custody on February 17 under dubious circumstances. When the churches, Anglican or Catholic, support such actions through their silence or pronouncements, they directly support the RPF's campaign to present a misleading narrative of Rwanda's history, a narrative that uses language, identity, and an idealized version of the past to support its monopolization of political power and repression of dissent. Yet, based on numerous conversations I had with people unaffiliated with the church, contemporary Rwandans are acutely aware of the identity of the new rulers and understand Rwanda's history better than the RPF thinks they do.[59]

In contemporary African states, new leaders have often "sought to generate new histories which legitimate their claims to power." Ruling through a form of enforced "amnesia points to the critical fact that history and memory can be manipulated to achieve certain goals" or the "construction of a collective identity to support their own agendas." For the RPF, the "rewriting of history has been a major academic and political project" that has occurred from nearly the outset of its reign. Before 1994 was over, the RPF "placed the rewriting of history books as a first priority." Most importantly, Kagame's government, with Anglican complicity, manipulates history to deny the existence of any precolonial Hutu/Tutsi differences with the aim of creating a new collective national identity. While the RPF's aim, the avoidance of classifying Rwandans as "Hutu" or "Tutsi," is an effective tool with outsiders who know little of Rwanda's history, to claim the distinction was a European invention supports Johan Pottier's argument that the government and its sympathizers in the Anglican Church have waged an extensive campaign to popularize misinformation about precolonial Rwanda, rewrite history, and make the world believe that ethnicity was and is a nonissue in RPF ranks. The first chapter of this book, and voluminous other writings by historians of Rwanda, demonstrates the distinction between "Tutsi" and "Hutu" was firmly established in the nineteenth century during Mwami Rwabugiri's reign, with roots dating back even earlier. Pottier makes the point that the portrayal of Rwanda's ethnic divisions as a European invention creates a "smoke-screen of sameness" that leads amateur observers of the country to read too much into the fact that Rwandans speak the same language, have the same religion, and inhabit the same space.[60]

The projection of an ethnically harmonious Rwanda before the European arrival serves two functions that play well with Western church audiences and the "Friends of the New Rwanda." First, as the introduction noted, blaming the Hutu-Tutsi division on the Europeans exacerbates the culture of guilt that exists in the West for not only failing to stop the genocide but also ultimately being responsible for creating the very conditions that caused it. The frequent statements of Kolini and other officials in PEAR that their "rescue" of American Anglicanism was born out of the West's failure to rescue Rwanda in 1994 serves this point explicitly. Second, as Pottier argues, this misleading depiction of Rwanda's history gives people unfamiliar with the country the false sense that "the clock can easily be turned back to those harmonious times" when the Tutsi elites benevolently ran the country.[61]

One example of PEAR's support of the RPF's revision of history is the "10-cows thesis." To explain the origins of the European classification system while obfuscating the fixed nature of the nineteenth-century Tutsi oligarchy, the RPF's spokespersons have resorted to the claim that "Tutsi" was solely an economic term meaning "one who owns ten or more cows," and the Europeans racialized what was merely a question of economics. These claims are ostensibly based on a Belgian census in the 1930s, without a single accompanying source, that those "possessing at least ten heads of cattle were considered Tutsi, thus showing the artificial nature of the claim." Reyntjens notes that as of 1949 there were simply not enough cows to make this mathematically possible, even assuming that "no Hutu possessed a single head of cattle." At the AMIA Winter Conference in 2005, I observed a representative of PEAR explain the "ten-cows thesis" to a large audience of American attendees. No one challenged the claim. Pottier noted that the ten-cows soundbite is an exceptionally effective way to convey to the world that the RPF is above ethnicity, while abundant evidence demonstrates that such is not the case.[62]

In such a light, the Tutsi elites presently in power appear as long-suffering Rwandan refugees who intervened to stop the killings and rebuild a once harmonious and united country. Rather, Ogenga Otunnu demonstrates that the RPA's invasion of Rwanda was calculated and well planned, fueled by the commencement of the genocide but originally timed by the citizenship crisis in Uganda. Lost in the culture of sympathy surrounding the Tutsi exiles is the observation that it was the initial RPF invasion of 1990 that gave "Hutu Power" proponents the opportunity to raise the specter of "Tutsi Power" returning to subjugate the populace, a specter reinforced by the RPF referring to itself as the Inkotanyi, the same name given to Mwami Rwabugiri's army when he advanced southward in the nineteenth century, an interesting choice of a name for an army seeking only to return and rebuild its homeland.[63]

The RPF's suppression of ethnic identification, a policy supported by PEAR, further serves to mask the prominence of Tutsi returnees and former RPF members' dominance of Rwandan government and society. Rwandan political power is presently in the hands of a few key men who grew up as refugees in Uganda and who are former RPF officers who maintain close business and political ties within a circle of civilian friends, family, and associates who monopolize all key posts in the country. Jean-Damascène Ntakirumana, a former Hutu member of the transitional government who defected in 1995, claims with firsthand insight, "The RPF denies that there is any ethnic problem today with the same energy it used in denouncing the ethnic imbalance of the old regime. . . . The RPF has simply installed a new form of Tutsi power."[64]

Elizabeth Sidripoulos supports the assertion, claiming Kagame's government enjoys support and legitimacy "among the new elite, many of whom are returnees. That support is evident among certain elements of the church as well." She further observes that "the perception that a small elite, primarily made up of Tutsi from Uganda, runs the country has alienated some segments of the population." Prunier further claims that even francophone, "interior Tutsi" (those who survived inside the country during the genocide) refer to the RPF as the "Gahini mafia," a small group of anglophone, Ugandan returnees who grew up as refugees "bent upon totally controlling the RPF structure." Moreover, the Anglicans and other Protestant churches enjoy an outsized role in the "Gahini mafia," occupying nearly 80 percent of the top political and administrative jobs in the RPF. The observation is especially interesting in its symbolism for PEAR when one remembers that Gahini was the alleged starting point for the Ruanda Mission and the East African Revival.[65]

For those familiar with Rwanda's precolonial history, the Anglican Church's mutual embrace with the ruling authorities and the subsequent rewriting of history is neither new nor unique. David Newbury notes that religious movements have always been associated with periods of political stress in Rwandan history. Throughout its history, the Nyiginya monarchy affirmed its legitimacy by drawing upon spiritual belief systems. Ruganzu Ndori made use of the Gihanga Myth to establish divine origins for his reign. Mwami Rujugira called on the Ryangombe Cult when he changed the rules of royal succession after he usurped power from Mwami Rwaka in the mid-eighteenth century. When Anglican Church leaders proclaim the returning revival will bring healing and reconciliation, they are knowingly (or unknowingly, depending upon their knowledge of Rwanda's history) using the rhetoric of Christianity to buttress the political legitimacy of the RPF, a legitimacy that has gone unchallenged for more than two-and-a-half decades since the genocide. Regardless of the well-known genocidal horrors that ended when the RPF ousted the Hutu Power regime, Kagame effectively usurped power through armed force and shows no sign of relinquishing it any time soon. Reminiscent of Rujugira's use of the Ryangombe Cult, PEAR is essentially affirming Kagame's legitimacy and ongoing "re-elections" to its parishioners, encouraging them through the lens of the East African Revival to accept the RPF's suspect claim to be building a new, ethnically inclusive state.[66]

PEAR's complicity in endorsing the RPF's false narrative of Rwandan history is in the same vein. As noted in the first chapter, following Rujugira's altering of the rules of succession, the keepers of the court rituals, the *biru*, were elevated to the role of court historians so the past could be bent to endorse the present. By joining the ruling authorities in espousing a Rwanda that was ethnically harmonious prior to the European arrival, the new Balokole have become the new *biru*. History is being revised again in Rwanda for the benefit of outsiders who see the RPF as above ethnicity. The facade of a new, politically inclusive Rwanda, but one in which minority rule continues to prevail, justifies Kagame's hold on power, and the West is erroneously reminded again of its guilt in creating the two groups. Within Rwanda, a new generation, with little access to an alternative and accurate narrative of the past, has little choice but to accept the pronouncements of those who are

authorized to speak on behalf of the regime, the new Anglican leadership among them. Once again, as in the past, historical remembrance has become the ultimate justification for political actions, a de facto weapon in the hands of the new Anglican *biru*.

Rwanda's embrace by Western churches, the former AMIA among them, has historical precedent as well. When Musinga's power was weakening in the 1920s, young Tutsi elites embraced the advantages offered by the Catholics. Access to Western education and resources offered new "sources of ritual legitimation" as the very notion of kingship was in crisis. When present Western church bodies, with little understanding of Rwanda's historical and cultural dynamics, heap aid dollars and resources on the county without questioning the political climate, they are unwittingly legitimizing the RPF's hold on power and affirming its supposed success in rebuilding the state. Throughout Rwanda's history, from Ndori to Rujugira and beyond, religious movements were incorporated for political capital with scant influence on behavior or ethics among the rulers. The Anglican Church in postgenocide Rwanda, with its Western partners, has been put to the same use.[67]

Numerous former AMIA pastors, congregants, and other supporters frequently travel in Rwanda under the watchful eye of PEAR to observe various social projects to which they can lend their support and resources, acting more as "ethical tourists" than missionaries. In so doing, they are subjected to an idealized portrayal of contemporary Rwanda's history and political culture. A convenient, albeit misleading, narrative is offered that presents the following: first, the RPF were suffering refugees who returned to end the genocide, a genocide ultimately caused by the Europeans, who then ignored it when it happened; second, the RPF, headed by Kagame, is above ethnicity and rules Rwanda strongly only for the purpose of rebuilding a country disheveled by the West; and third, the Anglican Church is above it all and seeks only Rwanda's development and recovery. Rarely if ever do the "Friends of the New Rwanda," and especially those in the American church, question what they are told. Nor are they welcome to. When I publicly questioned various aspects of this narrative in 2007, I was, as communicated by AMIA, no longer welcome in Rwanda by Kolini. As it happens, the RPF's misrepresentation of Rwanda's history, carried out in collusion with PEAR, has allowed the country to benefit richly from its embrace of American evangelicals without having attention called to any program of real political reform.[68]

Owing to its close alignment with the ruling RPF, the church has allowed itself to become a domestic political mouthpiece for the regime at home at the same time that it has become unwilling to challenge the RPF's own violent history and its aggressiveness toward Rwanda's neighbors. One case in point is the church's unwillingness to call attention to the many killings and human rights violations committed by the RPA during the war and afterward. When the RPA began its campaign southward in 1994 at the onset of the genocide, as many as 100,000 civilians were massacred. The most well-known allegation of RPA atrocities after the war, of which the Anglican Church makes no mention, were the killings that occurred at Kibeho in 1995. Kibeho was where several alleged apparitions of the Virgin Mary appeared in the 1980s, making it a place of pilgrimage. During the genocide, the church at Kibeho was the scene of a massacre of roughly 17,500 people. In the aftermath of the RPF invasion, an IDP camp was established there, housing as many as 100,000 people, some of whom were *génocidaires* hiding from the army but many of whom were innocent Hutu who feared the RPA for good reason.[69]

When the decision was made in April 1995 to close the camp and separate the guilty from the innocent, chaos ensued over the course of several days, with RPF forces firing indiscriminately into the crowd with guns, mortars, and rocket-propelled grenades. Former *génocidaires* also attacked those trying to flee the camp, while others were crushed to death by panicked crowds. Although the RPF claims the number killed was less than 400, two Australian medics on the ground counted more than 4,000 dead and 650 wounded when they were stopped after the RPA realized what they were doing. Other observers agree with the figure of 4,000 people killed. Regardless of what transpired, the RPF has never admitted responsibility for its role in the deaths that undeniably occurred.[70]

Moreover, while it was pointed out to the AMIA attendees at the Ruhengeri Crusade in 2004 that the area was home to many genocide perpetrators, no mention was made of the fact that the RPA killed tens thousands of people, roughly 6,000 of whom were unarmed civilians, during an insurrection in northwest Rwanda between January and August 1997. In 1999 hundreds of thousands of civilians in the Gisenyi and Ruhengeri prefectures were forcibly moved to "deplorable" relocation camps. Nor the does the church speak of how the RPF invasion in 1991 resulted in similar reprisals against interior Tutsi in the lead-up to the 1994 genocide. Rather, the RPF invasion is presented to outsiders as a noble attempt to stop the genocide once it was underway. A full and truthful account of the events leading to the genocide would present it in the context of the larger civil war, sparked in 1990 by the RPF invasion, wherein in the RPF was viewed in Rwanda through the lens of them being new *inyenzi*, seeking to restore Tutsi monarchism.[71]

The same holds true for many documented killings and atrocities by the RPF in its campaigns in Eastern Congo. Throughout the genocide and afterward, more than two million Rwandan Hutu, fearing reprisals by the RPF, fled westward to Zaire (now DRC) creating a severe refugee crisis. Among their numbers were tens of thousands of former Interahamwe and ex-FAR forces who were organizing themselves to continue the war and return "Hutu Power" to Rwanda. Already riddled with guilt over the genocide, the Western powers accepted the RPF's contention that its enemies were preparing for war and looked the other way when Rwanda invaded in 1996, along with Uganda, and again in 1998. While it's true enough that Rwanda still had enemies in the Congo, documented research shows that plundering the DRC's rich resources was a primary aim as well. In 2000, for example, the added values of coltan, gold, and diamonds stolen from Congo amounted to 190 percent of Rwanda's military budget and 110 percent of the foreign aid it received.[72]

The effects of Rwanda's interventions in eastern Congo were catastrophic. The invasions generated a civil war that brought more than half a dozen neighboring African countries into the conflict on one side or the other and precipitated a regime change in Kinshasa. The human toll was appalling. By most estimates, nearly two million people were killed as a result of the wars between 1996 and 2000. The breakdown of political order and the ongoing social devastation wrought in the east has accounted for roughly three million more deaths and an untold number of sexual assaults, with a corresponding rise in HIV infections. While thousands of innocent civilian Hutu were repatriated to Rwanda, hundreds of thousands more locals became displaced within Congo. In addition to the war deaths, Prunier has documented numerous massacres of civilians and extrajudicial killings committed by the RPA. As this book has claimed, the same can be said of many massacres and killings of Hutu by the RPF during and after its invasion of Rwanda itself. Many, if not most, in the Hutu majority have firsthand knowledge of such unaccounted-for crimes by the RPA. At issue here for the process of reconciliation is that "grievances surrounding unacknowledged, or unsettled, historical memories are likely to increase in intensity with time. Unacknowledged emotional (or physical) wounds could be powerful motivations for vengeance, including violence. In Rwanda, lack of acknowledgment of memories of members of the Hutu majority may be especially problematic."[73]

American evangelicals, largely unaware of such crimes, remain strongly attracted to PEAR's efforts in Rwanda. As a result, to paraphrase Pottier, Western supporters have joined the ranks of numerous groups in the "aid industry" who prefer to accept the authorities' easy reading of an extraordinarily complex situation and have actively reproduced and spread, wittingly or unwittingly, a vision of Rwanda that bears the RPF's seal of approval. Forgotten is Lemarchand's warning that "there can be no reconciliation without justice and no justice without truth." As such, American supporters are blinded both to the divisions that still plague Rwanda and the region and to the autocratic nature of its rulers. Especially troubling was Rick Warren's 2006 proclamation that Kagame is a "man who does what is right; he is a great leader who will save Rwanda. He stopped the genocide and thereafter installed reconciliation; he is a servant leader." Considering the history of the Ruanda Mission, to which the present Anglicans are heirs, none of this should elicit surprise.[74]

Anglican spokespersons in Rwanda frequently proclaim that they have "revival in their spiritual DNA." However much this may or may not be metaphorically true, a disturbing tendency exists to disregard or ignore other tendencies in their "spiritual DNA." From its inception, the missionaries of the Ruanda Mission were consistently unwilling to challenge the political and social framework in which they lived and worked. As this work has demonstrated, the *Ruanda Notes* from the colonial period frequently spoke of the desire for reconciliation and unity between Hutu and Tutsi, even while they endorsed the Hamitic Myth and gushed admiration for the Tutsi. Often, they condemned the servile role and mistreatment of the Hutu and privately opposed the identity cards following Belgian rule. Yet they remained publicly silent on these questions, hoping Gospel conversion alone would transform society. Roger Bowen, one of the few Anglican voices to take a critical approach, writes of how the Ruanda Mission always prioritized the spiritual over the political and social. Christine Schliesser agrees, noting that the East African Revival "focused primarily on personal conversion and spiritual life, Christian engagement in public and political life played hardly any role." As a result, the first generation of indigenous Anglican leadership was disinclined and ill-prepared to confront the oppression and violence occurring in their midst in the years between independence and the genocide. Much the same can be observed and said of the new, postgenocide generation of Anglican leaders. Evidently, an unwillingness to challenge the pronouncements of those in power is also in PEAR's "spiritual DNA."[75]

Understandably, speaking truth to power is no small act of courage, but a full and honest recognition of the past would be a strong start. For example, Kolini's claim that the Revival left Rwanda with the refugees is somewhat at odds with the most recent scholarship on the church's history prior to the genocide. Longman noted that while nearly all of the pregenocide Anglican leadership was vocal in its support of the Habyarimana regime, many rank-and-file parishioners remained a part of what he calls a new Abarokore movement that reemerged in the 1980s, drawing support from both the East African Revival and many charismatic North American churches. Throughout the pregenocide years, the Abarokore was often at odds with their own church leaders by insisting upon a code of moral conduct that condemned corruption and political involvement. They often defied church expectations by openly criticizing pastors and church leaders, calling them to task for the "immorality they saw within the churches," and presented "an alternative vision of church life."[76]

In 1986 three hundred members of the Abarokore and several other Christian sects were brought to trial for refusing to pay the state-required membership dues in the ruling MRND party and for failing to venerate the Rwandan state and its symbols of sovereignty. Danielle de Lame notes that the Pentecostal churches, which grew dramatically from the beginning of the 1980s, remained "moderate" during the "worst of the torment" and were not implicated in "acts of genocide." When the killings began, a disproportionate number of the Abarokore, including soldiers and policemen, refused to participate. Several witnesses reported to Longman how Hutu sometimes saved Tutsi from the genocide because they were *umurokore*, a member of the Abarokore. Several Anglican interviewees admitted to me that some Hutu affected by the Revival spirit did not participate in the genocidal killings. Paul Conway also wrote of many Hutu "influenced by religious principles" who tried to rescue and save Tutsi. So, despite Kolini's claims, elements of the Revival survived in pregenocide Rwanda, with parishioners doing what their leaders would not, questioning the policies of Habyarimana's regime and their church's collusion with said policies.[77]

More troubling is that Kolini's message undergirds the RPF's assertion of the "total complicity of the churches" in the years prior to the genocide. While in general the churches remained silent, exceptions abound that contradict such a one-sided argument. As early as December 1991, the Catholic bishop of Kabgayi, Thaddée Nsengiyumva (1949–94), and the president of the ecumenical Rwanda Episcopal Conference wrote a letter calling for the church to acknowledge its own responsibility in creating and sustaining ethnic divisions. When Nsengiyumva called for the killings to stop during the genocide, he was murdered on June 5, 1994. In February 1992, Catholic and Protestant church leaders created an ad hoc Contact Committee, with the aim of mediation between the different political parties. Four months before the genocide started, in January 1994, thousands of Christians marched for peace in Kigali, Butare, and Gisenyi. The Presbyterian Church of Rwanda also took a strong stance against ethnic strife. Popularizing such information in the churches might generate wonder as to why the current Anglican hierarchy cannot do the same in the pursuit of a more open society and of a more accurate accounting of the past for both sides.[78]

On one level, the church does recognize its own role in Rwanda's history. In 2004 Kolini admitted that the church must seek forgiveness. He stated, "The failure of the church in the genocide is an opportunity for the church to cleanse itself and ask for forgiveness." Here, at least, PEAR recognizes the power of history, symbolism, and language in its own messages. In a keynote sermon at the Ruhengeri crusade, Rucyahana proclaimed a common theme heard throughout the week. He extolled, "It is not the blood of Hutu or the blood of Tutsi that will make you free, but the blood of Jesus!" By invoking the graphic imagery of blood, Rucyahana reminded the audience of Rwanda's violent past while, at the same time, urging reconciliation in the name of Christ.[79]

Moreover, in their program guide for the crusade, as well as in conversations with me, the church and its clergymen avoided categorizing genocide victims as "Hutu Moderates and Tutsi," as is often done in much of the literature elsewhere. Nigel Eltringham warned of such constructions in *Accounting for Horror*. By referring to Hutu victimized by the genocide as "Hutu Moderates," the implication is that all Hutu who survived are extremists, culpable to some degree in the killings. Eltringham wrote, "Depicting moderate Hutu [as] an 'extinct category' contributes to a portrayal of contemporary Rwanda according to a crude, binary framework, composed only of 'victim-*rescapé*-Tutsi' and 'perpetrator-*génocidaire*-Hutu.' This binary segmentation echoes the imagined Manichean construction of Rwandan society found in genocidal propaganda."[80]

In conversations with me, Anglican pastors usually avoided making those references as well but still adopted a genocidal framework from which to characterize their society. Church leaders often referred to a Rwanda inhabited by people of different categories, among them "genocide survivors, genocide perpetrators, and those indifferent." The implication being that the genocide produces the only politically correct categories for identification and reference. The dangers of this construction are either unknown or ignored by Rwanda's supporters and the wider evangelical community in America.[81]

In its admissions and pronouncements on Rwanda's history, as well as its own, other problematic issues remain for the Anglicans, including their remembrance of the Revival as an organizing framework for their new identity and program of reconciliation. A prominent theme in the church's recounting of the Revival's history was the alleged harmony between Hutu and Tutsi. Nearly always, when asked what the Revival means for Rwanda, the first point made was the unity it brought between the two groups and how the same revival spirit would unite Rwanda again. The supposed unity brought about by the Revival was remembered far more than the specific practices. For example, several of the interviewees were unclear and in disagreement about whether the so-called sign gifts of the Holy Spirit were practiced by the Balokole at the start of the Revival.[82]

While instances of unity and harmony certainly occurred "at the foot of the cross," to use Revival language, the Belgian racialization of Rwanda society was becoming more pronounced than ever during these same years. A more accurate and forthcoming account of the Revival would include a recognition that spirituality alone was insufficient to transform society and challenge political injustices. In a perhaps unexpected way, the contention by many Anglican Church figures of the Revival bringing unity between Hutu and Tutsi serves to undermine the official version of Rwanda's history, a version that PEAR does not challenge otherwise. Church figures publicly contend there are no more Hutu and Tutsi, only Rwandans. Privately, they know otherwise. At a dinner conversation in Byumba Diocese with Archbishop Onesphore Rwaje, I was corrected and gently chastised on this point when I used the terms "Hutu" and "Tutsi." Later, and privately, Rwaje admitted he "used to be a Hutu," the only bishop then in Rwanda, incidentally, of whom this was true.[83]

These conversations and the very memory of the Revival itself support the conclusions of many observers that, despite the public claims of the RPF, Hutu and Tutsi identities not only existed prior to colonialism but remain intact and privately recognized. None of this per se means the Revival was not a time of Hutu-Tutsi unity in the churches, but as the church presently promotes this history, it's also contradicting the official version of Rwanda's past so assiduously maintained by the government. In this, one sees a reflection of Lars Waldorf's argument of there being "an inherent tension between the government's forward-looking reconciliation narrative, which seeks to erase ethnicity, and its backward-looking genocide narrative, which inevitably emphasizes ethnicity." Thus, while Kolini and other key figures in the current Anglican leadership were not present in Rwanda in the years prior to the genocide, they obfuscate their identity, and the RPF's, by blaming ethnicity on colonialism and erroneously present a "new Rwanda" in which there is no Tutsi or Hutu, even as they know otherwise.[84]

In addition to its association with the RPF, the Ugando-Tutsi origins of the Anglican hierarchy present several barriers to the church being an effective mouthpiece for reconciliation and political inclusiveness. Apart from the obvious identity of Kagame and the RPF, PEAR is essentially a Tutsi organization, and returnees occupy nearly every significant political, social, and ecclesiastical post in the country, and the observation is not lost on either the wider Hutu majority or the Anglican Church's largely Hutu congregants. While church leaders and pastors repeatedly refer to themselves as "Rwandan," the Hutu populace, still poor and without access to power, know otherwise. A researcher touring the country needs only to gain the confidence of his or her driver to privately find out anyone's ethnic identity, usually voiced in a whisper. Questions can also be raised about how many Anglican church leaders, who "have access to foreign currency for projects," have "developed lifestyles that have alienated them from the struggles of common people and make them appear part of the exploitive upper class," in a nation where the mass of people are still "very poor, peasant farmers."[85]

Moreover, the prevalence of English in church functions, in accordance with state policy, serves as a perpetual reminder of this. When the RPF took power, English was adopted as an official language "facilitating the transition for the returnees as well as the work of international NGOs and donors from the English-speaking world." Most of the ruling elites in both the government and the church, raised in anglophone Uganda, speak French as a third language if at all. For most Rwandans, this presents a barrier to the church's program of reconciliation. As the historian Phyllis Martin writes, the effect of the church "in contributing to perceptions of ethnicity and language should not be minimized, especially when coupled with official policy." Despite Anglicanism's long history in the country, the use of English in many church functions reminds Rwandans that PEAR, in its present form, is essentially an outside institution, fostered in Uganda.[86]

Considering both the importance of language in creating a sense of identity and the primacy of the church in African civil society, this is not a minor hurdle on Rwanda's road to overcoming the ethnic divisions of the past. The role of language in the construction of states is more crucial than many non-specialists realize, and "just as verbal communication is essential to the initiation and conduct of conflict, so it is essential to its prevention." As the use of English in Rwanda is not likely to change, PEAR's bishops and pastors would be wise to remember that "speech acts . . . uttered by certain authorized people . . . alter social relationships between people," and anyone concerned with genocide especially needs to "monitor specifically the use (and misuse) of religious language and symbolism in theologically framing the image of 'other' peoples." Additionally, PEAR's present association with high-profile English-speaking American supporters carries added weight and reinforces the prerogatives of the rulers.[87]

Symbolically, the central role of the Revival in Anglican history and its association with Gahini reminds Rwandans of the Tutsi monarchy. In Gahini, the generally acknowledged birthplace of the East African Revival, several interviewees privately spoke glowingly of their Tutsi heritage. One diocesan official, quietly and with evident pride, pointed out Kagame's private retreat home, overlooking the parish grounds from across Lake Muhazi, and claimed it was the site of the first Tutsi kingdom in the sixteenth century. He was generally correct in this. Kagame's home, and Gahini Parish, is indeed very close to Buganza, where the ruling Nyinginya Dynasty was born in the sixteenth century. With its proximity to Buganza, it is an interesting choice for a retreat home, as Kagame himself is from the Bega clan.[88]

When Mwami Rwabugiri died in 1895, following his expansion of the Nyiginya Kingdom and the subsequent entrenchment of Hutu-Tutsi identities, his son and designated successor, Rutarindwa, was overthrown (and killed) in the Rucunshu Coup, orchestrated, as discussed earlier, by members of the Bega clan. Rutarindwa's murder was carried out by Musinga's uncle, Kabare. Paul Kagame himself is a descendant of Kabare's younger brother, both men being matrilineal descendants of Mwami Yuhi Gahindiro. According to Longman, "Many people have said that his [Paul Kagame] rise to power represents the final victory of the Abega over the Nyiginya clan." To outsiders unfamiliar with Rwandan history, the Lake Muhazi region represents the Rwanda projected to the outside world by the RPF: peaceful, quiet, and bucolic. To Rwandans and scholars who know otherwise, Lake Muhazi, and Kagame's home there, is a powerful symbol of the Tutsi monarchy. Christopher Taylor found indications that "President Kagame continues to be perceived by many Rwandans as a leader who acts much like a divine king." As a Hutu informant said to the researcher Anuradha Chakravarty regarding Kagame's coming to power, "we could not refuse . . . a King who came back."[89]

In one sense, it is understandable that so many in the church are unwilling to speak against the regime. Numerous historians and academics who have questioned the RPF's preferred version of Rwanda's past and challenged its conduct have frequently been publicly decried. Kagame himself proclaimed, "The revisionists must receive justice for their crimes against historical truth and the affront of their fraudulent narratives." To such end, he even inserted himself into "international academic work" after he was invited to write the preface for Phil Clark and Zachary Kaufman's edited book *After Genocide: Transitional Justice, Post-conflict Reconstruction, and Reconciliation in Rwanda and Beyond*. In his preface, Kagame attacked the preeminent historian René Lemarchand's chapter as being "mistaken, simplistic, and wrong." Gérard Prunier was "violently taken to task" after publishing a critical analysis of the regime in 1997. As noted in the introduction, Susan Thomson was detained for "re-education" during her field work for *Whispering Truth to Power*. Many others have experienced the same, been banned from the country, or worse. Numerous human rights lawyers, journalists, and academics have had accusations hurled at them by the regime or barred entry into the country. In 2018 the Canadian journalist Judi Rever was informed of threats to her life when researching her book *In Praise of Blood: The Crimes of the Rwandan Patriotic*

Front, the most damning account yet of massacres she alleges were committed by the RPF in 1994 and afterward. As Kagame himself has said, "If you say things that destroy the Rwanda we are trying to build, we shall destroy you." In this, Kagame's approach to dissent bears striking parallels to Mwami Rudahigwa's 1958 pronouncement on the Hutu-Tutsi question, when he declared: "These are just destructive rumors propagated by a small group . . . under foreign influence whose intention is to divide the country. The entire country is united in the search of the bad tree that produces these sour fruits of division. When it is found, it will be cut, uprooted, and burned, so that it disappears and leaves no trace."[90]

This is the Rwanda the Anglican Church and the "Friends of the New Rwanda" support, defend, and act as apologists for, a nation governed by a regime that has "massacred its own citizens, eliminated spaces for the articulation of dissident narratives, installed a radical dictatorship, imposed collective guilt on the majority of its population, engineered radically new social and economic relations and again introduced a new 'premise of inequality,'" in reference to the classic work *The Premise of Inequality in Rwanda*, by J. J. Maquet. Under such a regime, the Tutsi returnees themselves and the hierarchy of the present Anglican Church understandably occupy a precarious position. They make up a formerly oppressed and victimized minority living again among a Hutu majority, a majority largely denied access to power and governed by a dictatorial regime. Many genuine efforts and achievements by the Anglicans and others have been made toward recovery and the rebuilding of a new Rwanda. Most Anglican pastors and parishioners are presumably sincere in their efforts. Yet, regardless of the personal sincerity of PEAR's clergymen and their Western supporters, reconciliation and recovery must take place in the context of a thorough and unbiased presentation of Rwanda's history. Without this, the efforts made toward reconciliation and development will be seen as support for the ruling RPF oligarchy, hindering any progress on genuine political reform, further endangering Rwanda's future, and likely engendering violence again across the country and region. For the Anglicans and their friends, they would do well to remember the words of Roger Bowen and Malachi Munyaneza in 1995: "A church too closely identified with a regime shares its fate."[91]

Conclusion

History Faces the Present

I N THE 2011 work *Remaking Rwanda: State Building and Human Rights after Mass Violence*, David Newbury recounts and summarizes a passage from the late Alison Des Forges's dissertation, wherein the German physician Richard Kandt is introduced to a phony stand-in for Musinga, the new *mwami* following Mwami Rwabugiri's death in 1895. In an act of deception, the "surrogate sovereign leads the gullible German into a parody of blood brotherhood." As each tied a strand of grass around the other's waist, the German was "left happy in his ignorance," having satisfyingly taken part in an *exotic African ritual* while the court mocked him for his "naïve participation in a sham ceremony." As a result, no one at the court, the real Mwami Musinga included, was under any obligation to meet the requirements normally "expected of blood brotherhood."[1]

The scene described here calls to mind much of my thinking and arguments about contemporary Rwanda and its Anglican Church. Richard Kandt was the first Westerner to interact with the court of Rwanda following years of bloodshed and violence at the hands of Rwabugiri. Following the bloodshed and violence of the genocide, roughly a century later, scores of Western church-goers, missionaries, aid workers, and diplomatic officials journey to the various "courts" of present-day Rwanda, including those of the Anglican Church. Beguiled by speeches and fed pabulum about reconciliation, development, and a "new Rwanda," they travel around an "exotic" country and wave at villagers who are compelled to smile and wave back. They often finish with a stop to see the gorillas at Virunga or do a game drive to see wildlife at Akagera, and then board planes to return home in happy ignorance about the real challenges facing a nation they want to support, but much of which is a phony presentation of democracy and a sham of inclusiveness. Many of the "Friends of the New Rwanda" and Western supporters of the Anglican Church ask no questions of what they are told. They make no investigations into the political realities at work in Rwanda. They largely do not read Rwandan history. Very, very few of them speak Kinyarwanda and are therefore at the mercy of their Anglican guides and overseers. Kandt at least studied the language. As a result, the RPF and the Anglican hierarchy find themselves under no obligation to meet the requirements of the outside Western world and donor community for political inclusiveness and a fair accounting of the past and present.[2]

In fairness, the viewpoint put forth here is not the only one concerning Rwanda. Rather, two opposing perceptions exist. One view focuses on Kagame's technocratic/bureaucratic governance and extols the economic and social progress made since 1994, including improvements in education, health care, agriculture, and women's empowerment. Indeed, in 2008 Rwanda became the first country in the world with a female-majority parliament. As Timothy Longman points out, though, "The dark side of the otherwise laudable extensive engagement of women . . . is the reality that men are much more vulnerable to genocide charges, forcing many out of active political participation." Nonetheless, Kagame, who received a Global Citizen Award in 2009, is seen as a visionary leader, hailed by the likes of "Bono, Rick Warren, Bill Clinton, and Tony Blair." This is the view shared by many churchgoers and evangelicals in the West, who often take their cues without question from PEAR. The regime, in the eyes of the "Friends of the New Rwanda," still enjoys the "genocide credit" earned by the "feelings of guilt over international inaction in 1994." The same "guilt feeling of the international community" enabled the country to also become a "donor darling" in its receipt of financial aid, despite a record on "political rights and civil liberties" that has yet to be better "than in 1992–1993."[3]

The opposing view focuses on the autocratic nature of the RPF's hold on power since the genocide. Those who share this view emphasize the gross human rights abuses under Kagame; unaccounted-for crimes and killings committed by the RPF before, during, and after the genocide; persistent inequality and lack of an inclusive democracy; and implicit "victimization of the Hutu majority." While those who hold this view recognize Rwanda's nearly miraculous achievements since the devastation of 1994, they do so with trepidation and worry that the "structural violence" and lack of transparency in politics, the dearth of an independent civil society (to include the churches), and a profound and persistent ignorance of the country's history is endangering Rwanda's future. Taking on the appearance of an African "Potemkin's village" to outsiders, Rwanda's progress can easily be seen in the building boom underway in Kigali with its unusually safe and clean streets. Off the beaten path, in the rural countryside, and minus the carefully articulated reconciliation narrative proffered by the RPF and its spokespersons in the Anglican Church, Rwanda calls to mind a "volcano waiting to erupt," with the possibility of "renewed violence" and the loss of so many achievements made from donor dollars "when mass bloodshed spills across its borders." If not apparent by now, this is the view of Kagame and the RPF presented in this book and held by me.[4]

In addition to offering a much-needed academic history of the Anglican Church of Rwanda, this work also offers another viewpoint, one that holds that regardless of the admirable developmental contributions made by the Ruanda Mission in the early history of the church, the nature of its approach left an indigenous church leadership too closely aligned with power. Be it with the Tutsi monarchy in the colonial period or the Hutu presidencies afterward, the church hierarchy was unable, unwilling, and ill-equipped to confront political extremism and oppression. Critically analyzing the early Anglican Church's role in leaving its postmissional leadership unprepared to play a constructive political role contributes to Rwandan historiography and the enlargement of its history by offering a new understanding of why the genocidal mentality so easily found a foothold in 1994.

In so doing, this work also finds the present Anglican leadership too closely aligned with power in the postgenocide period, power in the form of Kagame and the RPF's dictatorship. Explaining why the habit of being too close to power became the modus operandi of PEAR today is a primary aim of this book. The reason for this habit lies in an understanding of the church's history and that of its founders in the Ruanda Mission, who from the start remained largely uncritical when facing injustices as they sought influence with the reigning powers in the pursuit of their objectives, which included Christian conversions and social development in the form of health care and education. While there is no reason to doubt the sincerity of PEAR's efforts at Christian conversions in Rwanda today, in its desire to also contribute to reconciliation and development, the church has returned to an unself-examining, apolitical posture like its founders, leaving it aligned with a regime that has also returned to a past habit of political repression along ethnically tense lines.

Ironically, many of Rwanda's much-celebrated developmental achievements after the genocide have exposed the nation to renewed ethnic tensions, one of which is the result of "human geography." Following the RPF's victory in 1994, most of the new elites installed themselves in the capital for security reasons, as the countryside was still decidedly unstable. Most of the "old case load" Tutsi returnees also ensconced themselves in Kigali and other urban developments, as they had long since "lost ties with their 'hill of origin' and had little incentives to go to the rural areas." The return of the Tutsi, coupled

with natural growth, increased the urban population of Rwanda from 6 percent of the total population to 17 percent between 1991 and 2002 alone. As a
result, the "population in the countryside is mostly Hutu." The very success of
Kigali as a municipality, held forth as a model for urban development across
Africa, belies the reality of life in the (Hutu) rural areas where poverty remains
endemic and numerous villages lack access even to clean water or health care,
as I observed firsthand. In addition, many urban Hutu residents of Kigali were
forced into squalid, informal housing settlements on the city's fringe or into
the countryside when the government destroyed their properties in the name
of urban "cleanliness" and new business development, most notably a large
swath of the densely populated neighborhood of Kiyovu Cya Abacyene. As a
result, ethnic divisionism, brought on by political exclusion and geography,
was resurfacing by 2008. *Ibuka* reported on the "deepening of ethnic divisions." The same year, a BBC report found teachers in rural schools preaching
to their students the "ideology of the old regime."[5]

   None of this is surprising when one considers the effect of the RPF's engagement in the "social engineering of the rural sector," an effort to upgrade "rural
life" but that in reality "hides the extent of the poverty and inequality" present
in the villages. Rwanda has experienced impressive economic growth since
1994, even outperforming its donor-set goals, but such growth has inordi-
nately benefited a small clique of agricultural entrepreneurs. Most of the Hutu
peasantry lives in worsening conditions, conditions compounded by the RPF's
ostensibly progressive reforms of the countryside. In 2006 the government
mandated compulsory monocropping of cash crops, which increased production but "sharply" raised the price of staple foods as "agricultural diversity has
plummeted." Recall that one of the critical issues facing the Habyarimana
regime "was the growing fissure between its rural population (over 90 percent)
and its urban based elites." The RPF has continued this pattern, ostensibly in
the name of progress, but with a "new ethnic overlay."[6]

   For example, when traditional brickmaking was banned in 2006 to protect
the environment, the effect on the rural labor force was significantly negative.
Most local entrepreneurs cannot afford the expensive modern ovens for brickmaking, the only ones allowed after the 2006 ban, and the result has been a
great increase in the price of bricks at the hands of the few who can afford to
make them. As a result of polices such as these, Chris Huggins has documented how "only a small percentage of the population can afford to build
using government-approved materials, and that the vast majority are trapped
in a housing crisis." Additionally, the RPF has imposed modernistic reforms on
the countryside regarding "dress and behavior." Other mandates require the
wearing of shoes and the use of mosquito nets and dictate the making of

compost pits and the requirement to dry dishes on tables rather than the grass . . . all of which provides for "cosmetic upgrading of rural life," but which in reality "only hides the true extent of poverty and inequality in the countryside." Bert Ingelaere provides a list of twenty-nine common activities for which Rwandans can be fined, highlighting the RPF's detachment from the lives of ordinary people in the countryside. As has happened before in Rwanda's history, geographic and economic antagonisms, in this case between urban and rural Rwandans, coupled with rising ethnic tensions, can provide tinder for political demagogues opposed to the regime.[7]

Moreover, the rural majority's ability to express their legitimate economic grievances is suppressed by the RPF's overreach into society. Political authority in Rwanda is "present in all domains of life: education of children, cattle breeding, cultivating, heritage distribution, commercial activities, etc." Virtually all local authority figures are RPF members, suggesting that the regime's authority has penetrated even the "intimacy of the household." Opinions, grievances, and complaints cannot be voiced openly "since public space is policed by laws and public declarations on genocide ideology." The RPF considers "unscripted comments to be suspect and interprets them as a sign of disobedience," allowing it to not only orchestrate obedience but also shape the discussion about life in Rwanda. The actions and pronouncements of PEAR aid in orchestrating the discussion to many outsiders. Such intense monitoring, verging on the level of a police state, creates a coercive and suffocating state presence with the potential for a destructive release of rural discontent, discontent that is already being expressed in subtle, quiet ways.[8]

In her book *Whispering Truth to Power*, Susan Thomson demonstrates myriad ways in which ordinary Rwandans among the rural peasant population engage in subtle acts of everyday resistance to reconciliation. Her research found many in the rural areas who understand that the "policy of national unity and reconciliation is a mechanism of state power that reinforces the power of the RPF rather than alleviating Rwandan's deep-rooted feelings of fear, anger, and despair as they struggle to rebuild their lives." Her conclusions, and the conclusions of others, including myself, is that suppression of rural discontent "reveals that the same social, political, and economic trends that contributed to the 1994 genocide are reemerging." Nor has the RPF's, and PEAR's, misrepresentation of politics and history been effective in ameliorating the discontent. In Reyntjen's words, they have "privileged the public transcript of the powerful, although it has, of course, not eliminated the hidden transcript of the oppressed. In all likelihood, in the privacy of their homes . . . in discreet conversations . . . the powerless construct their own truth, which may well be more radical than the RPF believes."[9]

For the Anglican Church's part, in the countryside, its well-heeled diocesan centers, cathedrals, and churches are often the center of life and activity for rural dwellers. Admirably, the Anglicans provide much in the way of schools, vocational training, and poverty relief. The church's Western supporters have made possible numerous beneficial development projects. At the same time, the church hierarchy's close association with the regime enables it to also serve as monitors over the peasant populace. Field research by myself and others has demonstrated that the rural population is very much aware of the church's alignment with the RPF, an observation that could have serious repercussions for the church if conflict returns.[10]

Further exacerbating the church's disconnect with the people it claims to serve and to proclaim reconciliation over are "questions about the lifestyle of bishops and church leaders and whether they lead to an alienation from the mass of people who are very poor, peasant farmers." I observed in numerous dioceses that church leaders, who have "access to foreign currency for projects," have frequently developed lifestyles that appear to have alienated them from the struggles of common people and make them appear a part of an exploitive, and possibly corrupt, upper class. At an outdoor church banquet held by Bishop Rwaje in Byumba in 2007, curtains were drawn around the table as hungry and impoverished villagers disturbingly looked on. While doing research in Gahini, I was treated to a brief visit to Bishop Bilindabagabo's home, which looked like a veritable mansion in comparison to his neighbors. As Roger Bowen colorfully noted, "One might ask whether a church leader visiting his diocese in Rwanda in a chauffeur-driven Mercedes really gives the right message about servant leadership modelled on the servanthood of Christ?" One might also ask: Do these scenarios best position the church to preach about a reconciled and politically inclusive new state?[11]

Whether carried out by the agents of the state or church, the surveillance of Rwanda society goes far beyond the rural villages. The Rwanda of the RPF is often praised for its investment in the telecommunications sector, an African "Singapore," and its investment has paid off in more ways than one. The memory of the genocide and the need for "greater securitization of everyday life" led to a 2013 revision of the 2008 Law Relating to the Interception of Communications, providing for state officials "to listen and read private communications, both online and offline. Communication providers are required to use state-designed technologies such as keyboard scanners." Email and phone communications are tracked. The regime relies upon blogs, listservs, and social media to maintain an online presence to denigrate its critics and glorify its policies. In 2012, to demonstrate the level of close monitoring carried out by the RPF for my students at Longwood University, I sent a tweet from the classroom calling for Rwanda to account for its crimes in Congo. Both "Kagame" and "Rwanda" were hash-tagged. The next day, I was attacked, to the amusement of my students, as a "genocide denier" by several Twitter accounts from Kigali; it was amusing because the students were aware of my writing of a chapter on genocide for a previous textbook.[12]

Additionally, from early on, the "RPF established close control over foreigners working or traveling in areas under its authority." Journalists and aid workers can travel the country only in the company of designated officials. Thomson writes of a "24/20" rule, meaning, according to her source, "You say something wrong and you get 24 hours to leave the country with 20 kilos worth of stuff." When visitors and missionaries travel the country, the Anglican Church's supporters included, they are nearly always in the presence of handlers and minders. With the complicity of the Anglican Church and similar bodies, the "RPF's surveillance mechanisms keep a watchful eye on all religious leaders, monitoring their dealings" with foreigners. The consternation of Anglican officials was painfully obvious when I would occasionally "escape" and make observations and engage in unsupervised conversations. I suspect this was one reason I was not welcomed back after 2007.[13]

While such intense monitoring of everyday life can be directed against any perceived opponent or critic of the regime, it weighs most heavily upon the predominately Hutu majority, vis-à-vis the Tutsi-led RPF. Yet surveillance of the population by those in power is another antecedent in Rwanda's past, but one that provides for a common historical experience between both groups and cuts "across Hutu- and Tutsi-dominated epochs." Historically, as the precolonial Nyiginya Kingdom expanded, both "seeing and being seen was fundamental to its exercise of power." In the nineteenth century, "overlapping authority structures" were established in the districts "under the kingdom's control." The effect assured the court's authority as each appointee oversaw the actions of the others, preventing any of them from accumulating too much power. Both then and currently, being present "rather than simply overseeing has formed an important 'state effect' in the central state's feedback loop of control." Moreover, the Rwanda of today closely resembles the Second Republic of Habyarimana in its approach to surveillance. Thus, the nature of the state's "coercive and overbearing" presence has spanned its history, through projections of "benevolent leadership" and with "references to service provisions and security." The way "care and coercion have been tightly intertwined" by the RPF is apparent enough. Less noticeable is that the presence of the Anglican Church, aligned with the regime, serves the presence of the state nearly perfectly, and the same "highly top-down, authoritarian, and non-democratic set of institutional structures and exercise of power . . . [that] was of crucial importance in the administration of genocide. Such forces are still present and potentially destructive." One wonders if the Anglican Church is aware that the Potemkin's village it has helped construct more closely resembles "Nero's Rome"?[14]

The surveilling presence of the state and its accomplices in the church has made it possible for the RPF to close down "space for debate" at all levels of society, limiting the opportunities to challenge the ruling party on fundamental aspects of politics and society and threatening "the long-term prospects for a peaceful and stable Rwanda." Additionally, the RPF's careful monitoring of society has allowed it to carefully orchestrate ways of putting off outside donors' and Western aid agencies' pressures for democratic reforms and more openness "without sacrificing its own position in Rwandan politics." Yet the longer Rwanda avoids these pressures, the greater is the risk of a "violent backlash in the future as the perceived exclusion of the Hutu majority from political power could provide an opportunity for future manipulation of ethnic identities by opponents of the current regime." When the churches, media, and other institutions of civil society are denied the opportunity to offer counter-viewpoints and criticisms, it makes it more likely that the state will undertake policies that aggravate structural and geographic tensions in the Hutu rural areas. When policy mistakes and ethnic tensions accumulate, and grievances are unheard, repression of dissent grows, and the ruling regime becomes discredited. In Silva-Leander's words, "This is a well-rehearsed scenario that has already turned many African success stories into unenviable news headlines."[15]

As it now appears to many in Rwanda that the regime operates with impunity, and as the "post-genocidal legal framework has allowed the regime to equate criticism of the RPF government with support for the genocide, and thereby to delegitimize its critics and opponents," does any path forward exist? As this work has demonstrated, Rwanda's history is facing and defining its present, both for the church and the state, but still remains subject to competing interpretations and revisions with much of it either unknown or unspoken of. If political truth cannot yet be spoken to those in power, it is suggested here that historical truth could suffice to create more unity and reconciliation in the hope that such realizations could diminish the dangers of ethnic conflict in the future. The ruling authorities in the RPF, and the Anglican Church and its supporters, would be wise to note "that the origins of collective violence lie in repressing memory and mis-constructing the past." If the ruling authorities are unwilling to speak of any history apart from their preferred version, the Anglican Church and other long-established and respected organs in Rwandan society could begin to do so, perhaps in whispers and in the presence of their supporters, without fear of undue retaliation. If not, the church will continue to join the state, leaving the country "vulnerable to opportunistic Hutu elites who seek to sow the seeds of discord with their calls for collective action in 'self-defense,' as has happened in the past" so poorly understood.[16]

The teaching of history, in a form that the population participates in creating rather than receiving from above, allows for an exploration of "multiple perspectives and multiple identities." To do otherwise, to receive only one unchallenged history from the authorities, in this case aided by the Anglican Church, "allows no capacity for critical thinking and independent analysis." This is especially critical in Rwanda's case. As William Easterly has argued, repression can "work with a poor, disorganized population, but it gets more and more costly (and less likely to succeed) as the majority gets more educated and has more politically active" researchers, a point not lost on the elites who "often block mass education." Many have suggested that the genocidal ideology in 1994 and the willingness to quickly and wantonly exterminate neighbors, friends, and even family members for simply being Tutsi without hesitation stemmed from a "culture of obedience" and an "unwillingness to question those in authority." While the notion that Rwandans are inherently obedient to authority is an unverifiable cultural assumption befitting an earlier narrative of the genocide, it remains true that "any history which is not *multifaceted, analytical* and *inclusive* of all opinion, and arrived at through *challenging myths* and critically *deconstructing* received truths, could easily mutate into an *absolutist* history [as has happened numerous times in Rwanda's past and currently] of the kind that motivated and perpetuated past violence."[17]

The history of ethnicity lies at the core of Rwanda's past troubles and its prospects for the future. As such, a debate about this and the nature of the country's history is central in the process of political reconstruction and reconciliation. This book has shown that Hutu-Tutsi identities were evolving long before colonial rule and, in every period of Rwandan history, "elites have strategically manipulated ethnic identity to justify resorting to violence" and maintain power. Currently, the RPF presents a "self-serving version of history and manipulates the language of ethnicity to justify and maintain policies of exclusion in much the same way that previous regimes have done." Religious figures and institutions, be they spokespersons for precolonial mythologies or Western church bodies, have always been used by those in power to shape history and manipulate ethnic understandings. The argument made in this book is that the Anglican Church, both in its past and presently, has proven to be a useful voice.[18]

Church leaders in PEAR today, like its founders in the Ruanda Mission, propagate pronouncements from those in power, even in the face of evidence to the contrary. As the second chapter showed, the missionaries who arrived in the 1920s endorsed the Hamitic Myth and viewed the Tutsi as the natural-born rulers without question. Understandably, then, they supported the Belgian colonial state in its support of the Tutsi monarchy and acquiesced in the formation of pseudoracial categories based on earlier, precolonial identities, which themselves were frequently manipulated by the monarchy in its pursuit of power. Naively hoping that Gospel conversion and Revival enthusiasm alone, brought to light in the third chapter, were enough to heal the divisions, they maintained their support for the monarchy even when their own mission stations were aflame in the Muyaga, leaving behind a church that lacked the tools and willingness to challenge the policies of the First and Second Republics. Upon the formation of a new church hierarchy after the genocide, the present leadership of PEAR accepts and endorses a new RPF manipulation of ethnic identity and history, one that seeks an *integrationist* approach and a new Rwanda by proclaiming ethnicity no longer exists while denying voice to the very ones it seeks to integrate. In accordance with the legacy left to it by its founders, PEAR seems to hope that Gospel conversions alone and urging Rwandans to reconcile with one another and the past in the name of Christ will suffice to prevent future violence. By demonstrating the close alignment of PEAR with the RPF, even in the face of atrocities by the latter, chapter 5 heaps doubt upon this hope.

    Thus, most scholars, including myself, are skeptical about the prospects of this integrationist approach, and whether it will lead to the "desired assimilation and to the creation of one new national identity." If not, the current system will lead to "structural grievances and horizontal inequalities" among the Hutu rural populace, contributing again, as it has in the past, to renewed violence along ethnic lines. An open conversation about Rwanda's history and ethnic identities, it is argued here, would unsettle the integrationist approach but would more likely lead to a new understanding of what it is to be Rwandan. Ethnicity cannot be ignored in Rwanda's past, but as David Newbury reminds readers, "Ethnicity is not primordial—something received blindly from a long-forgotten past; it is a created classification—created both by the nature of state power and by the individual placement within that political order." Thus, relations among ethnic groups are not in essence confrontational, and "ethnic diversity does not necessarily lead to secession or armed conflict." History has proven time after time, however, that oppression, marginalization, and impoverishment at the hands of political elites often does lead eventually to confrontation, secession, and armed conflict.[19]

    Unsettling the integrationist approach would call for a new, albeit *revised* once again, presentation of Rwanda's history by those in the church and state.

This would be neither a new endeavor nor an invention. As the first chapter showed, Rwanda was "invented many times over before European rule," after which it was reinvented again by the colonialists. The concept of identity in precolonial Rwanda was inherently ambiguous, as this book demonstrates, and "such ambiguity was beneficial not only to those without power but to the powerful as well." Group identity and history are learned elements—and therefore culturally defined. As such, the people of this region have always been engaged in a long process whereby they must, to use Diop's words, "learn to become" Rwandan, including its characteristics and "relationships among its constituents." A more productive "invention" of postgenocide Rwanda, as opposed to a historically misleading "integrationist invention," would call for an acknowledgment of past episodes of violence and oppression by both sides, including by the RPF, a realization that ethnic and social categories do not have to be "irrevocably opposed to each other and inevitably in conflict," and that both sides have been subject to the same historical revisions and surveillances in the name of elite oppression. One starting point could be an understanding and teaching of Rwandan history in a way that searches for "universal themes in situations of ethnic conflict around the world," reminding Rwandans that ethnic conflict is neither unique nor unavoidable.[20]

With such understandings in hand, the way opens for a more democratic and inclusive Rwanda along the lines of the 1993 Arusha Accords. Lasting peace, social stability, economic development, and genuine progress could become a reality, and the historical debate over Rwanda could move from an "ideological terrain dominated by ethnicity" to a full and robust understanding of the past. Here again, the Anglican Church can play a more constructive role. Institutions can indeed make a difference in "preventing societal, identity-based divisions from turning violent[,] and a recourse to institutional processes rather than to violence can be a way of resolving differences between societal groups." The Anglican Church can contribute mightily to this process by first abandoning its own past habit, bequeathed to it by its predecessors, of towing the line held by those in power and turning a blind eye toward the false revision of history currently underway. As *Partners Together* stated in 1995, "The church needs to be a community of forgiveness modelling the honesty of facing the truth of the past, examining itself, and through its leaders making public confessions where there has been sin committed. To forgive is not to forget and the church can help in the process of forgiveness." Onesphore Rwaje himself said, "We shouldn't say we are concerned with reconciliation but not justice." If speaking truth to those in power is too fearsome, truth could be proclaimed from the pulpit and in the presence of its congregants and outside supporters. As Paul Gready contends, "Civil society actors can learn to balance and shift between collaboration on the one hand, and monitoring, lobbying, critique, and outright confrontation on the other."[21]

PEARS's Western supporters could assist by educating themselves about Rwanda's history and reigning political order to challenge the pronouncements they hear. Unfortunately, though, this has not generally been the case. From the outset, spokespersons and churches within AMIA and other evangelical bodies have resembled most of the international donor agencies who have been more willing to "engage the developmental side of the Rwandan government than penalize it for its misdemeanors." Like the first Anglican missionaries who arrived in the kingdom, they accept without question the dictates of those in authority, including figures within PEAR. They see "decent technocratic/bureaucratic governance but ignore flawed governance, whereas the latter risks destroying the former." Research by political scientists demonstrates that development dollars blindly given strengthen democracies when democracy is present, but strengthen dictatorial regimes when dictatorship is present, as in the Rwanda of Kagame.[22]

In this sense, the international community, including Western church supporters, bear "overwhelming responsibility in allowing the RPF to deploy its skills" and impose a radical, deceptive dictatorship over the country. Without a change in course and without genuine reform, both of which could be encouraged by a departure from its historical habits on the part of the Anglican Church and its Western supporters, Rwandans will see "no peaceful political ways of changing the government, thus leaving them only the option of violent means." At such time, to the extent that donors have funded and legitimized the government and its allies in PEAR, they will be considered "in part responsible for serious problems that will probably result from the government policies they support." The pressure will build inside the volcano until it erupts and the dictatorship breaks, causing more than development projects and dollars to be lost . . . lives will be lost. Should Kagame's government fall from power, it is likely that members of the RPF power structure, and perhaps other supporting structures as well, will be investigated and perhaps prosecuted. Major embarrassment will ensue for those in "politics, academia, the press or the business community—who have given him [Kagame] a red-carpet treatment for so many years," including numerous churches and evangelical figures in the United States. Pursuing a different path would be unsettling and fraught with risks, as much for the Anglican Church of Rwanda as any. The alternative, it is feared, is more so.[23]

Notes

Introduction

1. Jan Vansina, *Antecedents to Modern Rwanda: The Nyiginya Kingdom* (Madison: University of Wisconsin Press, 2004), 35. For a classically romantic, albeit colonial, vision of Rwanda, see Rosamond Halsey Carr and Ann Howard Halsey, *Land of a Thousand Hills: My Life in Rwanda* (New York: Penguin Books, 1999).

2. "For West, Rwanda Is Not Worth the Political Candle," *New York Times*, April 15, 1994; "Tribes Battle for Rwandan Capital," *New York Times*, April 16, 1994; "Americans Are Out of Rwanda," *Washington Post*, April 11, 1994; "Rwandan Tells of Horrors, Cannibalism," *Los Angeles Times*, July 24, 1994. Human Rights Watch places the total close to five hundred thousand, while the government of Rwanda claims a figure of over one million. The most commonly cited number is roughly eight hundred thousand.

3. Two of the most popular survivor's testimonials are both by Immaculé Ilibagiza: *Led by Faith: Rising from the Ashes of the Rwandan Genocide* (Carlsbad, CA: Hay House, 2008) and *Left to Tell: Discovering God amidst the Rwandan Holocaust* (Carlsbad, CA: Hay House, 2007). See also Omar Ndizeye, *Life and Death in Nyamata: Memoir of a Young Boy in Rwanda's Darkest Hour* (Amsterdam: Amsterdam Publishers, 2020). The genocide has also spawned a genre of historical novels, including Boubacar Boris Diop, *Murambi, The Book of Bones* (Bloomington: Indiana University Press, 2000); Élisabeth Combres, *Broken Memory: A Novel of Rwanda* (Toronto: Groundwood Books, 2011); and Gil Courtemanche, *A Sunday at the Pool in Kigali* (New York: Vintage Books, 2003). For an academic treatment of fictional writing about the genocide by Rwandans, see Olivier Nyirubugara, *Novels of Genocide: Remembering and Forgetting the Ethnic Other in Fictional Rwanda*, Memory Traps 2 (Leiden: Sidestone Press, 2017).

4. Timothy Longman, *Memory and Justice in Post-genocide Rwanda* (Cambridge: Cambridge University Press, 2017), 37.

5. Author's field notes, Kigali, Rwanda, 2004.

6. The present government in Rwanda is so determined to maintain its narrative of an ethnically united and harmonious precolonial past, one can face criminal charges for espousing a different viewpoint. The authorities have even tried to erase the words "Hutu" and "Tutsi" from the Rwandan language. Several Western historians and

academics have been barred from entering the country for publicly questioning these assertions.

7. Gérard Prunier, *Africa's World War: Congo, the Rwanda Genocide, and the Making of Continental Catastrophe* (Oxford: Oxford University Press, 2009), 466n101, 466n104; Filip Reyntjens, *Political Governance in Post-genocide Rwanda* (Cambridge: Cambridge University Press, 2013), xiv. For a full bibliographic list of works on Rwanda prior to 1987, see Marcel d'Hartefelt and Danielle de Lame, eds., *Société, culture et historie du Rwanda: Encyclopédie bibliographique, 1863–1980/1887*, 2 vols. (Tervuren: Koninklijk Museum voor Midden-Afrika, 1987).

8. J. J. Carney, *Rwanda before the Genocide: Catholic Politics and Ethnic Discourse in the Late Colonial Era* (Oxford: Oxford University Press, 2014); Timothy Longman, *Christianity and Genocide in Rwanda* (Cambridge: Cambridge University Press, 2010). The terms "old case-load" and "new case-load" scholars were first coined to me by Danielle de Lame, author of *A Hill among a Thousand: Transformations and Ruptures in Rural Rwanda* (Madison: University of Wisconsin Press, 2005). Interview with de Lame at the Koninklijk Museum voor Midden-Afrika, Tervuren, Belgium, July 9, 2012.

9. Longman, *Memory and Justice*, 34; Sarah Warshauer Freedman et al., "Confronting the Past in Rwandan Schools," in *My Neighbor, My Enemy: Justice and Community in the Aftermath of Mass Atrocity*, ed. Eric Stover and Harvey Weinstein (Cambridge: Cambridge University Press, 2004), 248, 250; conversation with the former bishop of Shyira John Rucyahana, Ruhengeri, Rwanda, June 7, 2007. Rucyahana's request was an awkward undertaking, as I do not agree with the RPF's official version of Rwanda's history, a version that Rucyahana himself espouses. For a book-length treatment of educational policy in postgenocide Rwanda, see Elisabeth King, *From Classrooms to Conflict in Rwanda* (Cambridge: Cambridge University Press, 2015).

10. Reyntjens, *Political Governance*, 131; Helen Hintjens, "Post-genocide Identity Politics in Rwanda," *Ethnicities* 8, no. 1 (2008): 7, 12–13; Susan Thomson, *Whispering Truth to Power: Everyday Resistance to Reconciliation in Postgenocide Rwanda* (Madison: University of Wisconsin Press, 2013), xvii.

11. Author's field notes, Rwanda, 2004 and 2007.

12. David Newbury, "Trick Cyclists? Recontextualizing Rwandan Dynastic Chronology," *History in Africa* 21 (1994): 197.

13. African Rights, *Death, Defiance, and Despair*, rev. ed. (London: African Rights, 1995), 865.

Chapter 1. False Narratives of a Disputed Past

1. David Newbury, "Jan Vansina—In Memory." Provided to the author by David Newbury.

2. Jan Vansina, "Historical Tales (Ibiteekerezo) and the History of Rwanda," *History in Africa* 27 (2000): 375–414; Jan Vansina, *Living with Africa* (Madison: University of Wisconsin Press, 1994), 65. Vansina published numerous books on Central African history, including *Oral Traditions as History* (Madison: University of Wisconsin Press, 1985), a groundbreaking work that has shaped the field. Supervising more than fifty doctoral dissertations at Wisconsin, he is regarded as a towering figure in the field of African history. Translated into French, the nearly seven thousand pages of oral tales

of the *Ibiteekerezo* are housed at the Africa Museum (formerly the Royal Museum for Central Africa) in Tervuren, Belgium.

3. Reyntjens, *Political Governance*, 196n52. For some well-known earlier studies that make an erroneous assumption about Hutu-Tutsi identities, see Helen Codere, *The Biography of an African Society, Rwanda 1900–1960: Based on Forty-Eight Rwandan Biographies* (Tervuren: Koninklijk Museum voor Midden-Afrika, 1973); J. J. Maquet, *The Premise of Inequality in Rwanda: A Study of Political Relations in a Central African Kingdom* (London: Oxford University Press, 1961); and the early court historian Alexis Kagame, *Les organisations socio-familiales de l'ancien Rwanda* (Brussels: Académie Royale des Sciences Coloniales, 1954).

4. The earlier myth of a singular Bantu migration was dispelled by Jan Vansina in "Bantu in the Crystal Ball, I," *History in Africa* 6 (1979): 287–333, and "Bantu in the Crystal Ball, II," *History in Africa* 7 (1980): 293–325. The distinct Kinyarwanda language developed among the Bantu inhabitants prior to the Rwandan state. Combined with the Kirundi language to the south in Burundi (which are 80 percent cognate), they are the most widely spoken Bantu tongues outside of Kiswahili.

5. Jan Vansina, *Paths in the Rainforest: Toward a History of Political Tradition in Equatorial Africa* (Madison: University of Wisconsin Press, 1990), 61; David L. Schoenbrun, "Cattle Herds and Banana Gardens: The Historical Geography of the West Great Lakes Region, ca AD 800–1500," *African Archaeological Review* 11, no.1 (1993): 50.

6. Jean-Pierre Chrétien, *The Great Lakes of Africa: Two Thousand Years of History*, trans. Scott Straus (New York: Zone Books, 2003), 64; Schoenbrun, "Cattle Herds and Banana Gardens," 53.

7. Vansina, *Paths in the Rainforest*, 185–86. For more in-depth reading in the nature of kingship in the region, see David Newbury, *King and Clans: Ijwi Island and the Lake Kivu Rift, 1780–1840* (Madison: University of Wisconsin Press, 1991), 219–24.

8. John Hanning Speke, *Journal of the Discovery of the Source of the Nile* (1969; repr., London: J. M. Dent & Sons, 1975), 201–4. While Speke is generally blamed for these ideas, he may not be entirely responsible. His publishers wrote most of the final version of the book (personal communication with Jan Vansina).

9. Charles Gabriel Seligman, *Races of Africa* (Oxford: Oxford University Press, 1930); Genesis 9:20–27 (King James Version); Chrétien, "Les deux visages de cham," in *L'Idée de race dans la pensée politique française contemporaine*, ed. Pierre Guiral and Emile Témime (Paris: Editions du Centre National de la Recherche Scientifique, 1977), 195.

10. Edith R. Sanders, "The Hamitic Hypothesis: Its Origin and Functions in Time Perspective," *Journal of African History* 10, no. 4 (1969): 521. Sanders offers the best general historical overview of the Hamitic Hypothesis/Myth.

11. "Leonard Sharp to Friends of Ruanda," September 14, 1922, *Mid-Africa Ministry Papers* [MAM Papers], Cadbury Research Library, University of Birmingham, Birmingham, England (E11). The terms used here by Sharp, "Batutsi" and "Bahutu," reflect a Bantu linguistic practice of using the prefix "Ba-" to speak of the group in the plural. As with most current writers, I do not make use of the prefix.

12. David L. Schoenbrun, *A Green Place, a Good Place: Agrarian Change and Social Identity in the Great Lakes Region to the 15th Century* (Portsmouth, NH: Heinemann, 1994), 71; Chrétien, *Great Lakes*, 67–69.

13. Longman, *Memory and Justice*, 43–44, emphasis added; David Newbury, "The Invention of Rwanda: The Alchemy of Ethnicity," paper presented at the African Studies Association Annual Meeting, Orlando, FL. 1995. Mahmood Mamdani, in *When Victims Become Killers: Colonialism, Nativism, and the Genocide in Rwanda* (Princeton, NJ: Princeton University Press, 2001), provides a more elaborate explanation of these deceptive genetic differences. Interestingly, the genetic blood trait that provides heightened resistance to malaria also causes the disease known as sickle cell anemia. The blood trait and the resulting sickle cell anemia occurs in higher rates among African Americans, most of whom have West-Central African origins, as opposed to Americans of European ancestry.

14. André Guichaoua, *From War to Genocide: Criminal Politics in Rwanda, 1990–1994* (Madison: University of Wisconsin Press, 2015), 7.

15. Guichaoua, *From War to Genocide*, 8.

16. David Newbury, "Augustinian Models in Rwanda: Religious Movements and Political Transformations," *Kyrkan och krisen i central afrika. SMT: Svensk Missionstidskrift* 83, no. 3 (1995): 18; Joseph Rwabukumba and Vincent Mudandagizi, "Les formes historiques de la dépendance personnelle dans l'État rwandais," *Cahiers d'études africaines* 14, no. 53 (1974): 7.

17. Karel Arnaut and Hein Vanhee, "History Facing the Present: An Interview with Jan Vansina," in *Annexe 1: Interview avec Jan Vansina, par Karel Arnaut et Hain Vanhee en 2001. Inventaire des archives de Jan Vansina, 1929–2017* (Tervuren: Koninklijk Museum voor Midden-Afrika, 2018), 8.

18. Arnaut and Vanhee, "History Facing the Present," 8.

19. Vansina, *Antecedents*, 36–37. As a caveat to this, while the term "Tutsi" is almost nonexistent in contemporary Rwanda, the term "Hima" can still be found. In 2007, traveling in the northern town of Nyagatare, established as a refuge for Tutsi returning after the genocide, I noted a regional business chain called "Hima Cement," a small but clear refutation of the notion that the terms Hutu, Tutsi, and Hima no longer have any meaning. Owing to its more obscure nature and meaning, "Hima Cement" appears meaningless to outsiders, but to the majority who understand the implications of the term, it is loaded with historical pejorative. I compare it to a hypothetical business chain in the American south calling itself "Dixie Cement," meaningless to those unfamiliar with the history of the term but with undeniable historical baggage for African Americans.

20. Arnaut and Vanhee, "History Facing the Present," 8, emphasis added.

21. David Newbury, "Precolonial Burundi and Rwanda: Local Loyalties, Regional Royalties," *International Journal of African Historical Studies* 34, no. 2 (2001): 290.

22. Vansina, *Antecedents*, 45–47.

23. Vansina, *Antecedents*, 63–65.

24. Twagiramungu, cited by Susan Thomson, *Rwanda: From Genocide to Precarious Peace* (New Haven, CT: Yale University Press, 2018), 232. For a lengthier discussion of Rwanda's military culture and the role of the army in fostering national unity around the king, see Frank K. Rugasara, *Resilience of a Nation: A History of the Military in Rwanda* (Kampala: Fountain, 2009).

25. Chrétien, *Great Lakes*, 78; Vansina, *Antecedents*, 56–57. According to the tale, Gihanga determined the vocations of his three sons, Gatutsi, Gahutu, and Gatwa, and

their children. After the passing of various skill tests from the founding father Gihanga, Gatutsi and his children were allocated with cattle herds because of their attentiveness. Gahutu's descendants, clumsy and awkward in the mythology, were designated as farmers, and the children of Gatwa were to be hunters, providing a supposedly ancient and predetermined basis for the social categories defining the region.

26. Vansina, *Antecedents*, 56–57; Ilaria Buscaglia and Shirley Randell, "Legacy of Colonialism in the Empowerment of Women in Rwanda," *Cosmopolitan Civil Societies Journal* 4, no. 1 (2012): 76.

27. David Newbury, *King and Clans*, 88–89; Vansina, *Antecedents*, 90–91; David Newbury, "Augustinian Models," 19. Upon Rugujira's accession to the throne, the kingdom was threatened by a combined military alliance of Rwanda's three most powerful enemies in the region: Ndorwa to the north, Gisaka to the east, and Burundi to the south.

28. Vansina, *Antecedents*, 103–5.

29. Vansina, *Antecedents*.

30. Interview with Paul Rusesabagina, Longwood University, Farmville, Virginia, February 24, 2010; author's field notes, Rwanda, 2007.

31. Vansina, *Antecedents*, 93–94.

32. Vansina, *Antecedents*, 95.

33. Catherine Buckley-Zistel, "Remembering to Forget: Chosen Amnesia as a Strategy for Local Coexistence in Post-genocide Rwanda," *Africa* 76, no. 2 (2006): 136; Vansina, *Antecedents*, 96.

34. Vansina, *Antecedents*, 121. For Nahimana's views, see *Le blanc est arrivé, le roi est parti* (Kigali: Printer Set, 1987). He also founded the *Radio Télévision Libre des Mille Collines*, which broadcast hate-filled propaganda against the Tutsi throughout the genocide.

35. One should note here that the final expansion of the kingdom did not fully occur until the early twentieth century, with European help.

36. Vansina, *Antecedents*, 127.

37. Vansina, *Antecedents*, 127–28; Catharine Newbury, "*Ubureetwa* and *Thangata*: Catalysts to Peasant Political Consciousness in Rwanda and Malawi," *Canadian Journal of African Studies* 14, no. 1 (1980): 99.

38. C. Newbury, "*Ubureetwa* and *Thangata*," 99; Rwabukumba and Mudandagizi, "Historical Forms," 10.

39. Catharine Newbury, *The Cohesion of Oppression: Clientship and Ethnicity in Rwanda, 1860–1960* (New York: Columbia University Press, 1988), 40.

40. David Newbury, "Precolonial Burundi and Rwanda," 308–9.

41. Catharine Newbury, "*Ubureetwa* and *Thangata*," 100–101.

42. Rwabukumba and Mudandagizi, "Historical Forms," 21.

43. Vansina, *Antecedents*, 135.

44. Vansina, *Antecedents*.

45. Johan Pottier, *Re-imagining Rwanda: Conflict, Survival and Disinformation in the Late Twentieth Century* (Cambridge: Cambridge University Press, 2002), 9.

46. Alison Liebhafsky Des Forges, *Defeat Is the Only Bad News: Rwanda under Musinga, 1896–1931*, ed. David Newbury (Madison: University of Wisconsin Press, 2011), 10; Vansina, *Antecedents*, 183, 186, 289n107.

47. Villia Jefremovas, "Loose Women, Virtuous Wives, and Timid Virgins: Gender and the Control of Resources in Rwanda," *Canadian Journal of African Studies* 25, no. 3 (1991): 380–81.

48. Vansina, *Antecedents*, 77.

49. Thomson, Rwanda, 128; de Lame, *Hill among a Thousand*, 487. Genocide was defined in 1948 by the United Nations Convention on the Prevention and Punishment of the Crime of Genocide in Article II, Resolution 260A (III), as "any of the following acts committed with intent to destroy, in whole or in part, a national, ethnic, racial or religious group, such as killing members of the group, causing serious bodily harm to members of the group, creating conditions meant to cause loss of life or the prevention of births, and the transferring away of children from parents." Following the International Criminal Tribunal for Rwanda (ICTR) in 1997, rape and sexual assault were added as genocide crimes.

50. Vansina, *Antecedents*, 193, 137–38.

51. Philip Gourevitch, *We Wish to Inform You That Tomorrow We Will All Be Killed with Our Families: Stories from Rwanda* (New York: St. Martin's Press, 1998), 48.

Chapter 2. History Intervenes

1. Chrétien, *Great Lakes*, 195. The term "calico," in reference to the English-printed textiles, came from the Indian port city of Calicut, where the design originated.

2. Vansina, *Antecedents*, 157, 168, 176.

3. Mike Davis, in *Late Victorian Holocausts: El Niño Famines and the Making of the Third World* (London: Verso, 2001), links the rinderpest epidemic to a period of devastating drought brought on by two powerful El Niño weather cycles in the late 1880s and early 1900s. For a cataloging of Rwanda's catastrophes in these years, see Roger Botte, "Rwanda and Burundi, 1889–1930: Chronology of a Slow Assassination, Part 2," *International Journal of African Historical Studies* 18, no. 2 (1985): 289–314.

4. C. Newbury, *Cohesion*, 57–58.

5. C. Newbury, *Cohesion*, 59. The Coup of Rucunshu, a final reminder of the internecine violence so rife in precolonial Rwanda, looms large in its historical memory but is generally unknown to outsiders and nonspecialists. An early historian of Rwanda, Louis de Lacger, referred to the events at Rucunshu as a "holocaust" and noted that it was only the "arrival of the whites" that prevented the Nyiginya from disintegrating entirely. Louis de Lacger, *Le Ruanda*, 2nd ed. (Kabgayi: Imprimérie de Kabgayi, 1959), 367, 369. According to one of Rwanda's epic poems, some contemporary Rwandans refer to Rucunshu as "the first genocide," all of which is suggestive of a kingdom far from a golden age of harmony before the European arrival. Catharine Newbury, "Ethnicity and the Politics of History in Rwanda," *Africa Today* 45, no. 1 (1998): 23.

6. Des Forges, *Defeat*, 15; A. Gille, "Sandrart (Georges Victor)," in *Biographie Belge d'Outre-Mer*, VII, *Fascicule B* (Brussels: Académie Royale des Sciences D'Outre-Mer, 1977), 335.

7. Carol Rittner, "Chronology," in *Genocide in Rwanda, Complicity of the Churches?*, ed. Carol Rittner, John K. Roth, and Wendy Whitworth (St. Paul: Aegis, 2004), 5.

8. Des Forges, *Defeat*, 18; Vansina, *Antecedents*, 179; Kandt quoted in Des Forges, *Defeat*, 26.

9. In addition, it was Kandt who, against Musinga's wishes, constructed a house in 1907 on Nyarugenge Hill in present-day Kigali, transforming it into the administrative capital for both the Germans and the Belgians.

10. Phillip A. Cantrell, "'We Were a Chosen People': The East African Revival and Its Return to Post-genocide Rwanda," *Church History* 83, no. 2 (2014): 3–4.

11. For two early accounts of the missionary effort in Uganda, see C. P. Groves, *The Planting of Christianity in Africa*, vol. 3, *1878–1914* (Cambridge: Lutterworth Press, 1956); or John Vernon Taylor, *The Growth of the Church in Buganda: An Attempt at Understanding* (London: SCM Press, 1958). For more recent, general accounts of church history in Africa, see John Bauer, *2000 Years of Christianity in Africa: An African Church History* (Nairobi: Pauline Publications Africa, 1994); or Adrian Hastings, *The Church in Africa: 1450–1950* (Oxford: Clarendon, 1994).

12. Bauer, *2000 Years*, 106. The White Fathers was one of three Catholic missionary societies that originated in France in the nineteenth century. The other two were the Holy Ghost Fathers, founded by Francis Libermann (1804–52) in 1848, and the Fathers of Lyon, founded by Bishop Melchior de Marion Brésillac (1813–59) in 1856. Taken together, the three societies made France the leading Catholic country for missionary activity in East Africa, while Britain was the leading proponent of Protestant work.

13. Taylor, *Growth of the Church*, 71.

14. Carney, *Rwanda before the Genocide*, 21; Taylor, *Growth of the Church*, 263–68; John Ssebalugga, "The African Cross-Bearers," *Touchstone: A Journal of Mere Christianity*, October 2003, 17; Des Forges, *Defeat*, 219. The Catholic victims were beatified in 1920 and canonized in 1964. Along with the Anglicans, they are collectively known as the "Martyrs of Uganda" and are still commemorated every year with a national holiday on June 3.

15. For more on the conflicts in Buganda, see Michael A. Wright, *Buganda in the Heroic Age* (Oxford: Oxford University Press, 1971).

16. Hastings, *Church in Africa*, 376, 464.

17. Ian and Jane Linden, *Church and Revolution in Rwanda* (New York: Africana, 1977), 31. An apostolic vicariate, headed by a vicar, is a Roman Catholic missionary region where no formal diocese yet exists.

18. Anthony Court, "The Christian Churches, the State, and Genocide in Rwanda," *Missionalia* 44, no. 1 (2016): 57; Des Forges, *Defeat*, 28. The early tribulations of the Whites Fathers in establishing their post at Save are set out in considerable detail in Roger Heremans and Emmanueal Ntezimana, *Journal de la Mission de Save* (Ruhengeri: Editions Universitaires du Rwanda, 1987).

19. Des Forges, *Defeat*, 29; Court, "Christian Churches," 57; Linden, *Church and Revolution*, 35; Carney, *Rwanda before the Genocide*, 27; Bauer, *2000 Years*, 249.

20. Carney, *Rwanda before the Genocide*, 25; David Newbury, "Multiple Missionary Histories in Rwanda: Local Agency and Institutional Agendas," in *Lives in Motion, Indeed: Interdisciplinary Perspectives on Social Change*, ed. Christiana Panella (Tervuren: Koninklijk Museum voor Midden-Afrika, 2012), 159–89.

21. "Adventure in Faith: Reminiscences of the Early Days of the Ruanda Mission," *John E. Church Papers* [*Church Papers*], Cambridge Center for Christianity Worldwide, Westminster College, Cambridge University, Cambridge, England (9/2/42).

22. H. B. Thomas, ed., "Kigezi Operations, 1914–1917," *Uganda Journal* 30, no. 2 (1966): 165.

23. D. Newbury, "Augustinian Models," 26.

24. "Commissioner General of Rwanda to Bishop Willis," May 28, 1917; "Smith to Bishop Willis," June 21, 1917, *MAM Papers* (Y11).

25. Kevin Ward, "Revival, Mission, and Church in Kigezi, Rwanda, and Burundi," in *The East African Revival: History and Legacies*, ed. Kevin Ward and Emma Wild-Wood (Farnham: Ashgate, 2012),14; Des Forges, *Defeat*, 137. For a recent, popular account of the Rubber Terror, see Adam Hochschild, *King Leopold's Ghost: A Story of Greed, Terror, and Heroism in Central Africa* (New York: Houghton Mifflin, 1999).

26. "Leonard Sharp to G. T. Manley," April 2, 1917, *MAM Papers* (Y12).

27. "G. T. Manley to Leonard Sharp," July 16, 1920; "G. T. Manley to Stanley Smith," November 5, 1920, *MAM Papers* (Y12).

28. For an ethnography of the Bakiga of Kigezi, see May Edel, *The Chiga of Western Uganda* (London: Routledge, 2018).

29. Leonard Sharp, "Adventure in Faith," *Church Papers* (9/2/4); "Stanley Smith to Ruanda Friends," June 1, 1923, *MAM Papers* (E11); "Subjects for Prayer and Praise," *Ruanda Notes*, no. 37 (July 1931): 24; "L. Margaret Orpwood," *Partners Together*, no. 259 (June 1988): 3; "Stanley Smith to Ruanda Friends," May 7, 1921, *MAM Papers* (E11).

30. "Stanley Smith to Ruanda Friends," May 7, 1921, *MAM Papers* (E11).

31. Cantrell, "We Were a Chosen People," 8.

32. Kevin Ward, "'Obedient Rebels'—The Relationship between the Early 'Balo-kole' and the Church of Uganda: The Mukono Crisis of 1941," *Journal of Religion in Africa* 19, no. 3 (1989): 197–98; Roger W. Bowen, "Genocide in Rwanda 1994—An Anglican Perspective," in Rittne, Roth, and Whitworth, *Genocide in Rwanda*, 38.

33. "Smith to Friends of Ruanda," September 15, 1921, *MAM Papers* (E11); *Church Missionary Outlook* 51 (1924), Cadbury Research Library, University of Birmingham, Birmingham, England, 238.

34. "Smith to Friends of Ruanda," September 7, 1922; "Sharp to Friends of Ruanda," September 14, 1922, *MAM Papers* (E11).

35. "Smith to Friends of Ruanda," September 15, 1921, *MAM Papers* (E11).

36. "Memorandum by Dr. Leonard Sharp on the Start and Growth of the Ruanda Mission," January 22, 1924, *MAM Papers* (Y12).

37. Gordon Hewitt, *The Problems of Success: A History of the Church Missionary Society, 1910–1942*, vol. 1 (London: SCM Press, 1977), 270; "The Rev. J. E. L. Warren," *Ruanda Notes*, no. 28 (April 1929); "Memorandum by Dr. Leonard Sharp on the Start and Growth of the Ruanda Mission," January 22, 1924, *MAM Papers* (Y12); "Dr. Sharp Sounds the Call to Prayer," *Ruanda Notes*, no. 37 (July 1931): 8.

38. "Kosea Shalita," *Ruanda Notes*, no. 43 (January 1933).

39. Christine Tinling, "A Time of Refreshing," *The Christian* (October 14, 1937), *MAM Papers* (AC4); "Leonard Sharp to Friends of Ruanda," *Ruanda Notes*, no. 11 (January 1925), *MAM Papers* (E11); "Introduction to a New Worker," *Ruanda Notes*, no. 25 (July 1928): 23.

40. Joe Church, *Quest for the Highest: An Autobiographical Account of the East African Revival* (Exeter: Pasternoster, 1981), 22, 75, 88.

41. John C. T. Church, "A Personal Experience of the Revival," in Ward and Wild-Wood, *East African Revival*, 44; Ward, "Revival, Mission, and Church," 17.

42. Buscaglia and Randell, "Legacy of Colonialism," 72. For a wider analysis on colonial-era views of womanhood, see Anna Davin, "Imperialism and Motherhood," *History Workshop Journal* 5, no. 5 (1978): 9–65.

43. "Adventure in Faith," *Church Papers* (9/2/4); Tinling, "A Time of Refreshing"; Hewitt, *The Problem of Success*, 271. Elsewhere in Hewitt's book, published as late as 1977, he refers to the Tutsi having invaded the region from the north in the fifteenth century, indicating the resilience of the Nilotic invasion thesis.

44. "Origin of the Ruanda Council," *General Secretary's Department, Minutes of Ruanda Council* [MRC], (GYA112),107.

45. Sharp quoted in Ward, "Revival, Mission and Church," 16.

46. "W. Wilson Cash to the Ruanda Council," November 15, 1926, *MAM Papers* (Y12).

47. Phyllis M. Martin, *Leisure and Society in Colonial Brazzaville* (Cambridge: Cambridge University Press, 1995), 42.

48. "Stanley Smith to Friends of Ruanda," *Ruanda Notes*, no. 27 (January 1929): 14; Botte, "Rwanda and Burundi," 313; Des Forges, *Defeat*, 221.

49. "Joe Church to Friends of Ruanda," *Ruanda Notes*, no. 27 (January 1929): 16–17; H. L. Vis, C. Yourassowsky, and H. van der Borght, *A Nutritional Survey in the Republic of Rwanda* (Tervuren: Koninklijk Museum voor Midden-Afrika, 1975), 148; Des Forges, *Defeat*, 221. See also David Newbury, "The Rwakayihura Famine of 1928–1929: A Nexus of Colonial Rule in Rwanda," in *Historie Sociale de 'Afrique de l'Est* (Paris: Karthala, 1991), 269–77.

50. Titus Presler, "The History of Mission in the Anglican Communion," in *The Wiley-Blackwell Companion to the Anglican Communion*, ed. Ian S. Markham et al. (West Sussex: John Wiley & Sons, 2013), 16; Elizabeth Hopkins, "The Nyabingi Cult of Southwestern Uganda," in *Protest and Power in Black Africa*, ed. Robert I. Rotberg and Ali A. Mazrui (New York: Oxford University Press, 1970), 268.

51. "Mrs. Wilkinson to Friends of Ruanda," *Ruanda Notes*, no. 28 (April 1920): 25; "Geoffrey Holmes to Friends of Ruanda," *Ruanda Notes*, no. 26 (October 1928): 12; "Leonard Sharp to Friends of Ruanda," *Ruanda Notes*, no. 18 (November 1926): 6; Des Forges, *Defeat*, 49.

52. Bowen, "Genocide in Rwanda," 44.

53. "Leonard Sharp to Friends of Ruanda," *Ruanda Notes*, no. 18 (November 1926): 6; "Stanley Smith to Friends of Ruanda," *Ruanda Notes*, no. 24 (April 1928): 7.

54. Linden and Linden, *Church and Revolution*, 202–3.

55. M. J. Bessell, "Nyabingi," *Uganda Journal* 6, no. 2 (October 1938): 73–74; Hopkins, "Nyabingi Cult," 258–59; D. Newbury, "Augustinian Models," 31n7.

56. Hopkins, "Nyabingi Cult," 275–76, 286, 314–16.

57. "Stanley Smith to Friends of Ruanda," September 15, 1921; "Leonard Sharp to Friend of Ruanda," May 31, 1928, *Ruanda Notes*, no. 25 (July 1928): 8; Leonard Sharp, "Paul a Servant of Jesus Christ," *Church Missionary Outlook* 60, no. 714 (September 1933): 194; "Talbot Hindley to Friends of Ruanda," August 4, 1947, *Ruanda Notes*, no. 96 (May 1947): 12.

58. Linden and Linden, *Church and Revolution*, 202–3; Hopkins, "Nyabingi Cult," 318; confidential report quoted in Hopkins, "Nyabingi Cult," 319.

59. Presler, "History of Mission," 16.

60. Thomas Spear, "Towards the History of African Christianity," in *East African Expressions of Christianity*, ed. Thomas Spear and Isaria N. Kimambo (Athens: Ohio University Press, 1999), 4.

61. Bessell, "Nyabingi," 85. The Catholics to the south followed similar practices. The worship of Imana, a common deity in the region, was replaced by worship of the Christian God, or Mungu Baba (Father God) as he was called in the Swahili language of the mission stations. Local cult practices were labeled evil and animistic ceremonies were called "Devil's Sabbaths." Converts who continued to take part were punished or excommunicated.

62. "Joe Church to Friends of Ruanda," *Ruanda Notes*, no. 27 (January 1929): 17; "Adventures in Faith," *Church Papers* (9/2/4).

63. Des Forges, *Defeat*, 134. When the Belgians arrived at the court, they addressed the notables in Swahili. When the notables, who only spoke Kinyarwanda, did not obey immediately, the Belgians shot them, for their "insubordination." Des Forges, *Defeat*, 135.

64. Linden and Linden, *Church and Revolution*, 45.

65. Des Forges, *Defeat*, 135.

66. Des Forges, *Defeat*, 211–13.

67. Des Forges, *Defeat*, 220–21; 225; Longman, *Christianity and Genocide*, 53.

68. Des Forges, *Defeat*, 227.

69. Des Forges, *Defeat*, 227; Longman, *Christianity and Genocide*, 54. Hirth retired in 1921 and died ten years later in January. The Vicariate of Ruanda was created from the older Vicariate of Kivu, itself created from the Vicariate of South Nyanza in 1912 under Bishop Hirth.

70. Bauer, *2000 Years*, 347.

Chapter 3. Growth, Revival, and Conflict

1. Octave Ugirashebuja, "The Church and Genocide in Rwanda," in Rittner, Roth, and Whitworth, *Genocide in Rwanda*, 50. Linden quoted in the same.

2. Carney, *Rwanda before the Genocide*, 29; Longman, *Christianity and Genocide*, 55.

3. Bauer, *2000 Years*, 247, 347.

4. Carney, *Rwanda before the Genocide*, 36, 39; Longman, *Christianity and Genocide*, 55–56.

5. Carney, *Rwanda before the Genocide*, 36; Bauer, *2000 Years*, 238; Ward, "Revival, Mission, and Church," 25.

6. "P. J. Brazier to Friends of Ruanda," *Ruanda Notes*, no. 49 (July 1934).

7. "Report of Events in Connection with the Visit of the White Fathers to Gahini," November 11, 1933, *Church Papers* (4/10/5); "Dora Skipper," *Partners Together*, no. 250 (March 1986): 7.

8. "May Langley to Fellow-Labourers," *Ruanda Notes*, no. 39 (January 1932): 25; Stanley Smith, "Memorandum on the two new sites of the Ruanda Mission," *MRC* (GYA112), 1926–1935 (38); "Recruits," *Ruanda Notes*, no. 31 (January 1930): 7; "Jack Symonds to Friends of Ruanda," September 16, 1937, *Ruanda Notes*, no. 62 (October 1937): 22; Leonard Sharp, "Adventure in Faith," *Church Papers* (9/2/4).

9. "Retrospect and Thanksgiving from Dr. Leonard Sharp," *Ruanda Notes*, no. 44 (April 1933); Randall Fegley, *A History of Rwandan Identity and Trauma: The Mythmakers Victims* (Lanham, MD: Lexington Books, 2016), 13; *Ruanda Notes*, no. 47 (January 1934), no. 50 (October 1934), no. 41 (July 1932).

10. "Leonard Sharp to Friends of Ruanda," *Ruanda Notes*, no. 50 (October 1934).

11. "The Ruanda Family Album, February 1921–January 1939," Crowther Library, Church Mission Society, Oxford, England.

12. "Dr. Church Reports on the African Convention," *Ruanda Notes*, no. 48 (April 1934): 17.

13. "At the Home Base," *Ruanda Notes*, no. 56 (April 1936): 6.

14. "Archdeacon Pitt-Pitts to the Friends of Ruanda," *Ruanda Notes*, no. 56 (April 1936): 10; "E. L. Barham to the Friends of Ruanda," *Ruanda Notes*, no. 56 (April 1936): 12; "Joe Church to Friends of Ruanda," *Ruanda Notes*, no. 58 (October 1936): 9.

15. Rev. P. J. Brazier, "Some Characteristics of the Ruanda Revival Fellowship," *Church Missionary Society Papers* [*CMS Papers*], Cadbury Research Library, University of Birmingham, Birmingham, England (AF3549, G3A111, Subfile 9); Catherine Ellen Robbins, "Tukutendereza: A Study of Social Change and Sectarian Withdrawal in the Balokole Revival of Uganda" (PhD diss., Columbia University, 1975), 6.

16. Rev. P. J. Brazier, "Some Characteristics of the Ruanda Revival Fellowship," *CMS Papers* (AF3549, G3A111, Subfile 9).

17. "Joe Church to Friends of Ruanda," *Ruanda Notes*, no. 58 (October 1936): 9; Joe Church, "Revival and Reunion in the Mission Field, 1945," 1945, *MAM Papers* (E8/2); Joe Church, "The Story of the Ruanda Mission," 1945, *MAM Papers* (E8/1).

18. Joe Church, "A Call to Prayer," *Ruanda Notes*, no. 57 (July 1936).

19. Richard MacMaster and Donald R. Jacobs, *A Gentle Wind of God: The Influence of the East African Revival* (Scottsdale, AZ: Herald Press, 2006), 28–32; Zebuloni Kabaza interview quoted in same; F. B. Welbourn, *East African Rebels: A Study of Some Independent Churches* (London: SCM Press, 1961), 65, 73. Ensor, whose story is recounted by Welbourne in chapter 4 of *East African Rebels*, harbored very disparaging views of African culture, denouncing African music, dancing, and folklore as "works of the devil."

20. Church, *Quest for the Highest*, 66–68.

21. Ward, "Revival, Mission, and Church," 18–19.

22. "Yosea Kinuka to the Ruanda Friends," *Church Papers* (6/3/2).

23. Kinuka quoted in Smith, *Road to Revival*, 54; Joe Church, "The Story of the Ruanda Mission," 1945, *MAM Papers* (E8/1); "Joe Church to Friends of Ruanda," *Ruanda Notes*, no. 56 (April 1936):, 29; "The Passing of an African Pioneer," *The Church Missionary Outlook* 63 (June 1936): 134. Church later memorialized Kigozi in *Awake, Uganda! The Story of Blazio Kigozi and his Vision of Revival* (Kampala, 1957).

24. Derek R. Peterson, "Revivalism and Dissent in Colonial East Africa," in Ward and Wild-Wood, *East African Revival*, 107. Two autobiographical histories of the Revival are Church, *Quest for the Highest*; and Smith, *Road to Revival*. Among the sympathetic histories are Macmaster and Jacobs, *Gentle Wind of God*; James Katarikawe, *The East African Revival* (Delaware: Lydia Murungi, 2004); and two works by H. H. Osborn, *Fire in the Hills* (Crowborough: Highland, 1991) and *Revival:*

A Precious Heritage (Winchester: Apologia, 1995). The most scholarly analyses of the Revival thus far have been published in Ward and Wild-Wood, *East African Revival*.

25. Ward, "Introduction," in Ward and Wild-Wood, *East African Revival*, 3; Ward, "Revival, Mission, and Church," 11.

26. "Lawrence Barham to Friends of Ruanda," *Ruanda Notes*, no. 39 (January 1932): 12; "Leonard Sharp to Friends of Ruanda," *Ruanda Notes*, no. 45 (July 1933): 7; "Geoffrey Holmes to Friends of Ruanda," *Ruanda Notes*, no. 45 (July 1933): 20.

27. "Jim Brazier to Friends of Ruanda," *Ruanda Notes*, no. 42 (October 1932): 15; "Jim Brazier to Friends of Ruanda," *Ruanda Notes*, no. 43 (January 1933): 20.

28. Cantrell, "We Were a Chosen People," 9.

29. Cantrell, "We Were a Chosen People," 8.

30. Taylor, *Growth of the Church*, 62–63; Pilkington quoted in Katarikawe, *East African Revival*, 4.

31. Kevin Ward, "The Revival in an African Milieu," in Ward and Wild-Wood, *East African Revival*, 192; MacMaster and Jacobs, *Gentle Wind*, 33.

32. Tinling, "Time of Refreshing," *MAM Papers* (AC4); "Geoffrey Holmes to Friends of Ruanda," *Ruanda Notes*, no. 45 (July 1933): 20; Bowen, "Genocide in Rwanda," 38–39.

33. A brief biography of William Wadé Harris can be found in David A. Shank, "The Legacy of William Wadé Harris," *International Bulletin of Missionary Research* 10, no. 4 (1986): 170–76. For the origins of the Kimbanguist movement, see Cecilia Irvine, "The Birth of the Kimbanguist Movement in the Bas-Zaire 1921," *Journal of Religion in Africa* 6, no. 1 (1974): 23–76.

34. Spear, "Towards the History," 16.

35. Spear, "Towards the History," 17; Ward, "Revival in an African Milieu," 194.

36. Gregory Maddox, "African Theology and the Search for the Universal," in Spear and Kimambo, *East African Expressions of Christianity*, 31–32.

37. Taylor, in *Growth of the Church*, 99, saw the East African Revival as distinctive and "unusual" in that it represented a movement in the "third generation" of the church, with revivals being much more common in the "second generation," as in what happened after 1893 in Buganda.

38. Robbins, "Tukutendereza," 4. Details regarding the Revival's spread further afield can be found in Katarikawe, *East African Revival*; and MacMaster and Jacobs, *Gentle Wind of God*.

39. MacMaster and Jacobs, *Gentle Wind of God*, 119–54.

40. Simon Stuart, "A Review of the Whole Mission by the Bishop," *Ruanda Notes*, no. 59 (January 1937): 5; "Lawrence Barham to Friends of Ruanda," *Ruanda Notes*, no. 59 (January, 1937): 17; Arthur Pitt-Pitts, "Report to the Secretary of the Mission, Nov. 1936," *MRC* (GYA112); Welbourn, *East African Rebels*, 73; "Reginal Palin to Bishop Stuart," January 19, 1947 (Folder 191.7), *Record Group 1: Archives of the Bishop of Uganda [ABU]*, Uganda Christian University, Library, Mukono, Uganda.

41. Ward, "Revival, Mission, and Church," 17–18.

42. Arthur Pitt-Pitts, "Pitt-Pitts Report: Gahini," January 1936, *Church Papers* (4/10/5); Arthur Pitt-Pitts, "Revival Difficulties," April 13, 1939, *MRC* (GYA112).

43. Arthur Pitt-Pitts, "Revival Difficulties," April 13, 1939, *MRC* (GYA112).

44. Ward, "'Obedient Rebels,'" 198–200.

45. Ward, "'Obedient Rebels,'" 202.

46. Ward, "'Obedient Rebels.'"

47. Church, *Quest for the Highest*, 184; Ward, "'Obedient Rebels,'" 205–6. Nagenda quoted in Church, *Quest for the Highest*, 185.

48. Church, *Quest for the Highest*, 185.

49. Church, *Quest for the Highest*, 185; Ward, "'Obedient Rebels,'" 212–14.

50. "Copy of Letter Received from Bishop Stuart," October 10, 1942, *MRC* (GYA112).

51. Ward, "Revival, Mission, and Church," 22; Leonard Sharp, "Copy of Airgraph from Dr. L. Sharp," October 25, 1942, *MRC* (GYA112).

52. "Esther Sharp to Dorothy," March 19, 1946, *MRC* (AF3549, G3A118); Welbourn, *East African Rebels*, 73.

53. "To all Missionaries," October 13, 1942, *MRC* (AF3549, G3A112); "Extract of Dr. Sharp's Letter," January 2, 1944, *MRC* (AF3549, G3A112).

54. Stanley Smith, "A Summary of Answer to Questions at the Council Meeting," January 15, 1945, *MRC* (AF3549, G3A112).

55. Bishop Stuart, "The Root Problem in Ruanda," February 13, 1945, *MRC* (AF3549, G3A112); "Extract from Letter from Mr. K. L. Cooper," June 28, 1945, *MRC* (AF3549, G3A112).

56. "A Statement Specially Prepared for Consideration and Prayer," May 25, 1948, *MRC* (AF3549, G3A112); Bishop Stuart, "Comments on the Specially Prepared for Consideration and Prayer," May 25, 1948, *MRC* (AF3549, G3A112); G. C. Grimshaw, "Extracts from Report on Tour of Ruanda," September 1949, *MRC* (AF3549, G3A112).

57. Maddox, "African Theology," 38.

58. C. Newbury, "*Ubureetwa* and *Thangata*," 105.

59. Nigel Eltringham, *Accounting for Horror: Post-genocide Debates in Rwanda* (London: Pluto Press, 2004), 185n14; C. Newbury, "*Ubureetwa* and *Thangata*," 104–6. For a detailed study of Rwandan economy in these years, see Learthen Dorsey, "The Rwandan Colonial Economy, 1916–1941" (PhD diss., Michigan State University, 1983).

60. Eltringham, *Accounting for Horror*, 14–15.

61. Ugirashebuja, "Church and the Genocide," 51–52; Ian Linden quoted in the same; Eltringham, *Accounting for Horror*, 15; Des Forges, *Defeat*, 274.

62. Eltringham, *Accounting for Horror*, 18.

63. Laurent Mbanda, *Committed to Conflict: The Destruction of the Church in Rwanda* (London: Society for Promoting Christian Knowledge, 1997), 49–51.

64. Mbanda, *Committed to Conflict*, 49.

65. Ward, "'Obedient Rebels,'" 195; Bowen, "Genocide in Rwanda," 38; Taylor, *Growth of the Church*, 103; Longman, *Christianity and Genocide*, 59.

66. Longman, *Christianity and Genocide*, 58.

67. Quoted in Bowen, "Genocide in Rwanda," 40.

68. Church, *Quest for the Highest*, 116, 68; Bowen, "Genocide in Rwanda," 40.

69. Bowen, "Genocide in Rwanda," 42–43; Mbanda, *Committed to Conflict*, 133–34.

Chapter 4. The Unraveling

1. Longman, *Memory and Justice*, 50. Historically, the Flemish hailed from Flanders in the north of Belgium, a more working-class and mercantile-oriented region. The

Walloons came from Wallonia in the south, dominated by more aristocratic farmers and large landowners who looked down on the more "earthy" Flemish workers, provoking Flemish resentments toward them.

2. Carney, *Rwanda before the Genocide*, 36; Tharcisse Gatwa, *The Churches and Ethnic Ideology in the Rwandan Crises, 1900–1994* (Milton Keynes: Paternoster Press, 2005), 90.

3. Gatwa, *Churches and Ethnic Ideology*, 92–93.

4. As late as 1957, Belgium foresaw a thirty-year time frame for independence in Central Africa. In less than four years, its territories were out of its hands and independent.

5. Learthen Dorsey, *Historical Dictionary of Rwanda* (London: Scarecrow, 1994), 70–74.

6. Dorsey, *Historical Dictionary of Rwanda*.

7. Dorsey, *Historical Dictionary of Rwanda*, 74–75; C. Newbury, *Cohesion of Oppression*, 145–46.

8. Gerard Prunier, *The Rwanda Crisis: History of a Genocide* (New York: Columbia University Press, 1995), 43.

9. Dorsey, *Historical Dictionary of Rwanda*, 76; Prunier, *Rwanda Crisis*, 45.

10. Chrétien, *Great Lakes*, 301; Prunier, *Rwanda Crisis*, 46. In 2016 Mugesera was sentenced to life in prison for genocide crimes.

11. C. Newbury, *Cohesion of Oppression*, 189.

12. Marcel Kabanda, "Rwanda: The Catholic Church and the Crisis. Autopsy of a Legacy," in *The Recurring Great Lakes Crisis: Identity, Violence, and Power*, ed. Jean-Pierre Chrétien and Richard Banégas (New York: Columbia University Press, 2011), 62–63; C. Newbury, *Cohesion of Oppression*, 189. See also Emmanuel Ntezimana, "Kinyameteka, temps nouveaux d'Afrique et l'évolution socio-politique du Rwanda (1954–1959)," *Études Rwandaises*, special issue (March 1978): 1–29.

13. C. Newbury, *Cohesion of Oppression*, 188–89; Chrétien, *Great Lakes*, 302.

14. C. Newbury, *Cohesion of Oppression*, 102; Prunier, *Rwanda Crisis*, 47–48; Chrétien, *Great Lakes*, 302–3.

15. Kabanda, "Rwanda," 69. Alexis Kagame (no relation to Paul Kagame) was a Tutsi Catholic priest and historian who came from a line of court ritualists known as the *biru*. As a member of the royal court and a great-nephew to an important Tutsi commander under Rwabugiri, he published prolifically on royal history, royal culture, and royal literary genres; and his works have become foundational for the current regime. But to many he is seen as an ideologue for the monarchy and a devout proponent of the Hamitic Myth. Thomson, *Rwanda*, 43.

16. Kabanda, "Rwanda," 73; C. Newbury, *Cohesion of Oppression*, 193; Harroy quoted in Chrétien, *Great Lakes*, 408n35; and in Prunier, *Rwanda Crisis*, 47–48. Harroy had been with the Institut pour la Recherche Scientifique en Afrique Centrale (IRSAC) until 1955, when he left to assume the governorship. Presumably then he had some academic knowledge of Rwanda. Vansina, *Living with Africa*, 60.

17. Prunier, *Rwanda Crisis*, 46, 48; C. Newbury, *Cohesion of Oppression*, 194. The "winds of change" is a reference to a speech given by British prime minister Harold Macmillan (1894–1986) in Cape Town, South Africa, wherein he seemed to accede to decolonization across Africa.

18. David Newbury, "Canonical Conventions in Rwanda: Four Myths of Recent Historiography in Central Africa," *History in Africa* 39 (2012): 50–51.

19. A useful work for the perspectives of ordinary Hutu and Tutsi men and women in these years is the collection of interviews in the classic work by Helen Codere, *Biography of an African Society*. The reader should be cautioned, however, that Codere's work accepts the premise of the earlier colonial period of Hutu, Tutsi, and Twa being separate, distinct races, with the usual approbation about the Tutsi being born to rule.

20. Chrétien, *Great Lakes*, 303–4; Prunier, *Rwanda Crisis*, 48–49. *Muyaga* is the name Rwandans use to refer to the violent events marking the end of Belgian rule and the coming of independence.

21. Chrétien, *Great Lakes*, 303–4; Prunier, *Rwanda Crisis*, 52–53.

22. Chrétien, *Great Lakes*, 304.

23. Linden and Linden, *Church and Revolution*, 249; Kabanda, "Rwanda," 79; Prunier, *Rwanda Crisis*, 54–55. The term *inyenzi* ("cockroaches," or creatures who act "stealthily at night") was a source of admiration by many in the RPA (private communication from David Newbury).

24. Prunier, *Rwanda Crisis*, 54.

25. "Important Notice," *Ruanda Notes*, no. 91 (February 1946): 4; "At the Throne of Grace," *Ruanda Notes*, no. 67 (February 1939): 41; "In Memoriam," *Partners Together*, no. 288 (Autumn 1995): 10; "Subjects for Prayer and Praise," *Ruanda Notes*, no. 80 (September 1942): 10; "Jack Symonds," *Partners Together*, no. 281 (Winter 1993); "William Arthur Pitt-Pitts," *Ruanda Notes*, no. 72 (May 1940): 3; "Our Beloved Archdeacon," *Ruanda Notes*, no. 77 (August 1941): 4; "Papers of Philippa Guillebaud," Finding Aid, Cambridge Center for Christianity Worldwide, Westminster College, Cambridge University, Cambridge, England.

26. Marvin D. Markowitz, *Cross and Sword: The Political Role of Christian Missions in the Belgian Congo, 1908–1960* (Stanford, CA: Stanford University Press, 1973), 66; Carney, *Rwanda before the Genocide*, 41.

27. Linden and Linden, *Church and Revolution*, 209, 255, 259.

28. *Ruanda Notes*, no. 140 (1957–58): 22.

29. "P. J. Brazier to Friends of Ruanda," *Ruanda Notes*, no. 110 (November 1950–January 1951); Jim Brazier, "Yesterday, Today, and Tomorrow," *Ruanda Notes*, no. 124 (May–July 1954): 2.

30. "An Urgent Call to Prayer," *Ruanda Notes*, no. 146 (December 1959–February 1960): 1; Mbanda, *Committed to Conflict*, 24.

31. "P. J. Brazier to Friends of Ruanda," *Ruanda Notes*, no. 110 (November 1950–January 1951); "P. D. Guillebaud to Friends of Ruanda," *Ruanda Notes*, no. 104 (May 1949); Harold Adeney, "Signs of a Storm," *Ruanda Notes*, no. 119 (February–April 1953): 8. Adeney had been in the CiCCU camp at Cambridge and was recruited to the field by Leonard Sharp.

32. "Which Way?," *Ruanda Notes*, no. 103 (February 1949); "Canon Lawrence Barham to Friends of Ruanda," *Ruanda Notes*, no. 110 (November 1950–January 1951).

33. Mbanda, *Committed to Conflict*, 49; Gatwa, *Churches and Ethnic Ideology*, 102.

34. "Report on Rwanda," *Ruanda Notes*, no. 107 (February 1950).

35. H. H. Osborn quoted in Gatwa, *Churches and Ethnic Ideology*, 102–3; "Freedom for the Captives," *Partners Together*, no. 253 (December 1986): 6.

36. Linden and Linden, *Church and Revolution*, 261; *Ruanda Notes* quoted in the same.

37. Linden and Linden, *Church and Revolution*, 278n95.

38. Jim Brazier, "A Survey of the Situation in Ruanda," December 30, 1959, *MAM Papers* (G59 YA114).

39. Longman, *Christianity and Genocide*, 80.

40. "Max Warren to Kenneth Grubb," December 7, 1959; "Copy of Letter from Dr. H. W. Adeney," November 13, 1959, "Extract from the 'New Day,'" December 4, 1959, *MAM Papers* (G59 YA114).

41. "Copy of Letter from CMS Gahini (Joe Church)," November 11, 1959; "Max Warren to Kenneth Grubb," December 7, 1959, *MAM Papers* (G59 YA114).

42. "Alan and Catherine Lindsay to Our Dear Praying Friends," November 21, 1959, *MAM Papers* (G59 YA114); "Harold Adeney to the Friends of Ruanda," *Ruanda Notes*, no. 149 (September–November 1960); "Peter Guillebaud to the Friends of Ruanda," *Ruanda Notes*, no. 150 (December 1960–February 1961).

43. "Memorandum Related to the Events in Ruanda-Urundi in 1959," January 19, 1960, *MAM Papers* (G59 YA114); *Ruanda Notes*, no. 148 (1959–60): 11; "Extract from Minutes of Africa Committee Meeting," December 1, 1959, *MAM Papers* (G59 YA114).

44. *Ruanda Notes*, no. 154 (December 1961–February 1962): 10; "Peter Guillebaud to Friends of Ruanda," December 30, 1961, *Ruanda Notes*, no. 155 (March–May 1962); Rt. Rev. P. J. Brazier, "Ruanda-Urundi: Still a Sick Patient," *Ruanda Notes*, no. 156 (1961–62): 5.

45. Joe Church, "Gahini—The Storm Breaks," *Ruanda Notes*, no. 156 (1961–62): 18–19; "Joe Church to Friends of Ruanda," *Ruanda Notes*, no. 153 (September–November 1961): 7; *Partners Together*, no. 265 (December 1989): 6.

46. Katherine Makower, *Not a Gap Year but a Lifetime*, 252, 241; *Ruanda Notes*, no. 163 (March–May 1964); "Dora Skipper," *Partners Together*, no. 250 (March 1986): 7; "Jack Symonds," *Partners Together*, no. 281 (Winter 1993); "Ruanda Mission CMS," *Partners Together*, no. 203 (Spring 1974).

47. "Harold Adeney to Friends of Ruanda," *Ruanda Notes*, no. 155 (March–May 1962): 4; John Church, *Ruanda Notes*, no. 156 (1961–62): 21; Jim Brazier, "The Present Position in Rwanda and Burundi," *Ruanda Notes*, no. 158 (December 1962–February 1963): 10.

48. René Lemarchand, *Rwanda and Burundi* (New York: Praeger, 1970), 270; Thomson, *Rwanda*, 48–49.

49. Ogenga Otunnu, "An Historical Analysis of the Invasion by the Rwandan Patriotic Army (RPA)," in *The Path of a Genocide: The Rwanda Crisis from Uganda to Zaire*, ed. Howard Adelman and Astri Suhrke (Piscataway, NJ: Transaction, 1999), 42–43.

50. Catharine Newbury, "Rwanda: Recent Debates over Governance and Rural Development," in *Governance and Politics in Africa*, ed. Goran Hyden and Michael Bratton (Boulder, CO: Lynne Rienner, 1992), 195; Reyntjens quoted in same, 195.

51. Guichaoua, *From War to Genocide*, 14.

52. Jennifer Olson, "Behind the Recent Tragedy in Rwanda," *GeoJournal* 35, no. 2 (1995): 219; Sebastian Silva-Leander, "On the Danger and Necessity of Democratisation: Trade-Offs between Short-Term Stability and Long-Term Peace in Post-genocide

Rwanda," *Third World Quarterly* 29, no. 8 (2008): 1605; Stephen W. Smith, "Rwanda in Six Scenes," *London Review of Books* 33, no. 6 (2011): 2.

53. Smith, "Rwanda in Six Scenes," 2.

54. Olson, "Behind the Recent Tragedy," 218; Jared Diamond, *Collapse: How Societies Choose to Fail or Succeed* (New York: Penguin Books, 2005), 314–15.

55. Olson, "Behind the Recent Tragedy," 217, 244; C. Newbury, "Rwanda," 193.

56. Philip Verwimp, "Development Ideology, the Peasantry and Genocide: Rwanda Represented in Habyarimana's Speeches," *Journal of Genocide Research* 2, no. 3 (2000): 326; Olson, "Behind the Recent Tragedy," 219; Catherine André and Jean-Philippe Platteau, "Land Relations under Unbearable Stress: Rwanda Caught in the Malthusian Trap," *Journal of Economic Behavior & Organization* 34, no. 4 (1998): 3–4.

57. C. Newbury, "Rwanda," 196; Silva-Leander, "On the Danger and Necessity," 1603.

58. Diamond, *Collapse*, 314–15, 310–21; Peter Uvin, "Tragedy in Rwanda: The Political Ecology of Conflict," *Environment* 38, no. 3 (April 1996): 14; John F. May, "Policies on Population, Land Use, and Environment in Rwanda," *Population and Environment* 16, no. 4 (March 1995): 323; An Ansoms, "Re-engineering Rural Society: The Visions and Ambitions of the Rwandan Elite," *African Affairs* 108, no. 431 (2009): 298.

59. Uvin, "Tragedy in Rwanda," 11; Olson, "Behind the Recent Tragedy," 219; Colin Murray Parkes, "Genocide in Rwanda: Personal Reflections," *Mortality* 1, no. 1 (1996): 99; Helen Hintjens, "Explaining the 1994 Genocide in Rwanda," *Journal of African History* 37, no. 2 (1999): 256–57; Ansoms, "Re-engineering Rural Society," 199.

60. C. Newbury, "Rwanda," 212–13; Peter Uvin, "Prejudice, Crisis, and Genocide in Rwanda," *African Studies Review* 40, no. 2 (1997): 108; Chrétien, *Great Lakes*, 322. For an in-depth analysis of the politics of this period, see Guichaoua, *From War to Genocide*.

61. Hintjens, "Explaining the 1994 Genocide," 258.

62. Hintjens, "Explaining the 1994 Genocide," 259. Nahimana was apprehended in Cameroun in 1996 and convicted of conspiracy to commit genocide by the International Criminal Tribunal for Rwanda (ICTR).

63. "Jon and Sheila Henderson," *Partners Together*, no. 211 (March 1976): 8; "Letters from Rwanda," *Partners Together*, no. 215 (March 1977): 8; "Bread not Words," *Partners Together*, no. 245 (September 1984): 1.

64. "Pioneering Physiotherapy in Rwanda," *Partners Together*, no. 221 (September 1978): 12–13; "Rwanda Not Worst, But . . . ," *Partners Together*, no. 246 (December 1984): 7.

65. "The New Archbishop," *Partners Together*, no. 205 (September 1974); "Basis of the Ruanda Mission," *Partners Together*, no. 209 (September 1975): 13; "Tukutendereza," *Partners Together*, no. 216 (June 1977): 10.

66. Timothy Longman, "Church, Politics, and the Genocide in Rwanda," *Journal of Religion in Africa* 31, no. 2 (2001): 166, 171–72.

67. Saskia van Hoyweghen, "The Disintegration of the Catholic Church in Rwanda: A Study of the Fragmentation of Political and Religious Authority," *African Affairs* 95, no. 380 (July 1996): 385–86.

68. Guichaoua, *From War to Genocide*, 24–26; Ogenga Otunnu, "Rwandese Refugees and Immigrants in Uganda," in Adelman and Suhrke, *Path of a Genocide*, 3–4;

Silva-Leander, "On the Danger and Necessity," 1603. For a largely sympathetic biography of Paul Kagame, see Colin Waugh, *Paul Kagame and Rwanda: Power, Genocide, and the Rwandan Patriotic Front* (Jefferson, NC: McFarland, 2004). An even more glowing presentation of Kagame came from Stephen Kinzer, *A Thousand Hills: Rwanda's Rebirth and the Man Who Dreamed It* (Hoboken, NJ: John Wiley and Sons, 2008), although by 2011 Kinzer had second thoughts and feared, correctly, that his regime was slipping toward dictatorship. Reyntjens, *Political Governance*, xivn4.

69. *Partners Together*, no. 270 (March 1991): 6; *Partners Together*, no. 275 (Summer 1992): 12; Otunnu, "Rwandese Refugees," 3–4; Sarah Kenyon Lischer, "Civil War, Genocide, and Political Order in Rwanda: Security Implications of Refugee Return," *Conflict, Security and Development* 11, no. 3 (July 2011): 268; Marco Jowell, "Cohesion through Socialization: Liberation, Tradition and Modernity in the Forging of the Rwandan Defense Force (RDF)," *Journal of Eastern African Studies* 8, no. 2 (2014): 282.

70. Otunnu, "Historical Analysis," 16–17.

71. Bruce D. Jones, *Peacemaking in Rwanda: The Dynamics of Failure* (Boulder, CO: Lynne Rienner, 2001), 24. For further details on the nature of Tutsi refugee status in Uganda, see David Newbury, "Returning Refugees: Four Historical Patterns of 'Coming Home' to Rwanda," *Comparative Studies in Society and History* 47, no. 2 (2005): 252–85.

72. Alan J. Kuperman, "Provoking Genocide: A Revised History of the Rwandan Patriotic Front," *Journal of Genocide Research* 6, no. 1 (2004): 63.

73. Otunnu, "Historical Analysis," 32; Prunier, *Africa's World War*, 14; Thomson, *Rwanda*, 61. The atrocities in northern Uganda committed by the NRA/RPA forces against the Acholi and Langi account in large part for the Holy Spirit Rebellion of Alice Lakwena and the subsequent rebellion of Joseph Kony and the Lord's Resistance Army, the latter of which generated suffering and atrocities in the north into the 2000s.

74. Chrétien, *Great Lakes*, 320–23; C. Newbury, "Rwanda," 217; Uvin, "Prejudice, Crisis, and Genocide," 109.

75. Several works offer a more detailed analysis of the negotiations at Arusha, including Bruce D. Jones, "The Arusha Peace Process," in Adelman and Suhrke, *Path of a Genocide: The Rwanda Crisis from Uganda to Zaire*, 131–56, and his *Peacekeeping in Rwanda*. See also David Rawson, *Prelude to Genocide: Arusha, Rwanda, and The Failure of Diplomacy* (Athens: Ohio University Press, 2018).

76. *Africa Research Bulletin* (December 1–31, 2018): 22129, column B. See also Luc Reydams, "Politics or Pragmatism? The International Criminal Tribunal for Rwanda and the Burying of the Investigation into the Assassination of President Juvénal Habyarimana," *Human Rights Quarterly* 40, no. 4 (November 2018): 989–1013.

77. America's lack of response was driven in part by the public's lack of appetite for foreign interventions after the disastrous U.S. mission to Mogadishu, Somalia, in October 1993, wherein nineteen soldiers were killed (immortalized in the 2001 film *Black Hawk Down*). The 2005 Frontline Documentary *Ghosts of Rwanda* (PBS Home Video) provides a clear presentation of these events. For the most comprehensive account of the genocide, see Alison Des Forges, *Leave None to Tell the Story: Genocide in Rwanda* (New York: Human Rights Watch, 1999). Guichaoua, in *From War to Genocide*, provides a highly detailed account of the political dynamics in Rwanda

during the years 1990–94. See also Alex de Waal and Rakiya Omaar, *Rwanda: Death and Despair* (London: African Rights, 1995).

78. Paul Conway, "Righteous Hutu: Can Stories of Courageous Rescuers Help in Rwanda's Reconciliation Process?," *International Journal of Sociology and Anthropology* 3, no. 7 (2011): 219. Although the small Muslim community in Rwanda is often singled out with praise for its lack of participation in the killings, Anne Kubai offers a more balanced and nuanced account of their role in "Walking a Tightrope: Christians and Muslims in Post-genocide Rwanda," *Islam and Christian-Muslim Relations* 18, no. 2 (2007): 219–235. She suggests that Muslims usually refrained from killing fellow Muslims regardless of ethnicity, but not so much when it came to the killing of non-Muslim Tutsi. African Rights, *Death, Defiance, and Despair*, rev. ed. (London: African Rights, 1995), 865; Hoyweghen, "Disintegration," 394–95.

79. Phillip A. Cantrell, "The Anglican Church of Rwanda: Domestic Agendas and International Linkages," *Journal of Modern African Studies* 45, no. 3 (2007): 339.

80. Filip Reyntjens, "Rwanda: Ten Years On; From Genocide to Dictatorship," *African Affairs* 103, no. 411 (2004): 179.

Chapter 5. Revival and Reconciliation

1. Reyntjens, "Rwanda, Ten Years On," 178.

2. Chrétien, *Great Lakes*, 336; Christine Schliesser, "From 'a Theology of Genocide' to a 'Theology of Reconciliation'? On the Role of Christian Churches in the Nexus of Religion and Genocide in Rwanda," *Religions* 9, no. 34 (2018): 6.

3. For a sympathetic and positive portrayal of the reconciliation process and the role of the *gacaca* courts, see the 2010 documentary film *As We Forgive*, produced by Laura Waters Hinson. A critical review of the film can be found in Phillip A. Cantrell, "Reconciliation in Post-genocide Rwanda as Presented in the Film *As We Forgive*," in *The Rwandan Genocide on Film: Critical Essays and Interviews*, ed. Matthew Edwards (Jefferson, NC: McFarland, 2018), 109–18.

4. Timothy Longman, "An Assessment of Rwanda's Gacaca Courts," *Peace Review: A Journal of Social Justice* 21, no. 3 (July–September 2009): 307–8. See also Timothy Longman, "Trying Times for Rwanda: Reevaluating Gacaca Courts in Post-genocide Reconciliation," *Harvard International Review* 32, no. 2 (Summer 2010): 48–52.

5. Jennie Burnet, "The Injustice of Local Justice: Truth, Reconciliation, and Revenge in Rwanda," *Genocide Studies and Prevention* 3, no. 2 (August 2008): 188.

6. Longman, "Assessment," 310–11; Burnet, "Injustice," 188. For a less critical account of *gacaca*, see Phil Clark, "Bringing the Rwandans Back In, Again: State, Power, and Local Agency in Rwanda's Gacaca Courts," *Journal of Eastern African Studies* 8, no. 2 (2014): 193–213.

7. Author's field notes, Rwanda, 2007.

8. For a sympathetic biography of Kolini, see Mary Weeks Millard, *Emmanuel Kolini: The Unlikely Archbishop of Rwanda* (Colorado Springs: Authentic Publishing, 2008). Among those newly appointed by the Consultative Council in 1996 were John Rucyahana as Bishop of Shyria, Venuste Mutiganda as Bishop of Butare, Alexis Bilindabagabo as Bishop of Gahini, Prudence Ngarambe as Bishop of Kibungo, and Jered Kalimba as Bishop of Shyogwe. A British Anglican, Ken Barham, was appointed bishop of Cyangugu. *Partners Together*, no. 297 (Winter 1997): 8.

9. In addition to Kolini and Rucyahana, their present numbers include the new bishop of Shyira Diocese, Samuel Mugisha, Bishop Augustin Ahimana of the Kivu Diocese, Bishop Nathan Amooti of the Kigali Diocese, Bishop Mannasseh Gahima of the Gahini Diocese, Geoffrey Rwubusisi, former bishop of the Cyangugu Diocese, and Josias Sendegeya, former bishop of Kibungo Diocese. The most noteworthy exception is the former bishop of Gahini, Alexis Bilindabagabo, who remained in Rwanda and survived the genocide. I met and spoke with all the aforementioned figures during two field research visits to Rwanda in 2004 and 2007. I identify by name only the key figures in the church leadership. Ordinary Rwandans and parishioners with whom I spoke remain nameless for their security.

10. Longman, *Memory and Justice*, 46. Among these memoirs are Emmanuel Kolini and Philip Holmes, *Christ Walks Where Evil Reigned: Responding to the Rwandan Genocide* (Colorado Springs: Authentic, 2008); John Rucyahana and James Riordan, *The Bishop of Rwanda: Finding Forgiveness amidst a Pile of Bones* (Nashville: Thomas Nelson, 2007); and Alexis Bilindabagabo and Alan Nichols, *Rescued by Angels: The Story of Miracles during the Rwandan Genocide* (Durham, NC: Acorn Press, 2006).

11. Reyntjens, *Political Governance*, 261.

12. Author's field notes, Rwanda, June 2007.

13. Interview with retired headmaster (anonymous), Gahini, Rwanda, June 19, 2007.

14. Interview with Emmanuel Kolini, Kigali, Rwanda, June 16, 2007; Robbins, "Tukutendereza," 342–68; Zablon Nthamburi, *From Mission to Church: A Handbook of Christianity in East Africa* (Nairobi: Uzima Press, 1995), 97; author's field notes, Kabale, Uganda, May 23, 2017.

15. Interview with Nathan Amooti, author's field notes, Rwanda, June 2007.

16. Interview with Amooti, Rwanda, June 2007.

17. Interview with Amooti, Ruhengeri, Rwanda, July 26, 2004; author's field notes, Kibungo, Rwanda, June 16, 2007; author's field notes, Gahini, Rwanda, June 19, 2007; "Devastation at Gahini," *Partner Together*, no. 250 (March 1986); Jesse Zink, "'Anglocostalism' in Nigeria: Neo-Pentecostalism and Obstacles to Anglican Unity," *Journal of Anglican Studies* 10, no. 2 (2012): 232.

18. Author's field notes, Ruhengeri, Rwanda, July 25, 2004.

19. PEAR, "Programme Guide, International Evangelistic Crusade," Ruhengeri, Rwanda (July 21–25, 2004), copy on file with the author.

20. PEAR, "Programme Guide."

21. Uvin, "Prejudice, Crisis, and Genocide," 94; author's field notes, Ruhengeri, Rwanda, July 25, 2004.

22. Catherine Newhouse, "Pentecostal Renewal Transforms Rwanda after Genocide," *Christianity Today*, January 3, 2012.

23. Allan H. Anderson, "The Newer Pentecostal and Charismatic Churches: The Shape of Future Christianity in Africa?," *Journal of the Society for Pentecostal Studies* 24, no. 2 (Fall 2002): 168; Anne Kubai, *Being Church in Post-genocide Rwanda: The Challenges of Forgiveness and Reconciliation* (Uppsala: Life and Peace Institute, 2005), 29; Anne Kubai, "Post-genocide Rwanda: The Changing Religious Landscape," *Exchange* 36, no. 2 (2007): 199.

24. Kubai, "Post-genocide Rwanda," 199.

25. David Brown, *Contemporary Nationalism: Civic, Ethnocultural and Multicultural Politics* (London: Routledge, 2000), 20.

26. Rene Lemarchand, "Genocide in the Great Lakes: Which Genocide? Whose Genocide?," *African Studies Review* 41, no. 1 (April 1998): 7.

27. Liisa Malkki, *Purity and Exile: Violence, Memory, and National Cosmology among Hutu Refugees in Tanzania* (Chicago: University of Chicago Press, 1995), 105.

28. Author's field Notes, Gahini, Rwanda, June 18, 2007.

29. Author's field Notes, Gahini, Rwanda, June 18, 2007.

30. Chrétien, *Great Lakes*, 360n5; William F. S. Miles, "Hamites and Hebrews: Problems in 'Judaizing' the Rwandan Genocide," *Journal of Genocide Research* 2, no. 1 (2000): 111–12.

31. Malkki, *Purity and Exile*, 235, 113.

32. For a lengthier treatment of the Anglican schism in the United States and its global significance, although using Ugandan sources, see Miranda K. Hassett, *Anglican Communion in Crisis: How Episcopal Dissidents and Their African Allies Are Reshaping Anglicanism* (Princeton, NJ: Princeton University Press, 2007).

33. Author's field notes, Ruhengeri, Rwanda, July 25, 2004.

34. Philip Jenkins, *The Next Christendom: The Coming of Global Christianity* (Oxford: Oxford University Press, 2002), 203; Griswold quoted in the same.

35. Emmanuel Kolini, "Cheap Evangelism," *Christianity Today*, January 1996.

36. Lacey and Goodstein, "African Anglican Leaders Outraged over Gay Bishop in U.S.," *New York Times*, November 4, 2003, A21; Nzimbi and Akinola quoted in Cantrell, "Anglican Church of Rwanda," 345.

37. Obasanjo quoted in Cantrell, "Anglican Church of Rwanda," 345; Lynne Duke, "Mugabe Makes Homosexuals Public Enemies," *Washington Post*, September 1995; Farbrice Iranzi, "Burundi President Believes That Covid-19 Is a Curse Linked to Homosexuality," *Region Week*, August 2020.

38. Kolini quoted in Cantrell, "Anglican Church of Rwanda," 345.

39. Marc Epprecht, *Hungochani: The History of a Dissident Sexuality in Southern Africa* (Montreal: McGill-Queen's University Press, 2004), 224–25. See also Lisa Lindsay and Stephan Miescher, *Men and Masculinities in Modern Africa* (Portsmouth, NH: Heineman, 2003), for further explorations into the changing definitions and understandings of African masculinity.

40. Vansina, *Antecedents to Modern Rwanda*, 108.

41. Jenkins, *Next Christendom*, 203–4; Peers quoted in the same.

42. Jenkins, *Next Christendom*, 203.

43. Emmanuel Kolini, "A Tutsi's Hope: A Zairean Bishop Wants American Christians to Remember the Struggles of the Church in East Africa," *Christianity Today*, April 1997; Sendegeya quoted in Cantrell, "Anglican Church of Rwanda," 346; author's field notes, Ruhengeri, Rwanda, July 25, 2004.

44. Cantrell, "'We Were a Chosen People,'" 14.

45. Author's field notes, Rwanda, 2007; Anglican Mission in America Winter Conference, Myrtle Beach, SC, 2005.

46. Bobby Ross Jr., "Out of Africa: What AMIA's Exodus from Rwanda Portends for Global Christianity," *Christianity Today*, December 2011.

47. Timothy C. Morgan, "Purpose Driven in Rwanda," *Christianity Today*, September 2005.

48. Kagame quoted in Reyntjens, *Political Governance*, 255.

49. Filip Reyntjens, "Constructing the Truth, Dealing with Dissent, Domesticating the World: Governance in Post-genocide Rwanda," *African Affairs* 110, no. 438 (2010): 8–9; Reyntjens, "Rwanda, Ten Years On," 178; Waugh, *Paul Kagame and Rwanda*, 152–53; Smith, "Rwanda in Six Scenes," 7; Thomson, *Rwanda*, 277n41. For a complete account of Sendashonga's assassination, see Prunier, *Africa's World War*, "Appendix 1: Seth Sendashonga's Murder," 365–68; Reyntjens, *Political Governance*, 10–11. Sebarenzi's story is told by himself in "Justice and Humans Rights for all Rwandans," in *Remaking Rwanda: State Building and Human Rights after Mass Violence*, ed. Scott Straus and Lars Waldorf (Madison: University of Wisconsin Press, 2011), 343–53. He is also the author of *God Sleeps in Rwanda: A Journey of Transformation* (New York: Atria Books, 2009).

50. Jowell, "Cohesion through Socialization," 284. For an analysis of Karegeya's assassination and its implications, see Michela Wrong, *Do Not Disturb: The Story of a Political Murder and an African Regime Gone Bad* (New York: Public Affairs, 2021).

51. Guichaoua, *From War to Genocide*, 146, 378n5.

52. Reyntjens, "Constructing the Truth," 3, 12, 13, 15; Longman, *Memory and Justice*, 62–63; Reyntjens, "Rwanda: Progress or Powder Keg?," *Journal of Democracy* 26, no. 3 (2015): 22–23; Kagame quoted in Chakravarty, "Navigating the Middle Ground," 233; Reyntjens, *Political Governance*, 92. For Sibomana's own account, see André Sibomana, *Hope for Rwanda: Conversations with Laure Guilbert and Hervé Deguine* (London: Pluto Press, 1999).

53. Reyntjens, *Political Governance*, 255; Reyntjens quoted in Rachel Hayman, "Funding Fraud? Donors and Democracy in Rwanda," in Straus and Waldorf, *Remaking Rwanda*, 118.

54. Timothy Longman, "State, Civil Society, and Genocide in Rwanda," in *State, Conflict and Democracy in Africa*, ed. Richard Joseph (Boulder, CO: Lynne Rienner, 1999), 354; Reyntjens, *Political Governance*, 57; Mamdani, *When Victims Become Killers*, 271; Longman, *Memory and Justice*, 147.

55. Reyntjens, *Political Governance*, 127.

56. Ted Olsen, "Bowing to Kigali," *Christianity Today*, November 2007; interview with Paul Rusesabagina, Longwood University, Farmville, VA, February 24, 2010; "'Hotel Rwanda' Hero, Paul Rusesabagina, Is Held on Terrorism Charge," *New York Times*, August 31, 2020; Morgan Winsor, "Jailed Hero of 'Hotel Rwanda' Claims He Was Tortured at 'Slaughter House' after Arriving in Kigali," ABC News, May 25, 2021, https://abcnews.go.com/International/jailed-hero-hotel-rwanda-claims-tortured-slaughterhouse-arriving/story?id=77748884.

57. Thomson, *Rwanda*, 253; "The Road Out of Hell: Rwanda since the Genocide," *Economist*, 2004.

58. Author's field notes, Kigali, Rwanda, July 24, 2004.

59. Thomson, *Rwanda*, 240. Mihigo's song, accessible on YouTube, is titled "Igisobanuro Cy'urupfu" (The Meaning of Death) and calls upon Rwandans to honor all lives, Hutu and Tutsi, lost in the genocide.

60. Cyprian F. Fisiy, "Of Journeys and Border Crossings: Return of Refugees, Identity, and Reconstruction in Rwanda," *African Studies Review* 41, no. 1 (1998): 19; Villia Jefremovas, "Contested Identities: Power and the Fictions of Ethnicity, Ethnography and History in Rwanda," *Anthropologica* 39, nos. 1–2 (1997): 91–92; Pottier, *Re-Imagining Rwanda*, 116.

61. While the distinction between Hutu and Tutsi preexisted European intervention, the allegation that the West was guilty of failing to stop the genocide is valid. Extensive analysis and writings have demonstrated the unwillingness of the Clinton administration and the United Nations to intervene in Rwanda in the face of undeniable evidence that massive killings were taking place. For an insiders' view of the UN's response, see Michael N. Barnett, "The UN Security Council, Indifference, and Genocide in Rwanda," *Cultural Anthropology* 12, no. 4 (1997): 551–78. For a lengthier account, see Samantha Power, *"A Problem from Hell": America and the Age of Genocide* (New York: HarperCollins, 2003); or Roméo Dallaire, *Shake Hands with the Devil: The Failure of Humanity in Rwanda* (New York: Carroll & Graf, 2004); Pottier, *Re-Imagining Rwanda*, 118.

62. Reyntjens, *Political Governance*, 195n46; Pottier, *Re-Imagining Rwanda*, 117.

63. Otunnu, "Historical Analysis," 31–49; Chrétien, *Great Lakes*, 413n80.

64. Eugenia Zorbas, "Reconciliation in Post-genocide Rwanda," *African Journal of Legal Studies* 1, no. 1 (2004): 45, 43.

65. Elizabeth Sidiropoulos, "Democratisation and Militarisation in Rwanda: Eight Years after the Genocide," *African Security Review* 11, no. 3 (2002): 5; Prunier, *Africa's World War*, 372n55, 435n75.

66. D. Newbury, "Augustinian Models," 21.

67. Longman, *Christianity and Genocide*, 55.

68. Author's field notes, Rwanda, 2007.

69. Longman, *Memory and Justice*, 84; Reyntjens, "Rwanda, Ten Years On," 194.

70. Terry Pickard, *Combat Medic: An Eyewitness Account of the Kibeho Massacre* (Wavel Heights: Big Sky, 2010), 81.

71. Lemarchand, "Genocide in the Great Lakes," 8; Reyntjens, "Rwanda, Ten Years On," 195–96.

72. Reyntjens, "Rwanda, Ten Years On," 190n51.

73. Elisabeth King, "Memory Controversies in Post-Genocide Rwanda: Implications for Peacebuilding," *Genocide Studies and Prevention: An International Journal* 5, no. 3 (2010): 304. Several works provide a more complete account of the RPF's actions in Congo, including Prunier, *Africa's World War*; Filip Reyntjens, *The Great African War: Congo, and Regional Geopolitics, 1996–2006* (Cambridge: Cambridge University Press, 2009); and Jason Stearns, *Dancing in the Glory of Monsters: The Collapse of Congo and the Great War in Africa* (New York: Public Affairs, 2011). Marie Beatrice Umutesi's *Surviving the Slaughter: The Ordeal of a Rwandan Refugee in Zaire* (Madison: University of Wisconsin Press, 2004) provides an excellent refugee perspective on the Congo crisis. For a scholarly analysis of Umutesi's work, placed in an academic context, see Phillip A. Cantrell, "Review Essay on *Surviving the Slaughter: The Ordeal of a Rwandan Refugee in Zaire*, by Marie Beatrice Umutesi, and *Accounting for Horror: Post-Genocide Debates in Rwanda*, by Nigel Eltringham," *Africa Today* 52, no. 1 (2005): 131–34.

74. Pottier, *Re-imagining Rwanda*, 47; Lemarchand, "Genocide in the Great Lakes," 3; Grace Mugabe, "Kagame Is Unique—Warren," *New Times* (Kigali), January 2006.

75. Bowen, "Genocide in Rwanda," 37–48; Schliesser, "From 'a Theology of Genocide,'" 6.

76. Longman, *Christianity and Genocide*, 113–14; Longman, "Church, Politics, and the Genocide," 175, 179. Longman uses the Kinyarwanda term *Barokore*, as opposed to *Balokole*, as it is known in Uganda, where the movement originated. Personal correspondence with Longman, January 17, 2011.

77. Danielle de Lame, "Mighty Secrets, Public Commensality, and the Crisis of Transparency: Rwanda through the Looking Glass," *Canadian Journal of African Studies* 38, no. 2 (2004): 303; Longman, *Christianity and Genocide*, 91–92, 195–96; author's field notes, Rwanda, 2007; Conway, "Righteous Hutu," 219.

78. Schliesser, "From 'a Theology of Genocide,'" 6.

79. Timothy C. Morgan, "Forgiveness 101," *Christianity Today*, April 2004; author's field notes, Ruhengeri, Rwanda, 2004.

80. Eltringham, *Accounting for Horror*, 76.

81. Author's field notes, Rwanda, June 2017.

82. Author's field notes, Gahini, Rwanda, June 19, 2007.

83. Interview with Onesphore Rwaje, author's field notes, Byumba, Rwanda, June 9, 2007.

84. Lars Waldorf, "Revisiting *Hotel Rwanda*: Genocide Ideology, Reconciliation and Rescuers," *Journal of Genocide Research* 11, no. 1 (2009): 104.

85. Bowen, "Genocide in Rwanda," 45.

86. Chukwuma Obidegwu, "Rwanda: The Search for Post-conflict Socio-economic Change, 1995–2001," World Bank Group, Africa Region Working Paper Series 59 (October 2003), 11; Martin, *Leisure and Society*, 42.

87. Paul Chilton, "The Role of Language in Human Conflict: Prolegomena to the Investigation of Language as a Factor in Conflict Causation and Resolution," *Current Issues in Language & Society* 4, no. 3 (1997): 177, 188, 183; Miles, "Hamites and Hebrews," 107.

88. Author's field notes, Gahini, Rwanda, June 2007; interview with Paul Rusesabagina, Longwood University, Farmville, VA, February 24, 2010.

89. Longman, *Memory and Justice*, 61–62; Christopher Taylor, "Kings or Presidents? War and the State in Pre- and Post-Genocidal Rwanda," *Social Analysis* 48, no. 1 (Spring 2004): 141; Chakravarty, "Navigating the Middle Ground," *African Affairs* 113, no. 451 (2014): 248. Taylor recounts in "Kings or Presidents?" a 2003 cartoon in the newspaper *Umuseso* that depicted Kagame as King Solomon holding a sword in one hand and a baby in the other, which represented the opposition party Mouvement Démocratique Républicain, intimating that only "King Kagame" can determine the political future.

90. Reyntjens, "Rwanda: Progress or Powder Keg?," 28; Paul Kagame, "Preface," in *After Genocide: Transitional Justice, Post-Conflict Reconstruction, and Reconciliation in Rwanda and Beyond*, ed. Phil Clark and Zachary Kaufman (London: Hurst, 2008), xxi–xxvi; Reyntjens, "Constructing the Truth," 4; Judi Rever, *In Praise of Blood: The Crimes of the Rwandan Patriotic Front* (New York: Random House, 2018); Kagame quoted in Thomson, *Rwanda*, 231; Rudahigwa quoted in Reyntjens, "(Re-)imagining

a Reluctant Post-genocide Society: The Rwandan Patriotic Front's Ideology and Practice," *Journal of Genocide Research* 18, no. 1 (2016): 65. Rever's book tends toward the sensational and is not without criticism. Written largely from private, confidential sources, her claims are difficult to verify. Still, her work demonstrates the hazards faced by critics of the RPF, even outside Rwanda.

91. Ryentjens, *Political Governance*, 254; Roger Bowen and Malachi Munyaneza, "Church & State," *Partners Together*, no. 287 (Summer 1995). Maquet viewed Rwanda as a feudal society in which the Tutsi were born to rule and Hutu to serve.

Conclusion

1. David Newbury, "The Historian as Human Rights Activist," in Straus and Waldorf, *Remaking Rwanda*, xxxvi.

2. I have firsthand experience with the "travel routine" in Rwanda and know many others who do as well.

3. Longman, *Memory and Justice*, 319; Reyntjens, *Political Governance*, xiii; Stefaan Marysse, An Ansoms, and Danny Cassimon, "The Aid 'Darlings' and 'Orphans' of the Great Lakes Region in Africa," *European Journal of Development Research* 19 (2007): 451. For more analysis on the role of Rwandan women during and after the genocide, see Jennie Burnet, *Genocide Lives in Us: Women, Memory, and Silence in Rwanda* (Madison: University of Wisconsin Press, 2012); or Sara E. Brown, "Female Perpetrators of the Rwandan Genocide," *International Feminist Journal of Politics* 16, no. 3 (2014): 448–469. While lacking in academic depth, see Patricia Crisafulli and Andrea Redmond, *Rwanda, Inc.: How a Devastated Nation Became an Economic Model for the Developing World* (New York: St. Martin's, 2012), for a glowing, business-oriented account of Rwanda's economic development since the genocide.

4. Reyntjens, *Political Governance*, xvi–xvii; Reyntjens, "Rwanda: Progress or Powder Keg?," 32.

5. Benjamin Chemouni, "Explaining the Design of the Rwandan Decentralization: Elite Vulnerability and the Territorial Repartition of Power," *Journal of Eastern African Studies* 8, no. 2 (2014): 255, 260n42; Jens Meierhenrich, "Topographies of Memory and Forgetting: The Transformation of *Lieux de Mémoire* in Rwanda," in Straus and Waldorf, *Remaking Rwanda*, 292; A. Durant-Lasserve, "Market-Driven Eviction Processes in Developing Country Cities: The Cases of Kigali in Rwanda and Phnom Penh in Cambodia," in *Informal Settlements: A Perpetual Challenge?*, ed. M. Huchzermeyer and A. Karam (Cape Town: University of Cape Town Press, 2006), 214–15; Ansoms, "Re-engineering Rural Society," 295; Thomson, *Whispering Truth to Power*, 134; Burnet, "Injustice of Local Justice," 186. One such example of an urban development apart from Kigali is the northeastern city of Nyagatare, designated after the genocide as a settlement town for Tutsi returnees. In 2002 the city's population was estimated at 8,500 people. Presently, the city claims more than 100,000, mostly as a result of the returnees.

6. An Ansoms, "Rwanda's Post-genocide Economic Reconstruction: The Mismatch between Elite Ambitions and Rural Realities," in Straus and Waldorf, *Remaking Rwanda*, 240; Reyntjens, "Rwanda: Progress or Powder Keg?," 29; Villia Jefremovas, *Brickyards to Graveyards: From Production to Genocide in Rwanda* (Albany: State University of New York Press, 2002), 125.

7. Chris Huggins, "Land Grabbing and Tenure Security in Post-genocide Rwanda," in *Losing Your Land: Dispossession in the Great Lakes*, ed. An Ansoms and Thea Hilhorst (Suffolk: James Corry Press, 2014), 149; Ansoms, "Rwanda's Post-genocide Economic Reconstruction," 246–47; Bert Ingelaere, "Do We Understand Life after Genocide? Center and Periphery in the Construction of Knowledge in Postgenocide Rwanda," *African Studies Review* 53, no. 1 (2010): 52. Huggins also documents extensive corruption in agricultural policies and rampant land-grabbing schemes in the countryside by high-level RPF officials.

8. Bert Ingelaere, "What's on a Peasant's Mind? Experiencing RPF State Reach and Overreach in Post-genocide Rwanda (2000–2010)," *Journal of Eastern African Studies* 8, no. 2 (2014): 220; Thomson, *Whispering Truth to Power*, 185. For a detailed analysis of the methods of state surveillance, see Andrea Purdeková, "'Even If I Am Not Here, There Are So Many Eyes': Surveillance and State Reach in Rwanda," *Journal of Modern African Studies* 49, no. 3 (2011): 475–97.

9. Thomson, *Whispering Truth to Power*, 185, 193; Reyntjens, *Political Governance*, 256.

10. Author's field notes, Rwanda, 2004 and 2007.

11. Author's field notes, Byumba, 2007; Bowen, "Genocide in Rwanda," 45; author's field notes, Rwanda, 2004 and 2007.

12. Andrea Purdeková, "'Mundane Sights' of Power: The History of Social Monitoring and Its Subversion in Rwanda," *African Studies Review* 59, no. 2 (2016): 69.

13. Reyntjens, *Political Governance*, 191; Thomson, *Rwanda*, 252–53, 185.

14. Reyntjens, *Political Governance*, 65, 68; Bert Ingelaere, "Peasants, Power, and Ethnicity: A Bottom-Up Perspective on Rwanda's Political Transition," *African Affairs* 109, no. 435 (2010): 292; Reyntjens, "Constructing the Truth," 28.

15. Danielle Beswick, "Managing Dissent in a Post-genocide Environment: The Challenge of Political Space in Rwanda," *Development and Change* 42, no. 2 (2010): 226–27; Silva-Leander, "On the Danger and Necessity," 1602, 1616.

16. Omer Bartov, *Erased: Vanishing Traces of Jewish Galicia in Present-Day Ukraine* (Princeton, NJ: Princeton University Press, 2007), 201; Chakravarty, "Navigating the Middle Ground," 253.

17. Marian Hodgkin, "Reconciliation in Rwanda: Education, History and the State," *Journal of International Affairs* 60, no. 1 (2006): 205, emphasis added; William Easterly, *The White Man's Burden: Why the West's Efforts to Aid the Rest Have Done So Much Ill and So Little Good* (New York: Penguin Books, 2006), 123. On this topic, see also Sarah Warshauer Freedman et al., "Teaching History after Identity-Based Conflicts: The Rwanda Experience," *Comparative Education Review* 52, no. 4 (2008): 663–90.

18. C. Newbury, "Ethnicity and the Politics," 7; Thomson, *Whispering Truth to Power*, 184.

19. Stef Vandeginste, "Governing Ethnicity after Genocide: Ethnic Amnesia in Rwanda versus Ethnic Power-Sharing in Burundi," *Journal of Eastern African Studies* 8, no. 2 (2014): 274, 266; David Newbury, "Understanding Genocide," *African Studies Review* 41, no. 1 (1998): 86.

20. D. Newbury, "Invention of Rwanda," 2; D. Newbury, "Understanding Genocide," 84; Diop, *Murambi*, 48; Freedman et al., "Confronting the Past," 259.

21. Guichaoua, *From War to Genocide*, 293; Vandeginste, "Governing Ethnicity," 266; "Reconciliation and Forgiveness," *Partners Together*, no. 288 (Autumn 1995): 3–4; Paul Gready, "Beyond 'You're with Us or against Us': Civil Society and Policymaking in Post-genocide Rwanda," in Straus and Waldorf, *Remaking Rwanda*, 87.

22. Rachel Hayman, "Abandoned Orphan Wayward Child: The United Kingdom and Belgium in Rwanda since 1994," *Journal of Eastern African Studies* 4, no. 2 (2010): 354; Reyntjens, *Political Governance*, 258.

23. Reyntjens, *Political Governance*, 257, 261, 254.

Bibliography

Periodicals

The Economist
Los Angeles Times
New Times (Kigali)
New York Times
Region Week
Washington Post

Unpublished Archival Sources

Cadbury Research Library, University of Birmingham, Birmingham, England.
  Church Missionary Outlook
  Church Missionary Society Papers
  General Secretary's Department, Minutes of Ruanda Council
  Mid-Africa Ministry Papers
  Mid-Africa Ministry News
  Partners Together: The Magazine of Mid-Africa Ministry
  Ruanda Notes
Cambridge Center for Christianity Worldwide, Cambridge University, Cambridge, England.
  John E. Church Papers
  Philippa Guillebaud Papers
Church Mission Society, Oxford, England.
  Crowther Library
Uganda Christian University Library, Archives Section, Mukono, Uganda.
  Archives of the Bishop of Uganda
Royal Museum for Central Africa, Tervuren, Belgium.

Published Primary Sources and Memoirs

Adeney, Harold. *Only One Weapon: Facing Difficulty and Danger with Christ in Rwanda.* London: Mission CMS, 1963.

Barham, E. L. *Ruanda: A Bird's Eye View.* London: Ruanda Mission of the Church Missionary Society, 1962.

Barham, E. L. *Rwanda, Burundi, Kigezi: A Look Ahead.* London: Ruanda Mission of the Church Missionary Society, 1965.

Bilindabagabo, Alexis, and Alan Nichols. *Rescued by Angels: The Story of Miracles during the Rwandan Genocide.* Durham, NC: Acorn Press, 2006.

Carr, Rosamond Halsey, and Ann Howard Halsey. *Land of a Thousand Hills: My Life in Rwanda.* New York: Penguin Books, 1999.

Church, Joe. *Awake, Uganda! The Story of Blazio Kigozi and His Vision of Revival.* Kampala, 1957.

Church, Joe. *Quest for the Highest: An Autobiographical Account of the East African Revival.* Exeter: Pasternoster, 1981.

Church, John C. T. "A Personal Experience of the Revival." In *East African Revival: History and Legacies*, edited by Kevin Ward and Emma Wild-Wood, 41–50. Farnham: Ashgate, 2012.

Ilibagiza, Immaculé. *Led by Faith: Rising from the Ashes of the Rwandan Genocide.* Carlsbad, CA: Hay House, 2008.

Ilibagiza, Immaculé. *Left to Tell: Discovering God amidst the Rwandan Holocaust.* Carlsbad, CA: Hay House, 2007.

Kolini, Emmanuel, and Philip Holmes. *Christ Walks Where Evil Reigned: Responding to the Rwandan Genocide.* Colorado Springs: Authentic, 2008.

Makower, Katharine. *Not a Gap Year but a Lifetime.* East Sussex: Apologia, 2008.

Ndizeye, Omar. *Life and Death in Nyamata: Memoir of a Young Boy in Rwanda's Darkest Hour.* Amsterdam: Amsterdam Publishers, 2020.

Osborn, H. H. *Fire in the Hills.* Crowborough: Highland, 1991.

Osborn, H. H. *Revival: A Precious Heritage.* Winchester: Apologia, 1995.

Rucyahana, John, and James Riordan. *The Bishop of Rwanda: Finding Forgiveness amidst a Pile of Bones.* Nashville: Thomas Nelson, 2007.

Sebarenzi, Joseph, and Laura Mullane. *God Sleeps in Rwanda: A Journey of Transformation.* New York: Atria Books, 2009.

Sibomana, André. *Hope for Rwanda: Conversations with Laure Guilbert and Hervé Deguine.* London: Pluto Press, 1999.

Smith, A. C. Stanley. *Road to Revival: The Story of the Ruanda Mission.* London: Church Missionary Society, 1946.

St. John, Patricia. *Breath of Life.* London: Norfolk Press, 1971.

Thomas, H. B., ed. "Kigezi Operations, 1914–1917." *Uganda Journal* 30, no. 2 (1966): 165–73.

Secondary Sources

Africa Research Bulletin (December 1–31, 2018).

African Rights. *Death, Defiance, and Despair.* Rev. ed. London: African Rights, 1995.

Anderson, Allan H. "The Newer Pentecostal and Charismatic Churches: The Shape of Future Christianity in Africa?" *Journal of the Society for Pentecostal Studies* 24, no. 2 (Fall 2002): 167–84.

André, Catherine, and Jean-Philippe Platteau. "Land Relations under Unbearable Stress: Rwanda Caught in the Malthusian Trap." *Journal of Economic Behavior & Organization* 34 (1998): 1–47.

Ansoms, An. "Re-engineering Rural Society: The Visions and Ambitions of the Rwandan Elite." *African Affairs* 108, no. 431 (2009): 289–309.

Ansoms, An. "Rwanda's Post-genocide Economic Reconstruction: The Mismatch between Elite Ambitions and Rural Realities." In *Remaking Rwanda: State Building and Human Rights after Mass Violence*, edited by Scott Straus and Lars Waldorf, 240–51. Madison: University of Wisconsin Press, 2011.

Arnaut, Karel, and Hein Vanhee. "History Facing the Present: An Interview with Jan Vansina." In *Annexe 1: Interview avec Jan Vansina, par Karel Arnaut et Hain Vanhee en 2001. Inventaire des archives de Jan Vansina, 1929–2017*, 1–30. Tervuren: Koninklijk Museum voor Midden-Afrika, 2018.

Barnett, Michael N. "The UN Security Council, Indifference, and Genocide in Rwanda." *Cultural Anthropology* 12, no. 4 (1997): 551–78.

Bartov, Omer. *Erased: Vanishing Traces of Jewish Galicia in Present-Day Ukraine.* Princeton, NJ: Princeton University Press, 2007.

Bauer, John. *2000 Years of Christianity in Africa: An African Church History.* Nairobi: Pauline Publications Africa, 1994.

Bessell, M. J. "Nyabingi." *Uganda Journal: The Organ of the Uganda Society* 6, no. 2 (October 1938): 73–86.

Beswick, Danielle. "Managing Dissent in a Post-genocide Environment: The Challenge of Political Space in Rwanda." *Development and Change* 42, no. 2 (2010): 225–51.

Botte, Roger. "Rwanda and Burundi, 1889–1930: Chronology of a Slow Assassination, Part 2." *International Journal of African Historical Studies* 18, no. 2 (1985): 289–314.

Bowen, Roger W. "Genocide in Rwanda 1994—An Anglican Perspective." In *Genocide in Rwanda: Complicity of the Churches?*, edited by Carol Rittner, John K. Roth, and Wendy Whitworth, 37–48. St. Paul: Aegis, 2004.

Brown, David. *Contemporary Nationalism: Civic, Ethnocultural and Multicultural Politics.* London: Routledge, 2000.

Brown, Sara E. "Female Perpetrators of the Rwandan Genocide." *International Feminist Journal of Politics* 16, no. 3 (2014): 448–69.

Buckley-Zistel, Catherine. "Remembering to Forget: Chosen Amnesia as a Strategy for Local Coexistence in Post-genocide Rwanda." *Africa* 76, no. 2 (2006): 131–50.

Burnet, Jennie. *Genocide Lives in Us: Women, Memory, and Silence in Rwanda.* Madison: University of Wisconsin Press, 2012.

Burnet, Jennie. "The Injustice of Local Justice: Truth, Reconciliation, and Revenge in Rwanda." *Genocide Studies and Prevention* 3, no. 2 (August 2008): 173–93.

Buscaglia, Ilaria, and Shirley Randell. "Legacy of Colonialism in the Empowerment of Women in Rwanda." *Cosmopolitan Civil Societies Journal* 4, no. 1 (2012): 69–85.

Cantrell, Phillip A. "The Anglican Church of Rwanda: Domestic Agendas and International Linkages." *Journal of Modern African Studies* 45, no. 3 (2007): 333–45.

Cantrell, Phillip A. "Reconciliation in Post-genocide Rwanda as Presented in the Film *As We Forgive*." In *The Rwandan Genocide on Film: Critical Essays and Interviews*, edited by Matthew Edwards, 109–18. Jefferson, NC: McFarland, 2018.

Cantrell, Phillip A. "Review Essay on *Surviving the Slaughter: The Ordeal of a Rwandan Refugee in Zaire*, by Marie Beatrice Umutesi, and *Accounting for Horror: Postgenocide Debates in Rwanda*, by Nigel Eltringham." *Africa Today* 52, no. 1 (2005): 131–34.

Cantrell, Phillip A. "'We Were a Chosen People': The East African Revival and Its Return to Post-genocide Rwanda." *Church History* 83, no. 2 (2014): 1–24.

Carney, J. J. *Rwanda before the Genocide: Catholic Politics and Ethnic Discourse in the Late Colonial Era.* Oxford: Oxford University Press, 2014.

Chakravarty, Anuradha. "Navigating the Middle Ground: The Political Values of Ordinary Hutu in Post-genocide Rwanda." *African Affairs* 113, no. 451 (2014): 232–53.

Chemouni, Benjamin. "Explaining the Design of the Rwandan Decentralization: Elite Vulnerability and the Territorial Repartition of Power." *Journal of Eastern African Studies* 8, no. 2 (2014): 246–62.

Chilton, Paul. "The Role of Language in Human Conflict: Prolegomena to the Investigation of Language as a Factor in Conflict Causation and Resolution." *Current Issues in Language & Society* 4, no. 3 (1997): 174–89.

Chrétien, Jean-Pierre. *The Great Lakes of Africa: Two Thousand Years of History.* Translated by Scott Straus. New York: Zone Books, 2003.

Chrétien, Jean-Pierre. "Les deux visages de cham." In *L'Idée de race dans la pensée politique française contemporaiene*, edited by Pierre Guiral and Emile Témime, 171–99. Paris: Editions du Centre National de la Recherche Scientifique, 1977.

Clark, Phil. "Bringing the Rwandans Back In, Again: State, Power, and Local Agency in Rwanda's Gacaca Courts." *Journal of Eastern African Studies* 8, no. 2 (2014): 193–213.

Clark, Phil, and Zachary Kaufman, eds. *After Genocide: Transitional Justice, Postconflict Reconstruction, and Reconciliation in Rwanda and Beyond.* London: Hurst, 2008.

Codere, Helen. *The Biography of an African Society, Rwanda 1900–1960: Based on Forty-Eight Rwandan Biographies.* Tervuren: Koninklijk Museum voor Midden-Afrika, 1973.

Combres, Élisabeth. *Broken Memory: A Novel of Rwanda.* Toronto: Groundwood Books, 2011.

Conway, Paul. "Righteous Hutu: Can Stories of Courageous Rescuers Help in Rwanda's Reconciliation Process?" *International Journal of Sociology and Anthropology* 3, no. 7 (2011): 217–23.

Court, Anthony. "The Christian Churches, the State, and Genocide in Rwanda." *Missionalia* 44, no. 1 (2016): 50–67.

Courtemanche, Gil. *A Sunday at the Pool in Kigali.* New York: Vintage Books, 2003.

Crisafulli, Patricia, and Andrea Redmond. *Rwanda, Inc.: How a Devastated Nation Became an Economic Model for the Developing World.* New York: St. Martin's, 2012.

Dallaire, Roméo. *Shake Hands with the Devil: The Failure of Humanity in Rwanda.* New York: Carroll & Graf, 2004.

Davin, Anna. "Imperialism and Motherhood." *History Workshop Journal* 5, no. 5 (1978): 9–65.

Davis, Mike, *Late Victorian Holocausts: El Niño Famines and the Making of the Third World*. London: Verso, 2001.

de Lacger, Louis. *Le Ruanda*. 2nd ed. Kabgayi: Imprimérie de Kabgayi, 1959.

de Lame, Danielle. *A Hill among a Thousand: Transformations and Ruptures in Rural Rwanda*. Madison: University of Wisconsin Press, 2005.

de Lame, Danielle. "Mighty Secrets, Public Commensality, and the Crisis of Transparency: Rwanda through the Looking Glass." *Canadian Journal of African Studies* 38, no. 2 (2004): 279–317.

Des Forges, Alison Liebhafsky. *Defeat Is the Only Bad News: Rwanda under Musinga, 1896–1931*. Edited by David Newbury. Madison: University of Wisconsin Press, 2011.

Des Forges, Alison Liebhafsky. *Leave None to Tell the Story: Genocide in Rwanda*. New York: Human Rights Watch, 1999.

de Waal, Alex, and Rakiya Omaar. *Rwanda: Death and Despair*. London: African Rights, 1995.

d'Hartefelt, Marcel, and Danielle de Lame, eds. *Société, culture et histoire du Rwanda: Encyclopédie bibliographique, 1863–1980/1887*. 2 vols. Tervuren: Koninklijk Museum voor Midden-Afrika, 1987.

Diamond, Jared. *Collapse: How Societies Choose to Fail or Succeed*. New York: Penguin Books, 2005.

Diop, Boubacar Boris. *Murambi, The Book of Bones*. Bloomington: Indiana University Press, 2000.

Dorsey, Learthen. *Historical Dictionary of Rwanda*. London: Scarecrow, 1994.

Dorsey, Learthen. "The Rwandan Colonial Economy, 1916–1941." PhD diss., Michigan State University, 1983.

Durant-Lasserve, A. "Market-Driven Eviction Processes in Developing Country Cities: The Cases of Kigali in Rwanda and Phnom Penh in Cambodia." In *Informal Settlements: A Perpetual Challenge?*, edited by M. Huchzermeyer and A. Karam, 207–30. Cape Town: University of Cape Town Press, 2006.

Easterly, William. *The White Man's Burden: Why the West's Efforts to Aid the Rest Have Done So Much Ill and So Little Good*. New York: Penguin Books, 2006.

Edel, May. *The Chiga of Western Uganda*. London: Routledge, 2018.

Eltringham, Nigel. *Accounting for Horror: Post-genocide Debates in Rwanda*. London: Pluto Press, 2004.

Epprecht, Marc. *Hungochani: The History of a Dissident Sexuality in Southern Africa*. Montreal: McGill-Queen's University Press, 2004.

Fegley, Randall. *A History of Rwandan Identity and Trauma: The Mythmakers' Victims*. Lanham, MD: Lexington Books, 2016.

Fisiy, Cyprian F. "Of Journeys and Border Crossings: Return of Refugees, Identity, and Reconstruction in Rwanda." *African Studies Review* 41, no. 1 (1998): 17–28.

Freedman, Sarah Warshauer, Déo Kambanda, Beth Lewis Samuelson, Innocent Mugisha, Immaculée Mukashema, Evode Mukama, Jean Mutabaruka, Harvey M. Weinstein, and Timothy Longman. "Confronting the Past in Rwandan Schools." In *My Neighbor, My Enemy: Justice and Community in the Aftermath of Mass Atrocity*, edited by Eric Stover and Harvey Weinstein, 248–64. Cambridge: Cambridge University Press, 2004.

Freedman, Sarah Warshauer, Harvey M. Weinstein, Karen Murphy, and Timothy Longman. "Teaching History after Identity-Based Conflicts: The Rwanda Experience." *Comparative Education Review* 52, no. 4 (2008): 663–90.

Gatwa, Tharcisse. *The Churches and Ethnic Ideology in the Rwandan Crises, 1900–1994.* Milton Keynes: Paternoster Press, 2005.

Gille, A. "Sandrart (Georges Victor)." In *Biographie Belge d'Outre-Mer*, VII, *Fascicule B*, 335. Brussels: Académie Royale des Sciences D'Outre-Mer, 1977.

Gourevitch, Philip. *We Wish to Inform You That Tomorrow We Will All Be Killed with Our Families: Stories from Rwanda.* New York: St. Martin's, 1998.

Gready, Paul. "Beyond 'You're with Us or against Us': Civil Society and Policymaking in Post-genocide Rwanda." In *Remaking Rwanda: State Building and Human Rights after Mass Violence*, edited by Scott Straus and Lars Waldorf, 87–100. Madison: University of Wisconsin Press, 2011.

Groves, C. P. *The Planting of Christianity in Africa.* Vol. 3, *1878–1914.* Cambridge: Lutterworth Press, 1956.

Guichaoua, André. *From War to Genocide: Criminal Politics in Rwanda, 1990–1994.* Madison: University of Wisconsin Press, 2015.

Hassett, Miranda K. *Anglican Communion in Crisis: How Episcopal Dissidents and Their African Allies Are Reshaping Anglicanism.* Princeton, NJ: Princeton University Press, 2007.

Hastings, Adrian. *The Church in Africa: 1450–1950.* Oxford: Clarendon, 1994.

Hayman, Rachel. "Abandoned Orphan Wayward Child: The United Kingdom and Belgium in Rwanda since 1994." *Journal of Eastern African Studies* 4, no. 2 (2010): 341–60.

Hayman, Rachel. "Funding Fraud? Donors and Democracy in Rwanda." In *Remaking Rwanda: State Building and Human Rights after Mass Violence*, edited by Scott Straus and Lars Waldorf, 118–31. Madison: University of Wisconsin Press, 2011.

Heremans, Roger, and Emmanueal Ntezimana. *Journal de la Mission de Save.* Ruhengeri: Editions Universitaires du Rwanda, 1987.

Hewitt, Gordon. *The Problems of Success: A History of the Church Missionary Society, 1910–1942.* Vol. 1. London: SCM Press, 1977.

Hintjens, Helen. "Explaining the 1994 Genocide in Rwanda." *Journal of African History* 37, no. 2 (1999): 241–86.

Hintjens, Helen. "Post-genocide Identity Politics in Rwanda." *Ethnicities* 8, no. 1 (2008): 5–41.

Hochschild, Adam. *King Leopold's Ghost: A Story of Greed, Terror, and Heroism in Central Africa.* New York: Houghton Mifflin, 1999.

Hodgkin, Marian. "Reconciliation in Rwanda: Education, History and the State." *Journal of International Affairs* 60, no. 1 (2006): 199–210.

Hopkins, Elizabeth. "The Nyabingi Cult of Southwestern Uganda." In *Protest and Power in Black Africa*, edited by Robert I. Rotberg and Ali A. Mazrui, 258–336. New York: Oxford University Press, 1970.

Huggins, Chris. "Land Grabbing and Tenure Security in Post-genocide Rwanda." In *Losing Your Land: Dispossession in the Great Lakes*, edited by An Ansoms and Thea Hilhorst, 141–62. Suffolk: James Corry Press, 2014.

Ingelaere, Bert. "Do We Understand Life after Genocide? Center and Periphery in the Construction of Knowledge in Postgenocide Rwanda." *African Studies Review* 53, no. 1 (2010): 41–59.

Ingelaere, Bert. "Peasants, Power, and Ethnicity: A Bottom-Up Perspective on Rwanda's Political Transition." *African Affairs* 109, no. 435 (2010): 273–92.

Ingelaere, Bert. "What's on a Peasant's Mind? Experiencing RPF State Reach and Overreach in Post-genocide Rwanda (2000–2010)." *Journal of Eastern African Studies* 8, no. 2 (2014): 214–30.

Irvine, Cecilia. "The Birth of the Kimbanguist Movement in the Bas-Zaire 1921." *Journal of Religion in Africa* 6, no. 1 (1974): 23–76.

Jefremovas, Villia. *Brickyards to Graveyards: From Production to Genocide in Rwanda.* Albany: State University of New York Press, 2002.

Jefremovas, Villia. "Contested Identities: Power and the Fictions of Ethnicity, Ethnography and History in Rwanda." *Anthropologica* 39, nos. 1–2 (1997): 91–104.

Jefremovas, Villia. "Loose Women, Virtuous Wives, and Timid Virgins: Gender and the Control of Resources in Rwanda." *Canadian Journal of African Studies* 25, no. 3 (1991): 378–95.

Jenkins, Philip. *The Next Christendom: The Coming of Global Christianity.* Oxford: Oxford University Press, 2002.

Jones, Bruce D. "The Arusha Peace Process." In *The Path of a Genocide: The Rwanda Crisis from Uganda to Zaire*, edited by Howard Adelman and Astri Suhrke, 131–56. Piscataway, NJ: Transaction, 1999.

Jones, Bruce D. *Peacekeeping in Rwanda: The Dynamics of Failure.* Boulder, CO: Lynne Rienner, 2001.

Jowell, Marco. "Cohesion through Socialization: Liberation, Tradition and Modernity in the Forging of the Rwandan Defense Force (RDF)." *Journal of Eastern African Studies* 8, no. 2 (2014): 278–93.

Kabanda, Marcel. "Rwanda: The Catholic Church and the Crisis. Autopsy of a Legacy." In *The Recurring Great Lakes Crisis: Identity, Violence, and Power*, edited by Jean-Pierre Chrétien and Richard Banégas, 61–98. New York: Columbia University Press, 2011.

Kagame, Alexis. *Les organisations socio-familiales de l'ancien Rwanda.* Brussels: Académie Royale des Sciences Coloniales, 1954.

Katarikawe, James. *The East African Revival.* Delaware: Lydia Murungi, 2004.

King, Elisabeth. *From Classrooms to Conflict in Rwanda.* Cambridge: Cambridge University Press, 2015.

King, Elisabeth. "Memory Controversies in Post-genocide Rwanda: Implications for Peacebuilding." *Genocide Studies and Prevention: An International Journal* 5, no. 3 (2010): 293–309.

Kinzer, Stephen. *A Thousand Hills: Rwanda's Rebirth and the Man Who Dreamed It.* Hoboken, NJ: John Wiley and Sons, 2008.

Kolini, Emmanuel. "Cheap Evangelism." *Christianity Today*, January 1996.

Kolini, Emmanuel. "A Tutsi's Hope: A Zairean Bishop Wants American Christians to Remember the Struggles of the Church in East Africa." *Christianity Today*, April 1997.

Kubai, Anne. *Being Church in Post-genocide Rwanda: The Challenges of Forgiveness and Reconciliation*. Uppsala: Life and Peace Institute, 2005.

Kubai, Anne. "Post-genocide Rwanda: The Changing Religious Landscape." *Exchange* 36, no. 2 (2007): 198–214.

Kubai, Anne. "Walking a Tightrope: Christians and Muslims in Post-genocide Rwanda." *Islam and Christian-Muslim Relations* 18, no. 2 (2007): 219–35.

Kuperman, Alan J. "Provoking Genocide: A Revised History of the Rwandan Patriotic Front." *Journal of Genocide Research* 6, no. 1 (2004): 61–84.

Lemarchand, René. "Genocide in the Great Lakes: Which Genocide? Whose Genocide?" *African Studies Review* 41, no. 1 (April 1998): 3–16.

Lemarchand, René. *Rwanda and Burundi*. New York: Praeger, 1970.

Linden, Ian, and Jane Linden. *Church and Revolution in Rwanda*. New York: Africana, 1977.

Lindsay, Lisa, and Stephan Miescher, eds. *Men and Masculinities in Modern Africa*. Portsmouth, NH: Heineman, 2003.

Lischer, Sarah Kenyon. "Civil War, Genocide, and Political Order in Rwanda: Security Implications of Refugee Return." *Conflict, Security and Development* 11, no. 3 (July 2011): 261–84.

Longman, Timothy. "An Assessment of Rwanda's Gacaca Courts." *Peace Review: A Journal of Social Justice* 21, no. 3 (2009): 304–12.

Longman, Timothy. *Christianity and Genocide in Rwanda*. Cambridge: Cambridge University Press, 2010.

Longman, Timothy. "Church, Politics, and the Genocide in Rwanda." *Journal of Religion in Africa* 31, no. 2 (2001): 163–86.

Longman, Timothy. *Memory and Justice in Post-genocide Rwanda*. Cambridge: Cambridge University Press, 2017.

Longman, Timothy. "State, Civil Society, and Genocide in Rwanda." In *State, Conflict and Democracy in Africa*, edited by Richard Joseph, 339–58. Boulder, CO: Lynne Rienner, 1999.

Longman, Timothy. "Trying Times for Rwanda: Reevaluating Gacaca Courts in Post-genocide Reconciliation." *Harvard International Review* 32, no. 2 (2010): 48–52.

MacMaster, Richard, and Donald R. Jacobs. *A Gentle Wind of God: The Influence of the East African Revival*. Scottsdale, AZ: Herald Press, 2006.

Maddox, Gregory. "African Theology and the Search for the Universal." In *East African Expressions of Christianity*, edited by Thomas Spear and Isaria N. Kimambo, 25–36. Athens: Ohio University Press, 1999.

Malkki, Liisa. *Purity and Exile: Violence, Memory, and National Cosmology among Hutu Refugees in Tanzania*. Chicago: University of Chicago Press, 1995.

Mamdani, Mahmood. *When Victims Become Killers: Colonialism, Nativism, and the Genocide in Rwanda*. Princeton, NJ: Princeton University Press, 2001.

Maquet, J. J. *The Premise of Inequality in Rwanda: A Study of Political Relations in a Central African Kingdom*. London: Oxford University Press, 1961.

Markowitz, Marvin D. *Cross and Sword: The Political Role of Christian Missions in the Belgian Congo, 1908–1960*. Stanford, CA: Stanford University Press, 1973.

Martin, Phyllis M. *Leisure and Society in Colonial Brazzaville*. Cambridge: Cambridge University Press, 1995.

Marysse, Stefaan, An Ansoms, and Danny Cassimon. "The Aid 'Darlings' and 'Orphans' of the Great Lakes Region in Africa." *European Journal of Development Research* 19 (2007): 433–58.

May, John F. "Policies on Population, Land Use, and Environment in Rwanda." *Population and Environment* 16, no. 4 (March 1995): 321–34.

Mbanda, Laurent. *Committed to Conflict: The Destruction of the Church in Rwanda.* London: Society for Promoting Christian Knowledge, 1997.

Meierhenrich, Jens. "Topographies of Memory and Forgetting: The Transformation of *Lieux de Mémoire* in Rwanda." In *Remaking Rwanda: State Building and Human Rights after Mass Violence*, edited by Scott Straus and Lars Waldorf, 283–96. Madison: University of Wisconsin Press, 2011.

Miles, William F. S. "Hamites and Hebrews: Problems in 'Judaizing' the Rwandan Genocide." *Journal of Genocide Research* 2, no. 1 (2000): 107–15.

Millard, Mary Weeks. *Emmanuel Kolini: The Unlikely Archbishop of Rwanda.* Colorado Springs: Authentic, 2008.

Morgan, Timothy C. "Purpose Driven in Rwanda." *Christianity Today*, September 2005.

Morgan, Timothy C. "Forgiveness 101." *Christianity Today*, April 2004.

Mugabe, Grace. "Kagame Is Unique—Warren." *New Times* (Kigali), January 2006.

Nahimana, Ferdinand. *Le blanc est arrivé, le roi est parti.* Kigali: Printer Set, 1987.

Newbury, Catharine. *The Cohesion of Oppression: Clientship and Ethnicity in Rwanda, 1860–1960.* New York: Columbia University Press, 1988.

Newbury, Catharine. "Ethnicity and the Politics of History in Rwanda." *Africa Today* 45, no. 1 (1998): 7–24.

Newbury, Catharine. "Rwanda: Recent Debates over Governance and Rural Development." In *Governance and Politics in Africa*, edited by Goran Hyden and Michael Bratton, 193–220. Boulder, CO: Lynne Rienner, 1992.

Newbury, Catharine. "*Ubureetwa* and *Thangata*: Catalysts to Peasant Political Consciousness in Rwanda and Malawi." *Canadian Journal of African Studies* 14, no. 1 (1980): 97–111.

Newbury, David. "Augustinian Models in Rwanda: Religious Movements and Political Transformations." *Kyrkan och krisen i central afrika. SMT: Svensk Missionstidskrift* 83, no. 3 (1995): 16–34.

Newbury, David. "Canonical Conventions in Rwanda: Four Myths of Recent Historiography in Central Africa." *History in Africa* 39 (2012): 41–76.

Newbury, David. "The Historian as Human Rights Activist." In *Remaking Rwanda: State Building and Human Rights after Mass Violence*, edited by Scott Straus and Lars Waldorf, xxvii–xxxix. Madison: University of Wisconsin Press, 2011.

Newbury, David. "The Invention of Rwanda: The Alchemy of Ethnicity." Paper presented at the African Studies Association Annual Meeting, Orlando, FL, 1995.

Newbury, David. "Jan Vansina—In Memory." Provided to the author by David Newbury.

Newbury, David. *King and Clans: Ijwi Island and the Lake Kivu Rift, 1780–1840.* Madison: University of Wisconsin Press, 1991.

Newbury, David. *The Land beyond the Mists: Essays on Identity and Authority in Precolonial Congo and Rwanda.* Athens: Ohio University Press, 2009.

Newbury, David. "Multiple Missionary Histories in Rwanda: Local Agency and Institutional Agendas." In *Lives in Motion, Indeed: Interdisciplinary Perspectives on Social Change*, edited by Christiana Panella, 159–89. Tervuren: Koninklijk Museum voor Midden-Afrika, 2012.

Newbury, David. "Precolonial Burundi and Rwanda: Local Loyalties, Regional Royalties." *International Journal of African Historical Studies* 34, no. 2 (2001): 255–314.

Newbury, David. "Returning Refugees: Four Historical Patterns of 'Coming Home' to Rwanda." *Comparative Studies in Society and History* 47, no. 2 (2005): 252–85.

Newbury, David. "The Rwakayihura Famine of 1928–1929: A Nexus of Colonial Rule in Rwanda." In *Historie Sociale de Afrique de l'Est*, 269–77. Paris: Karthala, 1991.

Newbury, David. "Trick Cyclists? Recontextualizing Rwandan Dynastic Chronology." *History in Africa* 21 (1994): 191–217.

Newbury, David. "Understanding Genocide." *African Studies Review* 41, no. 1 (1998): 73–97.

Newhouse, Catherine. "Pentecostal Renewal Transforms Rwanda after Genocide." *Christianity Today*, January 2012.

Ntezimana, Emmanuel. "Kinyamateka, temps nouveaux d'Afrique et l'évolution sociopolitique du Rwanda (1954–1959)." *Études Rwandaises*, special issue (March 1978): 1–29.

Nthamburi, Zablon. *From Mission to Church: A Handbook of Christianity in East Africa*. Nairobi: Uzima Press, 1995.

Nyirubugara, Olivier. *Novels of Genocide: Remembering and Forgetting the Ethnic Other in Fictional Rwanda*. Memory Traps 2. Leiden: Sidestone Press, 2017.

Obidegwu, Chukwuma. "Rwanda: The Search for Post-conflict Socio-economic change, 1995–2001." World Bank Group, Africa Region Working Paper Series 59 (October 2003): 1–53.

Olsen, Ted. "Bowing to Kigali." *Christianity Today*, November 2007.

Olson, Jennifer. "Behind the Recent Tragedy in Rwanda." *GeoJournal* 35, no. 2 (1995): 217–22.

Otunnu, Ogenga. "An Historical Analysis of the Invasion by the Rwandan Patriotic Army (RPA)." In *The Path of a Genocide: The Rwanda Crisis from Uganda to Zaire*, edited by Howard Adelman and Astri Suhrke, 31–49. Piscataway, NJ: Transaction, 1999.

Otunnu, Ogenga. "Rwandese Refugees and Immigrants in Uganda." In *Path of a Genocide: The Rwanda Crisis from Uganda to Zaire*, edited by Howard Adelman and Astri Suhrke, 3–29. Piscataway, NJ: Transaction, 2000.

Parkes, Colin Murray. "Genocide in Rwanda: Personal Reflections." *Mortality* 1, no. 1 (1996): 95–110.

Peterson, Derek R. "Revivalism and Dissent in Colonial East Africa." In *East African Revival: History and Legacies*, edited by Kevin Ward and Emma Wild-Wood, 105–18. Farnham: Ashgate, 2012.

Pickard, Terry. *Combat Medic: An Eyewitness Account of the Kibeho Massacre*. Wavel Heights: Big Sky, 2010.

Pottier, Johan. *Re-imagining Rwanda: Conflict, Survival and Disinformation in the Late Twentieth Century*. Cambridge: Cambridge University Press, 2002.

Power, Samantha. *"A Problem from Hell": America and the Age of Genocide*. New York: HarperCollins, 2003.

Bibliography 207

Presler, Titus. "The History of Mission in the Anglican Communion." In *Wiley-Blackwell Companion to the Anglican Communion*, edited by Ian S. Markham et al., 15–32. West Sussex: John Wiley & Sons, 2013.

Prunier, Gérard. *Africa's World War: Congo, the Rwanda Genocide, and the Making of Continental Catastrophe.* Oxford: Oxford University Press, 2009.

Prunier, Gérard. *The Rwanda Crisis: History of a Genocide.* New York: Columbia University Press, 1995.

Purdeková, Andrea. "'Even If I Am Not Here, There Are So Many Eyes': Surveillance and State Reach in Rwanda." *Journal of Modern African Studies* 49, no. 3 (2011): 475–97.

Purdeková, Andrea. "'Mundane Sights' of Power: The History of Social Monitoring and its Subversion in Rwanda." *African Studies Review* 59, no. 2 (2016): 59–86.

Rawson, David. *Prelude to Genocide: Arusha, Rwanda, and The Failure of Diplomacy.* Athens: Ohio University Press, 2018.

Rever, Judi. *In Praise of Blood: The Crimes of the Rwandan Patriotic Front.* New York: Random House, 2018.

Reydams, Luc. "Politics or Pragmatism? The International Criminal Tribunal for Rwanda and the Burying of the Investigation into the Assassination of President Juvénal Habyarimana." *Human Rights Quarterly* 40, no. 4 (November 2018): 989–1013.

Reyntjens, Filip. "Constructing the Truth, Dealing with Dissent, Domesticating the World: Governance in Post-genocide Rwanda." *African Affairs* 110, no. 438 (2010): 8–9.

Reyntjens, Filip. *The Great African War: Congo and Regional Geopolitics, 1996–2006.* Cambridge: Cambridge University Press, 2009.

Reyntjens, Filip. *Political Governance in Post-genocide Rwanda.* Cambridge: Cambridge University Press, 2013.

Reyntjens, Filip. "(Re-)imagining a Reluctant Post-genocide Society: The Rwandan Patriotic Front's Ideology and Practice." *Journal of Genocide Research* 18, no. 1 (2016): 61–81.

Reyntjens, Filip. "Rwanda: Progress or Powder Keg?" *Journal of Democracy* 26, no. 3 (2015): 19–33.

Reyntjens, Filip. "Rwanda, Ten Years On: From Genocide to Dictatorship." *African Affairs* 103, no. 411 (2004): 177–210.

Rittner, Carol. "Chronology." In *Genocide in Rwanda, Complicity of the Churches?*, edited by Carol Rittner, John K. Roth, and Wendy Whitworth, 5–21. St. Paul: Aegis, 2004.

Robbins, Catherine Ellen. "Tukutendereza: A Study of Social Change and Sectarian Withdrawal in the Balokole Revival of Uganda." PhD diss., Columbia University, 1975.

Ross, Bobby, Jr. "Out of Africa: What AMIA's Exodus from Rwanda Portends for Global Christianity." *Christianity Today*, December 2011.

Rugasara, Frank K. *Resilience of a Nation: A History of the Military in Rwanda.* Kampala: Fountain, 2009.

Rwabukumba, Joseph, and Vincent Mudandagizi. "Les formes historiques de la dépendance personnelle dans l'État rwandais." *Cahiers d'études africaines* 14, no. 53 (1974): 6–25.

Sanders, Edith R. "The Hamitic Hypothesis: Its Origin and Functions in Time Perspective." *Journal of African History* 10, no. 4 (1969): 521–32.

Schliesser, Christine. "From 'a Theology of Genocide' to a 'Theology of Reconciliation'? On the Role of Christian Churches in the Nexus of Religion and Genocide in Rwanda." *Religions* 9, no. 34 (2018): 1–14.

Schoenbrun, David L. "Cattle Herds and Banana Gardens: The Historical Geography of the West Great Lakes Region, ca AD 800–1500." *African Archaeological Review* 11, no. 1 (1993): 39–72.

Schoenbrun, David L. *A Green Place, A Good Place: Agrarian Change and Social Identity in the Great Lakes Region to the 15th Century.* Portsmouth, NH: Heinemann, 1994.

Sebarenzi, Joseph. "Justice and Humans Rights for all Rwandans." In *Remaking Rwanda: State Building and Human Rights after Mass Violence*, edited by Scott Straus and Lars Waldorf, 343–53. Madison: University of Wisconsin Press, 2011.

Seligman, Charles Gabriel. *Races of Africa.* Oxford: Oxford University Press, 1930.

Shank, David A. "The Legacy of William Wadé Harris." *International Bulletin of Missionary Research* 10, no. 4 (1986): 170–76.

Sidiropoulos, Elizabeth. "Democratisation and Militarisation in Rwanda: Eight Years after the Genocide." *African Security Review* 11, no. 3 (2002): 77–87.

Silva-Leander, Sebastian. "On the Danger and Necessity of Democratisation: Trade-Offs between Short-Term Stability and Long-Term Peace in Post-genocide Rwanda." *Third World Quarterly* 29, no. 8 (2008): 1601–20.

Smith, Stephen W. "Rwanda in Six Scenes." *London Review of Books* 33, no. 6 (2011): 3–8.

Spear, Thomas. "Towards the History of African Christianity." In *East African Expressions of Christianity*, edited by Thomas Spear and Isaria N. Kimambo, 3–24. Athens: Ohio University Press, 1999.

Speke, John Hanning. *Journal of the Discovery of the Source of the Nile.* 1969. Reprint, London: J. M. Dent & Sons, 1975.

Ssebalugga, John. "The African Cross-Bearers." *Touchstone: A Journal of Mere Christianity*, October 2003.

Stearns, Jason. *Dancing in the Glory of Monsters: The Collapse of Congo and the Great War in Africa.* New York: Public Affairs, 2011.

Taylor, Christopher. "Kings or Presidents? War and the State in Pre- and Post-genocidal Rwanda." *Social Analysis* 48, no. 1 (Spring 2004): 136–42.

Taylor, John Vernon. *The Growth of the Church in Buganda: An Attempt at Understanding.* London: SCM Press, 1958.

Thomson, Susan. *Rwanda: From Genocide to Precarious Peace.* New Haven, CT: Yale University Press, 2018.

Thomson, Susan. *Whispering Truth to Power: Everyday Resistance to Reconciliation in Postgenocide Rwanda.* Madison: University of Wisconsin Press, 2013.

Ugirashebuja, Octave. "The Church and the Genocide in Rwanda." In *Genocide in Rwanda, Complicity of the Churches?*, edited by Carol Rittner, John K. Roth, and Wendy Whitworth, 49–63. St. Paul: Aegis, 2004.

Umutesi, Marie Beatrice. *Surviving the Slaughter: The Ordeal of a Rwandan Refugee in Zaire.* Madison: University of Wisconsin Press, 2004.

Uvin, Peter. "Prejudice, Crisis, and Genocide in Rwanda." *African Studies Review* 40, no. 2 (1997): 91–115.

Uvin, Peter. "Tragedy in Rwanda: The Political Ecology of Conflict." *Environment* 38, no. 3 (April 1996): 6–17.

Vandeginste, Stef. "Governing Ethnicity after Genocide: Ethnic Amnesia in Rwanda versus Ethnic Power-Sharing in Burundi." *Journal of Eastern African Studies* 8, no. 2 (2014): 263–77.

van Hoyweghen, Saskia. "The Disintegration of the Catholic Church in Rwanda: A Study of the Fragmentation of Political and Religious Authority." *African Affairs* 95, no. 380 (July 1996): 379–401.

Vansina, Jan. *Antecedents to Modern Rwanda: The Nyiginya Kingdom.* Madison: University of Wisconsin Press, 2004.

Vansina, Jan. "Bantu in the Crystal Ball, I." *History in Africa* 6 (1979): 287–333.

Vansina, Jan. "Bantu in the Crystal Ball, II." *History in Africa* 7 (1980): 293–325.

Vansina, Jan. "Historical Tales (*Ibiteekerezo*) and the History of Rwanda." *History in Africa* 27 (2000): 375–414.

Vansina, Jan. *Living with Africa.* Madison: University of Wisconsin Press, 1994.

Vansina, Jan. *Oral Tradition as History.* Madison: University of Wisconsin Press, 1985.

Vansina, Jan. *Paths in the Rainforest: Toward a History of Political Tradition in Equatorial Africa.* Madison: University of Wisconsin Press, 1990.

Verwimp, Philip. "Development Ideology, the Peasantry and Genocide: Rwanda Represented in Habyarimana's Speeches." *Journal of Genocide Research* 2, no. 3 (2000): 325–61.

Vis, H. L., C. Yourassowsky, and H. van der Borght. *A Nutritional Survey in the Republic of Rwanda.* Tervuren: Koninklijk Museum voor Midden-Afrika, 1975.

Waldorf, Lars. "Revisiting *Hotel Rwanda*: Genocide Ideology, Reconciliation and Rescuers." *Journal of Genocide Research* 11, no. 1 (2009): 101–25.

Ward, Kevin. "'Obedient Rebels'—The Relationship between the Early 'Balokole' and the Church of Uganda: The Mukono Crisis of 1941." *Journal of Religion in Africa* 19, no. 3 (1989): 194–227.

Ward, Kevin. "Revival, Mission, and Church in Kigezi, Rwanda, and Burundi." In *The East African Revival: History and Legacies*, edited by Kevin Ward and Emma Wild-Wood, 11–29. Farnham: Ashgate, 2012.

Ward, Kevin. "The Revival in an African Milieu." In *The East African Revival: History and Legacies*, edited by Kevin Ward and Emma Wild-Wood, 187–200. Farnham: Ashgate, 2012.

Waugh, Colin M. *Paul Kagame and Rwanda: Power, Genocide, and the Rwandan Patriotic Front.* Jefferson, NC: McFarland, 2004.

Welbourn, F. B. *East African Rebels: A Study of Some Independent Churches.* London: SCM Press, 1961.

Winsor, Morgan. "Jailed Hero of 'Hotel Rwanda' Claims He Was Tortured at 'Slaughter House' after Arriving in Kigali." ABC News, May 25, 2021. https://abcnews.go.com/International/jailed-hero-hotel-rwanda-claims-tortured-slaughterhouse-arriving/story?id=77748884.

Wright, Michael A. *Buganda in the Heroic Age.* Oxford: Oxford University Press, 1971.

Wrong, Michela. *Do Not Disturb: The Story of a Political Murder and an African Regime Gone Bad.* New York: Public Affairs, 2021.

Zink, Jesse. "'Anglocostalism' in Nigeria: Neo-Pentecostalism and Obstacles to Anglican Unity." *Journal of Anglican Studies* 10, no. 2 (2012): 231–50.

Zorbas, Eugenia. "Reconciliation in Post-genocide Rwanda." *African Journal of Legal Studies* 1, no. 1 (2004): 29–52.

Index